DROUGHT AND WATER SUPPLY

DROUGHT AND WATER SUPPLY
Implications of the Massachusetts
Experience for Municipal Planning

Clifford S. Russell
David G. Arey
Robert W. Kates

With the assistance of
Duane Bauman
Donald J. Volk

Published for Resources for the Future, Inc.

by The Johns Hopkins Press
Baltimore and London

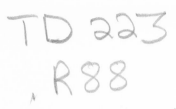
RESOURCES FOR THE FUTURE, INC.
1755 Massachusetts Avenue, N.W., Washington, D.C. 20036

Resources for the Future is a nonprofit corporation for research and education in
the development, conservation, and use of natural resources and the improvement of
the quality of the environment. It was established in 1952 with the cooperation of
the Ford Foundation. Part of the work of Resources for the Future is carried out by
its resident staff; part is supported by grants to universities and other nonprofit
organizations. Unless otherwise stated, interpretations and conclusions in RFF
publications are those of the authors; the organization takes responsibility for the
selection of significant subjects for study, the competence of the researchers,
and their freedom of inquiry.

This book is one of RFF's studies on water resources, which are directed by
Charles W. Howe. Research was conducted under an RFF grant to Clark University.
Clifford S. Russell is research associate with Resources for the Future; David G. Arey
is assistant professor of geography at the University of Pittsburgh; Robert W. Kates
is professor of geography at Clark University. The manuscript was edited by
Roma K. McNickle. Charts were drawn by Clare and Frank Ford. The index was
prepared by Adele Garrett.

RFF staff editors: Henry Jarrett, Vera W. Dodds, Nora E. Roots, Tadd Fisher.

Copyright © 1970 by The Johns Hopkins Press
All rights reserved
Manufactured in the United States of America
The Johns Hopkins Press, Baltimore, Maryland 21218
The Johns Hopkins Press Ltd., London
Library of Congress Catalog Card Number 72-123861
ISBN 0-8018-1183-X

FOREWORD

The unexpected enlivens human affairs. It often elicits behavior different from that which responds to likely and predictable events. The latter tend to be routinized by established institutions or management systems and their measurement results in clusters of only marginally differentiated observations. A dominant tradition in social science has been to seek an understanding of society by analyzing stimulus-response patterns within a system. Far less attention has been devoted to assessing the consequences of outside shocks which shake up that system. Yet such disturbances leave a legacy of effects on individuals and institutions which influences the future behavior of a community.

This book is about an unusual natural event and how communities and individuals respond to it. Following a period of well-watered years, New England experienced in the mid-1960's five years of very low rainfall. Clifford Russell, David Arey, Robert Kates, and their associates have used data covering the dry 1962–66 period to explore what happened when unexpected drought was encountered and what types of defensive response were taken by three New England communities. The authors use this unusual and rather extreme climatic event to explore the adequacy of community water supply systems in terms of both physical structure and operation, and to analyze the capacity of communities to adapt to drought conditions. The data developed were in turn used in a model depicting the efficient expansion of an existing water supply system.

This study is part of a small but growing literature which explores society's ability to cope with natural hazards. Much of the early work in this field, centering on flood problems, was undertaken at the University of Chicago under the direction of Professor Gilbert White. His analysis of land use activities on the flood plain suggested that insurance programs and land use zoning might provide more efficient alternatives for communities seeking protection from flood damage than the physical structures upon which they traditionally have relied. The present study substantially broadens our understanding of community water supply management, and suggests that expanding the physical system is not necessarily the most efficient response to anticipated shortage.

To exploit the research opportunities offered by a reasonably well documented extreme event, the authors found it necessary to elaborate a comprehensive framework of concepts and definitions as well as a methodology which could be made operational in their case studies. Their definition of adequacy of a water supply system is a welcome contribution to an area of substantial public expenditure for which no very firm investment criteria exist. The rules of thumb which the authors have developed for efficient water supply system planning help fill this void.

In making explicit the service capacity of a system under drought conditions, by considering the curtailment of water use as an investment, and by expressing "losses" in dollar terms, important options for future water system planning are developed. One may expect that similar types of studies will be undertaken in different areas of the country, and that the insights and specific information developed from them will lead to the improved management of community water supply systems.

Michael F. Brewer
Vice President, Resources for the Future

February 1970

ACKNOWLEDGMENTS

The authors wish to acknowledge their debts to many people whose contributions to this study cover a wide range.

For basic financial support we thank Resources for the Future, Inc., which also made it possible for the senior author to put the final touches on the manuscript as part of his duties as a research associate at RFF. At one stage, the Harvard Water Program provided secretarial, computational, and other support for the entire study.

A special debt is owed Duane Bauman who provided challenging ideas and hard work at every stage of the study and who prepared Chapter 8 on municipal response to drought. Donald Volk undertook a study of the Metropolitan District Commission from which we have taken much useful material. Charles W. Howe, director of the Water Resources Program at RFF, gave help ranging from advice and guidance at the beginning of the study through critical review of successive drafts. Blair T. Bower, also at RFF, generously took the time to review the study and to share with us his broad background in water resource problems. Early in the study, Myron Fiering of Harvard University provided us with simulation studies indicating the impact of the drought on the estimation of streamflow variability in Massachusetts.

In the area of data gathering, our largest debt is to the forty-eight water system managers and twenty-three private firm executives we interviewed at great length. These men cheerfully put up with our questioning and gave us the raw material for the study. This phase of the study would certainly have been far harder (and probably far less successful) had we not had the cooperation in Braintree, Fitchburg, and Pittsfield of the executives of the local Chambers of Commerce. In addition, we are grateful to Wayne Palmer of the U.S. Weather Bureau for providing us with data on climatic variation over long periods in Massachusetts. Hyman Steinhurst of the Massachusetts Department of Public Health assisted us greatly in obtaining, copying, and interpreting documents in that organization's custody.

In the initial stages of the formulation of the research report Roger Kasperson, then at Clark University with Arey and Kates, contributed many valuable insights into the political processes surrounding water supply decisions.

At Harvard, where Russell worked on the study as the basis of his thesis, Professors Robert Dorfman, Harold Thomas, and Henry Jacoby gave freely of their time in helping us over some of the rough spots. In particular, Professor Dorfman suggested the present form of the capacity expansion planning model and provided an exacting critique of the economic and econometric work. Professor Thomas assisted us whenever engineering problems arose. Professor Jacoby also served as a valuable critic but even more important, perhaps, as the keeper of the Water Program funds he smoothed our path by providing support during a critical period.

When it came time to try to solve the nonlinear programming problem defined by our planning model, we were fortunate to be able to turn to Douglas Shier. As part of the research for his B.A. Honors thesis in Applied Mathematics at Harvard, he undertook all the programming required in the solution of the model. His version of the method of feasible directions proved to be very efficient and quite robust in the face of the nonconvexity of our problem.

The testing and manipulation of our data on rainfall have been greatly improved thanks to the detailed comments on an earlier draft provided by Nicholas Matalas of the U.S. Geological Survey.

In final preparation of the manuscript we are grateful to Roma McNickle, our editor, and to Henry Jarrett of RFF, both of whom suggested important improvements in organization and presentation.

For secretarial and computational assistance we thank Ellen Berger, formerly of the Harvard Water Program, who typed most of the study in its earliest versions; Doris Stell of RFF, who efficiently made the seemingly endless string of modifications and corrections that resulted in the final version; and Betty Duenckel and Iris Long of RFF, who assisted with some of the statistical exercises undertaken late in the study.

CONTENTS

LIST OF TABLES

Table

LIST OF FIGURES

Figure

DROUGHT AND WATER SUPPLY

CHAPTER 1

RESEARCH AS AN AID TO
WATER SUPPLY PLANNING

The social sciences must depend largely on natural, uncontrolled experiments for obtaining data about the world they are attempting to describe and for testing theories they develop about cause-and-effect relations in that world. The economist, for example, is provided a rich source of data on prices, wages, and interest rates by the day-to-day functioning of the market economy.

But relying on the uncontrolled flow of the world's events presents a problem, because most of the systems being observed in the human social and economic world are seldom very far from equilibrium, and hence observations made on the parameters of these systems tend to be clustered in a small part of their potential ranges. This implies difficulty both in formulating and in testing theories to account for extreme events and forces the social scientist to question the generality of his results.

There is, however, one part of our world which, with some consistency, does introduce relatively extreme variation into the parameters of human social and economic systems. This is "nature," which through events such as floods, hurricanes, tornadoes, and blizzards disrupts production, transportation, and sales within the economy, introduces stresses into the general scheme of social relations, and produces pressures for both immediate and long-term actions by various levels of government. Thus it is not surprising, even on this very general level, that such events, often referred to as "natural hazards," have come to be recognized as fruitful fields of research for several branches of social science.[1]

[1] For an introduction to the existing natural-hazard research literature, see Ian Burton, Robert W. Kates, and Gilbert F. White, *The Human Ecology of Extreme Geophysical Events*, Working Paper No. 2, Natural Hazard Research Series (Toronto: University of Toronto, 1968, mimeo.). Examples of studies of specific hazards are:

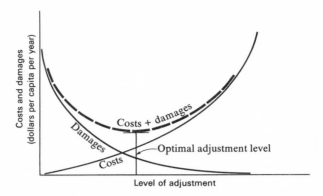

Figure 1. Adjustment to natural hazard: the problem.

Studies of natural hazards have a more tangible payoff than increased understanding of how various social systems function under stress. Any of these hazards imposes costs on society, most obviously in the forms of injury, loss of life, destruction of property, and diversion of effort to clean up and repair, but just as surely in the form of higher levels of tension and anxiety for the individual and for the group. Since certain natural events will continue to occur, the problem is to identify the best possible adjustment to these events on the part of society[2] and, since all adjustments have costs, to minimize the sum of these costs and the residual damages of the

---

(1) S. D. Flora, *Hailstorms of the United States* (Norman: University of Oklahoma Press, 1956); (2) R. Henrick and D. Freedman, "Potential Impacts of Storm Modification on the Insurance Industry" in *Human Dimensions of Weather Modification*, W. R. D. Sewell, ed., Department of Geography Research Paper No. 105 (Chicago: University of Chicago Press, 1966), which discusses hurricanes, tornadoes, hail, wind, thunderstorms, and extra-tropical windstorms; (3) U.S. Department of Commerce, Environmental Science Services Administration, *A Proposed Nationwide Natural Disaster Warning System* (Washington: U.S. Government Printing Office, 1965), especially pp. 25–37, which covers floods, hurricanes, tornadoes, lightning strikes and fire, earthquakes, and tsunamis; (4) U.S. House of Representatives, *A Unified National Program for Managing Flood Losses*, House Document 465, 89th Cong., 2nd Sess. (Washington: U.S. Government Printing Office, 1966), p. 3.

[2] "Adjustment" here is used in the widest sense to cover any action society or an individual may take to reduce the costs of an occurrence of the specific hazard in question, involving the construction of dams, dikes, or sea walls, the provision of warning systems and rescue units, the underwriting of insurance to affect the variance of losses, and many other actions. To assume that certain natural events will occur (probably according to some random distribution in time and space) is not to assume away such adjustments as weather modification; it is merely to move our concern back to levels at which we lose control. In this example, certain climatic patterns make weather modification seem attractive; we assume the climatic patterns are beyond man's control at least for the present.

event adjusted to. Clearly, then, one very important role of research in natural hazards is to provide data on the damages resulting under various levels of adjustment and, by extrapolation from the existing situation, on the damages to be avoided by further adjustments. This information is vital to any attempt to seek the optimal level of adjustment in the face of a given distribution of natural events.

Graphically, the situation may be characterized as in Figure 1. Damages are seen as a decreasing function of the level of adjustment and the costs of adjustment as an increasing function of that level. Observation of a specific occurrence (or series of occurrences) hopefully provides us with information on the extent of damages suffered under particular levels of adjustment, the costs of which are known. We are thus in principle able to estimate the two crucial functions and hence to find the optimal level of adjustment.[3]

This study is an example of such uses of the data generated by a natural event: the 1962–66 drought in Massachusetts, which was part of the drought experienced by the whole northeastern section of the country. The Northeast Drought began in 1961 or later, depending on location within the region. Rainfall had returned to normal by the end of 1966 for most of the region. The drought was, then, roughly 5 or 6 years in duration.

The amount of the precipitation shortage was also variable within the region. In general, the deficit amounted to about one year's rainfall over the 5- to 6-year period.[4]

The fact that a considerable proportion of the nation's population and industrial capacity is located in the Northeast had an important bearing on the widespread publicity about the drought. National concern was evidenced by hearings in the U.S. Senate and by a series of reports to the President by the Water Resources Council.[5] Several federal agencies assayed the situation as the drought deepened.[6]

[3] This discussion, in the interest of simplicity, does not deal with problems raised by uncertainty itself, with perception of hazard by individuals, or with "readjustment" by individuals to previous collective adjustment (such as in increased construction on plains behind flood walls).

[4] For example, at Pittsfield, the average annual precipitation is 40.6 inches, which would amount to 203.0 inches for a 5-year period. Over the years 1962 through 1966 the accumulated rainfall amounted to only 160.8 inches, making a deficit of 42.3 inches for the period.

[5] U.S. Water Resources Council, *Report to the President, Drought in Northeast United States*, July 21, 1965; *Report to the President, Reappraisal of Drought in Northeastern United States*, September 7, 1965; and *Report to the President, Drought in Northeastern United States, a Third Appraisal*, March 1, 1966 (Washington: U.S. Government Printing Office). The U.S. Water Resources Council is a cabinet level agency, established by the Water Resources Planning Act of 1965, to be responsible for coordinating federal water resources planning, policy-making, and action programs.

[6] A concise discussion of the hydrologic consequences of the drought, especially its

The drought's major impact was on municipal and industrial water supplies, since the Northeast is largely urban and industrialized, although damage to crops and livestock was heavy in limited areas of the region. Most widely publicized were the emergency conditions in New York City. But the same severe conditions existed throughout the region. Indeed, for most of the Northeast, the drought was the worst in recorded history when measured by the common hydrologic indices.

While it would have been highly desirable to study the effects of the drought on the whole Northeast, the research being reported was limited to Massachusetts primarily for reasons of convenience and economy. Two of the investigators (Kates and Arey) were then at Clark University in Worcester, which is in the approximate center of the state. Available time and travel funds promised to produce a maximum amount of data when expended within the relatively small area of Massachusetts. A number of other local characteristics were useful for a study of the drought. Long records of flow and runoff are available for several Massachusetts rivers, along with even longer series of rainfall records from stations over the state. The municipalities themselves are generally rather old and often have water systems records, including the reports of consulting engineers, reaching back into the 19th century. Most of these records are comparable over their lengths, for both the decision-making process of the local government and the hydrologic estimates which serve as guides in the process have remained unchanged for long periods.[7] In addition, there were available the records and planning experience of a much younger governmental entity, the Metropolitan District Commission, which, through a series of very large reservoirs and other works, supplies water to parts of the Boston metropolitan area, with an estimated total population of about 1,650,000.[8]

effects on streamflow and groundwater, is to be found in H. C. Barksdale, Deric O'Bryan, and W. J. Schneider, "Effect of Drought on Water Resources in the Northeast," *Hydrologic Investigations Atlas*, HA 243 (Washington: U.S. Government Printing Office, 1966). The U.S. Army Corps of Engineers instituted a program of status reports originated by the regional Engineer Divisions to the Chief of Engineers in Washington.

[7] The decision-making process has not changed substantially since the city fathers of Boston debated the merits of alternative plans by a consulting engineer in 1825. See Daniel Treadwell, *Report Made to the City of Boston, on the Subject of Supplying the Inhabitants of that City with Water* (Boston: True and Greene, 1825). Quoted in Nelson M. Blake, *Water for the Cities*, Maxwell School Series III, p. 174 (Syracuse: Syracuse University Press, 1956).

[8] The Metropolitan District Commission, hereinafter referred to as the MDC, is a governmental unit chartered by the Commonwealth of Massachusetts. The MDC has three main divisions, Parks and Recreation, Sewerage, and Water Supply. The Water Supply Division provides water for the city of Boston and 31 other municipalities, most of which are in the Boston suburban area. In addition to supplying water for its member communities, the MDC supplies water when needed on an emergency basis to several other municipalities where the physical facilities for such transfer exist.

METHODOLOGY OF THE STUDY

With such records available, what could the tools of social science produce from them that would be of significance in planning to meet such a natural hazard in the future? First, we extracted data on the losses to be expected from water shortage in a municipal water supply system at various levels of the "adjustment" of that system. Broadly speaking, adjustment was measured in terms of the amount of water storage in the system relative to the projected demand for water at the historically given price, assuming a particular distribution of natural events in terms of rainfall. Since the expected losses vary inversely with the size of storage relative to demand, and since it was possible to estimate the costs of providing storage and to project future demands, it was possible to generate the two functions required for determining the optimal level of adjustment.

Our second major step, then, was to combine our estimates of expected losses and of costs of adjustment (construction of storage) in the appropriate optimizing framework. Specifically, we constructed a planning model for which we sought combinations of timing and size of increments to water system storage which would minimize the discounted sum of construction costs and expected losses from water shortage.

These results were then used to construct sample rules of thumb for planning the expansion of water systems. That is, a method was indicated for translating the solutions of fairly complicated programming models into terms which could be summarized in handbook pages for the use of practical planners.

Finally, these rules of thumb for decisions on the size and timing of increments were compared to the records of actual expansion decisions made over about 70 years by several Massachusetts cities.

The 237 Massachusetts communities which have their own water supply system and are not served by the Metropolitan District Commission formed our universe. All were surveyed initially with a one-page questionnaire, to which 156 replies were received. Fifty communities were then chosen for intensive interview surveys which concentrated on the characteristics of the municipal water supply system. Forty-eight of these interviews were completed. Tables 1 and 2 summarize the stratification of this sample of intensively studied water supply systems by size of population served, type of source, and type of adjustment to drought chosen by the municipal government.[9] Figure 2 shows the location of the 48 study communities.

[9] When the original sample was chosen, it was not realized that groundwater sources would be so difficult to fit into the conceptual framework of the adjustment-impact model developed below.

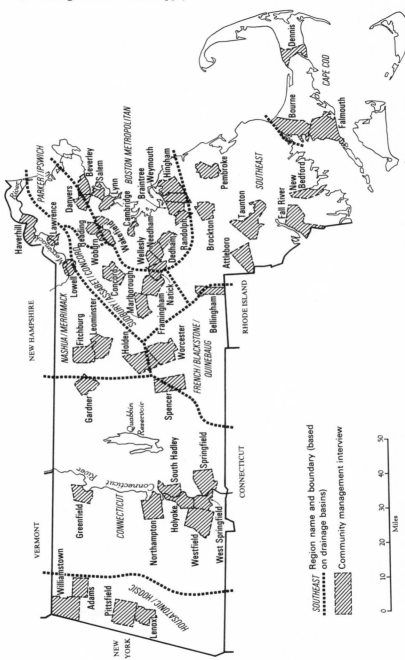

Figure 2. Location of 48 study sites.

TABLE 1. WATER SUPPLY SYSTEMS IN DETAILED SURVEY: BY POPULATION SERVED AND TYPE OF ADJUSTMENT

Population served	Number of systems	No adjustments	Restrictions on use	Increases in supply	Total number adopting some adjustment
5,000–25,000[1]	18	3	10	9	15
Over 25,000[1]	30	6	24	14	24
Total[1]	48	9	34	3	39

[1] Some communities adopted more than one type of adjustment; hence the totals do not check across the rows.

From these 48 communities, three were chosen for detailed investigation of drought losses. These were Braintree, Fitchburg, and Pittsfield. The survey methods included interviews with all managers of industrial and commercial firms of over 50 employees who claimed to have incurred costs or losses because of the drought; interviews with various public officials who had knowledge of municipal government expenditures in connection with the drought; and reviews of local newspaper files for the drought period. These several layers of sampling and the major studies conducted at each level are recorded in Table 3.

Finally, certain more specialized studies were conducted, as recorded in Table 4. The survey of the engineering reports made to the governments of 4 cities was conducted to give us a base of actual decisions on system expansion against which to compare our planning prescriptions.

THE PLAN OF THE BOOK

We begin by discussing in Part I the definition and measurement of the level of system adjustment. We use as a measure of system adjustment the ratio of system demand (at the historically given price set) to safe yield, a probabilistic measure of supply capability in the face of previously observed distribution of climatic events. This ratio is an indicator of the system's relative inadequacy. The higher the ratio, the smaller the supply capability relative to the predictable demand. After Chapter 2, which deals more carefully with this demand-supply measure of inadequacy, we spend two chapters discussing the components individually; in Chapter 3 we go into the concept of the safe yield of a surface water supply system,[10] while in Chapter 4 we explain our methods of measuring the demand for water

[10] We do not deal in this study with groundwater systems, primarily because of the difficulty of defining and measuring safe yields for them.

TABLE 2. Selected Characteristics of Water Supply Systems in Detailed Survey

Population served	Number of systems	Primary Source			Average Consumption			Average charge per 1,000 gallons[a] (cents)
		Surface water	Ground water	Combined groundwater and surface water	Total daily 1950–62 (million gallons per day)	Per capita daily 1950–62 (gallons per day)	Per capita daily 1963–66 (gallons per day)	
5,000–15,000	12	2	5	5	0.7	90	95	39.5 (6 systems)
16,000–25,000	6	3	3	0	1.6	94	100	21.0 (2 systems)
26,000–75,000	21	9	5	7	4.2	119	137	26.5 (13 systems)
Over 75,000	9	9	0	0	14.2	123	139	20.7 (4 systems)
Total	48	23	13	12		106[b]	118[b]	

Source: Interviews with 48 water system managers and the files of the Massachusetts Department of Public Health.
[a] Where data were available, the average charge per 1,000 gallons was derived by dividing total community water revenues by the number of gallons sold.
[b] Simple average.

TABLE 3. SUMMARY OF DATA SURVEYS

Public water supply Systems (Total in state: 237)	Water system characteristics	Drought impact and adjustment	Hydroclimatological data	Other socioeconomic data	Major sources
184 cities and towns	Safe yield; population served (where available)	Adequacy of system estimate	Monthly Palmer Drought Index for entire state 1929–66 (for 150 cities and towns, information on restrictions and emergency supplies)		Mail questionnaires; 1963 USPHS inventory[a]
48 cities and towns (including all over 25,000 not in Massachusetts District Commission)	Supply-demand characteristics; annual water use 1950–66; monthly water detailed use 1960–66; rates; financial structure	Adequacy of system; managerial perception; adjustments	Monthly Palmer Drought Index for entire state 1929–66 (for 150 cities and towns, information on restrictions and emergency supplies)	Estimated population; employment index 1950–66	Interview with water manager; Massachusetts Department of Public Health reports
Braintree Fitchburg Pittsfield	Demand, actual consumption, safe yield 1950–66	Detailed drought losses		Attitudes of community leaders and municipal decision-makers	Interviews with municipal, commercial, industrial leaders; newspaper files

[a] U.S. Department of Health, Education and Welfare, *1963 Inventory of Municipal Water Facilities,* USPHS Publication No. 775, rev. (Washington: U.S. Government Printing Office, 1964).

TABLE 4. SUMMARY OF SPECIALIZED DATA SURVEYS

System	Water system characteristics	Drought impact and adjustment	Hydroclimatological data	Socioeconomic data	Major sources
Fall River Fitchburg Pittsfield Worcester	See Table 3; demand, actual consumption, safe yield 1929–66		Annual precipitation 1867–1966 at 5 stations; streamflows as available	Municipal debt, 1907–62; employment, 1929–66	Interviews; Massachusetts Department of Public Health reports; engineering reports
Metropolitan District Commission (MDC)	Actual consumption, safe yield	Measure of restriction effects	None specific to MDC		Interviews, literature, public documents
Miscellaneous	Water-use/safe-yield ratios	Attitudes of state officials and consulting engineers	New Bedford Palmer Drought Index 1812–1967		U.S. Public Health Service inventory; interviews

at existing prices using the available data for the pre-drought period. We are interested here in identifying a relation for each community between the level of per capita demand and the values assumed by various explanatory variables.

In Chapter 5 of Part II, the empirical relations of Chapter 4 are used to project demand into the drought period. These projections, in turn, allow a working definition of the level of *water shortage* suffered in a year by a system: Shortage equals the difference between the *projected demand* for the year and the *amount of water actually delivered* by the system. (In looking into the future, actual deliveries are replaced by the amount of water available for delivery.)

The size of the shortage suffered in a dry year by a system having a given inadequacy level will naturally depend on the severity of the climatic event occurring in that year—how dry the dry year really is. In Part II, Chapter 6, we discuss the measures of climatic variation which are used in our model. Having defined and measured the physical severity of drought in a particular community and year, we set out a model linking these climatic conditions with water system inadequacy and the amount of shortage. This is the concern of Chapter 7. The evidence developed by this study on the relation between shortage, inadequacy, and climatic variation is then examined. Finally, in Chapter 8, we consider *possible* adjustments to impending shortages on the part of water system managers. Evidence is then presented on the adjustments *actually* adopted in Massachusetts during the recent drought.

Part III of the work deals with the measurement of losses attributed to the drought in three Massachusetts cities, and with the relation between these losses and the levels of potential water shortage which caused them. After discussing in Chapter 9 the methods used in obtaining raw-loss estimates from our sample communities and displaying these estimates, we apply, in Chapter 10, corrections for several important economic considerations: the returns to drought-induced investment, the appropriate accounting stance, and the effect of deferral or transferral of production and sales.

Chapter 11 presents a summary of corrected losses suffered by customers of the municipal system (and by the municipality itself) in annual per capita terms. These figures are then combined with probabilistic climatic data to derive expected-loss functions which can be used in the planning model. The expected-loss functions represent the ultimate payoff from the study of the drought itself. The remaining chapters of the book discuss the application of these results to the planning of municipal water supply systems.

In Part IV, we derive cost-of-safe-yield functions and combine these with the expected-loss functions to form a capacity expansion model designed to determine the optimal size and timing of increments to a water supply system.

The final part of the volume (V) deals with practical water system planning. We begin by deriving two sets of rules of thumb for practical planning based on the results obtained from the planning model. These rules permit managers to plan for approximate optimality (in terms of the capital-cost/drought-loss trade-off) for given estimates of the rate of growth of population and the appropriate discount rate. We then discuss the process of planning and decision-making for the water supply system as actually observed in the context of municipal government. Finally, we examine historical records to see what can be said about the actual paths of the five systems studied in comparison with the paths implied by the rules of thumb.

A final chapter summarizes our findings about the drought and gives our suggestions for improving the planning process. Here, as elsewhere, we touch briefly on some of the very real obstacles to planning solely on the basis of economic considerations. The brevity of the discussion should not be taken to imply that such obstacles can be assumed away.

PART I

WATER SUPPLY AND DEMAND: THE LEVEL OF SYSTEM INADEQUACY

AN INDEX OF WATER SYSTEM INADEQUACY: THE RELATION BETWEEN POTENTIAL DEMAND AND SUPPLY

As we have pointed out, the central variable in our progress from a study of the drought itself to prescription for optimal system expansion is the level of adjustment of a water system to the threat of water shortage. To this level we must attempt to relate losses incurred during the study period; on it will depend our extrapolation from the results of a single event to long-run expected-loss functions; and with it as the choice variable or policy instrument, we shall construct our planning model. It is thus important that we choose as the representation of level of adjustment a variable, or combination of variables, having at least the following useful properties:

We must be able to measure the actual levels of adjustment of systems observed during the drought;

We must be able to relate the level of adjustment directly to probability statements about the likelihood of climatic events of varying levels of severity; and

We must be able to show explicitly how the level of adjustment of a system will vary over time as a function of expansion decisions (and any other choice variables) and as a function of any time-dependent changes assumed to be exogenous.

With these requirements in mind, we have chosen for our index of adjustment level the ratio of potential demand for system deliveries at the existing price to the "safe yield" of the system, the measure of the probabilistic ability of the system to provide water.

Before we go on to discuss the nature of this index further, it may be worth while to bring out one implication of using such an index in discussing drought. That is, in general, for any group of independent water supply systems, the level of climatic severity (the amount of precipitation shortfall, say) that creates supply problems will be different for each system because each will, in general, face a different level of demand (determined by prices, customer composition, and the like) and have a different safe yield (determined by previous investment decisions). The relative adjustment level (relative inadequacy, in our terms) will be different for each system, and hence the level of natural variation in rainfall amounts at which each will begin to be unable to meet demand will be different. This means that what is a drought for one system will not be for another, and that even in the face of a rainfall shortage as severe as that of 1962–66 in Massachusetts, some systems may very well never face any difficulty in meeting demands for water. On the other hand, relatively common periods of rainfall shortage may be enough to drive other systems to the point at which restrictions will have to be instituted or emergency supplies tapped.

This illustrates the slipperiness of the concept of "drought" as it relates to municipal and industrial water supply systems. It is certainly not possible, from this point of view, to define "drought" in purely meteorological terms, except by choosing an arbitrary level of system adjustment as a base.

By the same argument, to refer to a particular system's problem as a "man-made" drought is to ignore the role of natural variation in bringing shortages even to relatively inadequate systems. This situation contrasts with that in such fields as agronomy and meteorology in which a definition of drought in physical terms may be possible, even if no entirely satisfactory one has been produced.[1]

We should also note that our choice of an index for the level of system adjustment was conditioned by our interest in relatively long-run problems of shortage, rather than in short-run peaking problems which, of course, may arise for various reasons quite unconnected with shortage of rainfall. For example, in the short run, demand may be highly variable relative to supply capability, and the importance of climatic variation will be its role in determining the probability distribution of levels of demand. Thus, an important influence in peak hourly and daily demands for water will be air

[1] For example, at a recent meeting this goal was described as follows: "A good objective definition of drought is wanted. It should be of such a nature that it describes a state of the hydrologic cycle and is separated from the assumed 'demand for water.'" See K. H. Jehn and Amos Eddy, *Summary Report of Workshop/Conference on Meteorological Drought*, Atmospheric Science Group Report No. 4, University of Texas (Austin: College of Engineering, May 1966).

temperature; and the probability of exceeding certain peak demands will be some complicated function of the probability of exceeding certain atmospheric temperatures. (There will, of course, be many other influences present here, most importantly those of the prevailing social habits.) Then, man's adjustment to short-run problems lies in two directions. First, he must decide what distributional capacity to maintain, i.e., what size pumps and mains to install. Second, he may consider construction of storage designed to allow the accumulation of a supply peak to match the demand peak—as, for example, when a water tower is constructed to allow collection of water from the source during slack periods for use during peaks. The efficacy of the latter adjustment depends, of course, on the existence of adequate distributional facilities.

On the other hand, average annual demand may be a fairly stable figure which can be estimated in advance from expected population growth and projections of per capita water use based on knowledge of social habits that change relatively slowly. But the naturally available annual supply will be more or less highly variable, depending on climatic and hydrologic conditions in the region, as year-to-year variations in total precipitation will be modified by groundwater and runoff conditions to produce variations in streamflows. Here, man's adjustment will take the form of the provision of overyear storage, aimed essentially at smoothing the variability of supply.

Thus, depending on whether our view is short- or long-run, we would be interested in different climatic variables and different forms of human adjustment, and we would hold a different view of the relative variability of demand and supply. Note also, that in either view shortage and hence losses will be random variables with distributions depending on the distribution of climatic events, though it will, in general, be true that the derivation of these distributions will be enormously complex.

To demonstrate the underlying conceptual similarity of the two cases, we first consider the ratio of the projected demand to some measure of the supply capability of the system for the period of interest. The measure of supply capability used may be more or less probabilistic in nature. For the short run, the distributional capacity of the system is of interest and depends on main and pump sizes, among other things. This capacity is probabilistic in the sense that there always exists some probability of breakdown, but this aspect of the problem is frequently not considered. (The probabilistic nature of peak capacity *is* explicitly recognized in the electric utility field.) A common longer-run measure of capacity is that flow which can be assured 95 percent of the time; here the probabilistic nature of the figure is obvious.

Contrast, for example, the ratio of *hourly* demand to system distributional capacity, and that of the *annual* demand to the 95 percent assured flow provided by system storage. Either ratio may be considered a measure of system inadequacy (for the appropriate run), in the sense that systems higher on the scale are less adequate than those lower on it, i.e., they have smaller supply capability relative to projected demand. The decision-maker for the system "chooses" the level of the demand-to-supply ratio for the appropriate run, over the planning horizon, generally by choosing a level of supply. In these circumstances, whether or not shortage occurs—and if it occurs, how serious it is—depends on the outcomes of the events produced by nature, i.e., on the climatic variation.

In the short-run situation, "the" projection of demand may be viewed as the mean (or some other measure) of a distribution of possible levels of demand depending on (we assume) the air temperature at the given hour. The level of supply is *chosen* in the form of the capacity of the distribution system. (This choice will, no doubt, be related to the projection of demand.) Thus, for a chosen demand-to-supply ratio, there will be a relation between the actual air temperature occurring and the level of short-run shortage. Since the actual air temperature occurring is a random variable, it will, in principle, be possible to find the expected shortage for any chosen level of the demand-supply ratio. If we also have information relating economic losses to level of shortage, we will be able to find expected losses for given levels of system adequacy.

Fundamentally, the long-run situation is the same in that our ultimate aim is a function relating levels of system adequacy to the losses we can expect to suffer as a result of climatic variation. Because this situation is the one dealt with in this book, it will be discussed here more fully than the short-run problem. In order to postpone discussion of the conceptual difficulties in defining "supply" in the long run, we shall adopt an approach that is somewhat artificial but will convey the essentials of the problem.

Let us say that a community projects its total annual demand for water as D million gallons. Let us, for simplicity, now assume that this level of demand is expected to last into the indefinite future. Let us further suppose that this town has available to it an infinite number of streams of different sizes which it can tap for a run-of-the-river supply. We assume that for each stream, annual streamflow (*SF*) is a random variable and, again for simplicity, we shall assume that it is serially independent and that the flows are all spatially independent as well. The distribution for each stream is essentially the same (as measured, say, by the ratio of a standard deviation to mean), and we shall distinguish between them on the basis of the "5 percent low flow" (*SF**), that level of streamflow than which the actual

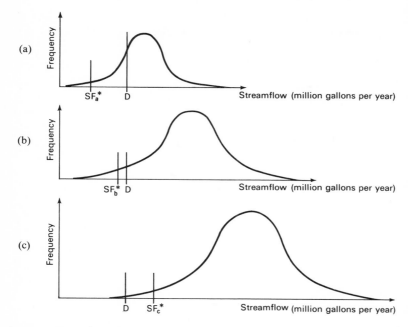

Figure 3. Illustrative supply source choices.

flow will be greater 95 percent of the time. In Figure 3 we have drawn three such streams. In each case, we show the projected demand (*D*) on the flow axis.

Now, it should be clear that the choice of a particular stream implies both a particular frequency function for shortages, where we define percentage shortage as $(D - SF)/D$ in any particular year, and a particular value for the ratio D/SF^*. We show in Figure 4 frequency distributions for shortages and surpluses corresponding to choice of streams (*a*), (*b*), and (*c*) in Figure 3.

Using these shortage-frequency functions we can find, for any particular stream, the expected annual shortage implied by that choice. Characterizing system inadequacy by the ratio D/SF^*, we can thus construct a relation showing expected annual shortage for each level of inadequacy (for each choice of source). Such a relation is shown in Figure 5. Since we are interested in the economic impact of shortage, we first transform shortages into annual losses through a shortage-loss relationship as illustrated in Figure 6. It seems reasonable to suppose that in such a relation, costs would increase with shortage, though it is not clear whether this increase should be linear or more than or less than proportional. For exposition,

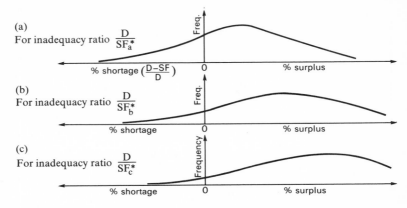

Figure 4. Supply reliability resulting from different choices of source.

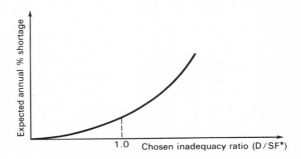

Figure 5. Illustrative expected shortage—system-inadequacy relation.[2]

we assume a more than proportional increase.[3] We are then in a position to derive the cost analog of Figure 5, an expected-loss/system-inadequacy relation. Functions of this type may, then, be used in making choices between various possible levels of system adequacy, as we describe below.

OBSERVED LEVELS OF ADJUSTMENT OF WATER SYSTEMS

Before turning to more careful definitions of the key demand and supply variables in our index of inadequacy, let us pause to examine actual distri-

---

[2] The claim that we adequately characterize each choice by the expected shortage it will produce is essentially equivalent to stating that the aim of the system is to meet all demand generated at the going price. System surpluses are indistinguishable from a just-adequate supply. Surplus water is of no use to system customers who cannot adjust to quantities greater than their intended demands.

[3] In this static situation (fixed demand into the future) and for illustration, total losses may be used without any problem. When, however, we work with the actual model and data, losses measured at one time are applied to future (different) situations. Then we shall need to express losses in per capita terms.

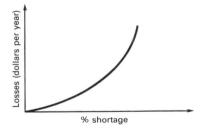

Figure 6. Illustrative loss-shortage relation.

butions of systems on this scale. Such an investigation should help to give us a better "feel" for the index and, in particular, should allow us to judge what range of index values is relevant for the application of our results. In what follows, we discuss such distributions determined both cross-sectionally (for many systems in each of several geographic regions of the United States at one point in time) and over time (for four Massachusetts cities over about 66 years). Since the "demand" estimates involved in all these data are merely point measurements of actual water consumed, we shall refer to the ratios as water-use/safe-yield ratios (WU/SY).

CROSS-SECTIONAL DISTRIBUTIONS OF WATER-USE/SAFE-YIELD RATIOS (WU/SY)

In constructing the distribution of WU/SY ratios, we have relied primarily on data gathered by the U.S. Public Health Service in 1962, just prior to the drought,[4] supplementing this information with data from our study wherever possible.

Because of the fundamental conceptual differences between the measures of capacity for groundwater as opposed to surface-water sources, we first separated the inventoried systems into three groups according to their degree of dependence on surface water.[5] As we have noted previously, our investigation centered on systems depending primarily on surface water.

As a first step, the WU/SY ratios were calculated and plotted for the population supplied by surface water in Massachusetts. Because of the relatively small number of such communities with complete data, gaps

[4] U.S. Department of Health, Education, and Welfare, *1963 Inventory of Municipal Water Facilities*, Public Health Service Publication No. 775, rev. (Washington: U.S. Government Printing Office, 1964).

[5] Systems are classified on the basis of the proportion of the "dependable"supply which comes from each source (the safe yield of surface -water supplies or the maximum dependable draft of groundwater supplies). If 80 percent or more is accounted for by surface supplies, the system is classified as surface; if 80 percent or more comes from groundwater supplies, the system is classified as groundwater. In combination systems, both surface and groundwater supplies account for 20–80 percent of the total.

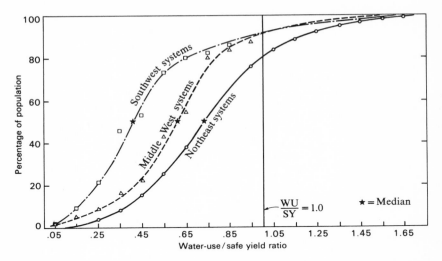

Figure 7. Interregional comparison of the distribution of population over the water-use/safe-yield scale.

appeared in the distribution. It was the existence of these gaps which led us to use the USPHS data for all of the northeastern states.[6]

The data for the Northeast are plotted as a cumulative distribution in Figure 7. In the same figure, we present for contrast similarly defined distributions for two other sections of the United States: the Middle West and the Southwest.[7]

From the distribution for the Northeast we note that the median system ratio is about 0.73. This means that in 1962, half of the population represented was served by systems with safe yields at least 37 percent greater than current water use.[8] About 20 percent of the population was served by systems with safe yields less than use. These people are the ones we would expect to suffer in a repetition of the design drought.[9]

[6] The additional states used were: Maine, New Hampshire, Vermont, Rhode Island, Connecticut, New York, Pennsylvania, New Jersey, and Delaware. Note that differing definitions of safe yield between states and between cities within each state, based on differences in consulting engineering practices, will tend to make the various WU/SY ratios not comparable. We have assumed that this problem is not particularly severe because of the prevalence of safe-yield definitions based either on the 1908–11 drought or on some measure of a "5 percent event."

[7] The Middle West distribution is based on USPHS inventory data for Illinois, Indiana, and Ohio. That for the Southwest is based on data for Texas, Oklahoma, and New Mexico.

[8] For those systems with $SY > WU$, we may write $SY = WU(1 + \alpha)$ and hence $WU/(WU)(1 + \alpha) \leq 0.73$ or $\alpha \geq 0.37$.

[9] "Design drought" is discussed in Chapter 3.

A comparison of the three distributions indicates the dramatic differences between the regions, differences which appear to be related to climate. Both the Middle West distribution and that for the Southwest lie everywhere above that for the Northeast; and the Southwest distribution is almost everywhere above that for the Middle West. This indicates that for any given inadequacy level a greater proportion of the population of the Southwest will be served by systems with at least that much capacity relative to demand (with WU/SY ratios less than or equal to the given level). For example, about 67 percent of the population represented by the Southwest curve is served by systems with WU/SY ratios less than or equal to 0.5, that is, by systems with safe yield at least twice as great as water use. The corresponding figure for the Middle West is 32 percent; for the Northeast, 20 percent. The median system inadequacy level for the Southwest is about 0.41; that for the Middle West, about 0.60.

These measures indicate that levels of system *adequacy* are generally highest in the Southwest and lowest in the Northeast. This corresponds to the interregional differences in the variability of precipitation and streamflow; such variability is greater in the Southwest than in the Middle West and greater in the Middle West than in the Northeast. Thus this measure is clear evidence of the reliance in the West on man-made systems as opposed to the tendency of the East to rely on its more regular rainfall.

We should note that safe yield is, in one sense, no "safer" in the Northeast than in the Southwest. In both areas, events worse than the safe-yield event may be expected about 5 percent of the time.[10] It may be, however, that because of shorter records (along with greater variability) the safe yield estimates available to western water system managers are considered by them to be particularly rough. This greater uncertainty might very well lead to the inclusion of substantial safety factors in system plans.

TIME SERIES DISTRIBUTIONS OF *WU/SY* RATIOS

Data have been gathered for four Massachusetts communities—Fall River, Fitchburg, Pittsfield, and Worcester—on the changes in water use and safe yield over the period from 1900 to 1966. A detailed analysis of these system histories is presented in Part V. At this point we are, however, interested only in the distribution on the inadequacy scale implied by the

---

[10] It is possible that in the area of greater variability (as measured, say, by the variance of annual precipitation totals) the physical severity of the 1 or 2 percent event is worse, relative to the safe-yield event. This, however, need not be true.

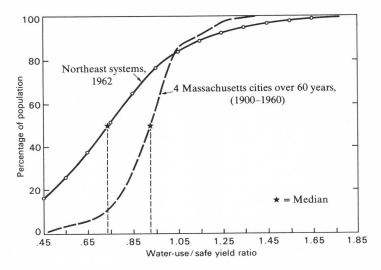

Figure 8. Historical distribution of 1900–1960 populations of 4 Massachusetts cities over water-use/safe-yield scale.

historic experience of these cities. Accordingly, the data are plotted in Figure 8.[11]

In comparison with the cross-sample of Northeast systems in 1962, the time series distribution is more compact and has a higher median adjustment level (the systems tended to be more inadequate). The compactness is probably largely accounted for by our method of construction. It is not clear to what we should attribute the other phenomenon.

This brief study of the observed behavior of water system decision-makers in terms of our inadequacy ratio suggests that a model of drought impact which is satisfactory for systems in the range $0.50 \leq PD/SY \leq 2.00$ will be covering the empirically important cases of chosen inadequacy levels. It is important to note this, particularly since our later evidence on drought impact is drawn from systems in this range, a range we may say includes virtually all systems.

---

[11] The following method was used to construct this distribution. First, WU/SY ratios were calculated for each city and year. Then the median WU/SY values were chosen for each city for 10-year intervals centered on the decennial census years. This median WU/SY ratio was weighted in each case by the city's population for the census year contained in the interval, and the combination of median WU/SY and population weight was considered as a separate system. The total population summed over all the census years and the four cities was taken as the base for calculating the percentage of population served by systems below the various WU/SY ratios.

CHAPTER 3

WATER SUPPLY SYSTEMS
AND THE LEVEL OF SUPPLY

Water supply systems are complex networks designed to collect, store, and distribute water. Our concern is with the functions of collection and storage, since these are most important to an understanding of the impact of long-term rainfall shortage.[1]

It is, of course, true that many urban water problems are distributional in nature; that is, while storage may be adequate, the annual, or more often the seasonal, daily, or hourly peak demands exceed the capacity of the pumps and lines that make up the distribution system. The problems raised by these demand patterns are serious, and it may be that drought-related uses such as lawn-sprinkling contribute significantly to the existence of shortages for towns on the border of distributional adequacy. It is, however, our purpose to study the shortages which arise from a lack of water to distribute rather than those resulting from inability to distribute available water in conformance with the pattern of peak demands.

Considered, then, from the point of view of collection and storage, the water supply system planning process is, in outline, a simple one. The planners, in response to actual and anticipated levels of demand for water, seek out and examine available alternative sources of supply.[2] In the genesis

---

[1] As a consequence of our emphasis on collection and storage aspects of water supply, our discussions of flows (annual, monthly, or daily) will almost invariably refer to average amounts over some particular period (e.g., mean long-term annual streamflow). The reader will be warned whenever it is necessary to discuss peak flows.

[2] The general philosophy of system managers and municipal governments is to meet all demands at the current price structure. The implications of this approach have been discussed by others, e.g., Jack Hirshleifer, James C. DeHaven, and Jerome W. Milliman, *Water Supply: Economics, Technology and Policy* (Chicago: University of Chicago Press, 1960). For the most part we accept this as given.

of the system, these alternatives may be limited by the myopic vision of the planners, and in existing systems further constraints are implied by past decisions. Nevertheless, there is almost always a choice of size and timing of development, and frequently of source as well (i.e., a choice between ground or surface water; location, size, and quality of stream). And, almost always, the size and timing problem is one of balancing the costs of expansion (usually under conditions of falling unit costs) against some notion of the costs of shortages to be expected in the absence of expansion. (See the discussion and planning model presented in Part IV below.)

Given these fundamental influences, then, the growth of a typical water system, when viewed in historical perspective, might take the form shown in Figure 9. Demand, as the product of innumerable individual decisions, varies nearly continuously and generally upwards, reflecting both a growing urban population and increases in per capita water use. (See Chapter 4.) On the other hand, the effect of the existence of economies of scale is to cause supply to move in large, discrete steps. Hence, the characteristic pattern of system growth involves the periodic introduction of "over-capacity," and the eventual elimination of that cushion through steady

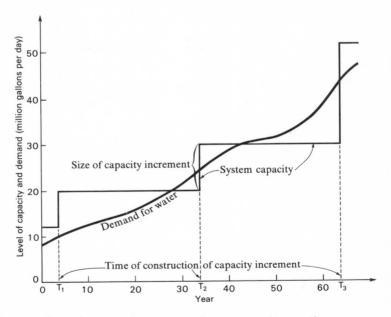

Figure 9. Illustrative trace of water use and system capacity over time.

demand growth, the latter in turn leading sooner or later to a further discrete increment to supply.[3]

Now, it is intuitively reasonable to suppose that the impact of any given climatic event (e.g., any given level of precipitation shortfall) will be different for systems with different relations between supply and demand. Thus, a system which has just completed a large addition to its capacity should probably be better able to meet the demands of its customers than one which has allowed demand growth to outrun available supply. This notion was already outlined schematically in Figures 3–5.

CAPACITY: THE SAFE YIELD OF SURFACE-WATER SOURCES

The basic supply capacity of a water system (as opposed to its distributional capacity) is a product of its flow and storage characteristics. Water inflow is randomly variable and is usually measured as precipitation, streamflow, runoff, or recharge. Storage, while not completely fixed, is much less varied and is usually measured by the volumetric capacity of reservoirs. Thus, the calculation of the safe yield of a surface-water supply system involves explicit dependence on probabilistic statements regarding rainfall and runoff. The conceptual difficulty here is that "supply" cannot be unambiguously defined except in reference to the probabilities of occurrence of a particular set of climatic events. Thus, we could for a given stream, readily construct a function relating to any particular streamflow the probability that at least that level of flow would be attained over any period. Then, in the absence of storage considerations, we could adopt some particular level of assurance (say 95 percent) and consider the corresponding flow as our "safe yield."[4]

Conceptually, the introduction of storage changes only the level of flow which can be attained with given assurance on the same stream (in, of course, the same climate). As the level of storage provided approaches infinity, the assured flow approaches the long-term mean flow of the stream. It is, however, important to bear in mind that the safe yield thus arrived at for a given stream and given storage is "safe" only to the extent that we consider the chosen probability level of assurance safe. There is no absolute safety here; the safe yield is *not* a minimum flow for the stream. Indeed, in principle the minimum flows for most streams are zero, although

[3] For the three water systems we studied which exhibited this characteristic pattern, new increments of supply were added, on the average, every 13 years, and the average size of the increments was 16 percent when measured against total safe yield existing at the time of addition.

[4] Here, too, we deal primarily with average annual flows.

the probabilities associated with extreme events in the neighborhood of zero flow are, for good-sized streams in humid areas, very small.

In practice, of course, we are not supplied with such complete information as that hypothesized above, and the practical difficulties of obtaining safe-yield estimates for particular streams are great. This is primarily the result of the fact that we have only a sample from the universe of possible streamflows for any particular stream. Hence, the best we can do is to estimate with more or less confidence the parameters of the streamflow frequency function. An additional important difficulty is, however, our lack of knowledge of the form of this frequency function. In particular, the question of the degree of serial correlation of streamflows has great bearing on the amount of storage needed to produce a given flow at a particular assurance level on a given stream.

In response to these difficulties, a number of methods of estimating storage/yield relations have been developed. The seminal work in the field was that of Rippl, in 1882.[5] His methods were subsequently extended by Hazen to cover more accurately the kind of problems actually faced by engineers.[6] These techniques have been further refined,[7] and now techniques are available for extracting a larger portion of the information from available streamflow records. One relatively new tool useful in this application is the estimation of complicated streamflow frequency functions from the records and the generation from these functions of long traces of "synthetic hydrology."[8]

More commonly used in practice is a method of estimating storage requirement which singles out a "design drought," or some specific period of historic low flows. Reservoirs are, then, designed to provide the required flow even under the precipitation/runoff conditions existing during the design drought. The required flow is then a "safe" yield in some probabilistic sense as discussed above, though here the probability statement remains implicit until the recurrence frequency of the design drought is analyzed.

[5] For an exposition of the Rippl method see Arthur Maass et al., *The Design of Water Resource Systems* (Cambridge: Harvard University Press, 1962), Ch. 3.

[6] Allen Hazen, "Storage to Be Provided in Impounding Reservoirs for Municipal Water Supply," *Transactions, American Society of Civil Engineers*, 77 (1914), 1539–1640.

[7] See, for example, Charles E. Sudler, "Storage Required for the Regulation of Streamflow," *Transactions, American Society of Civil Engineers*, 91(1927), 622; and M. B. Fiering, "Queuing Theory and Simulation in Reservoir Design," *Proceedings of the American Society of Civil Engineers, Journal of the Hydraulics Division*, 87, No. HY6 (1961), 39–70.

[8] M. M. Hufschmidt and M. B. Fiering, *Simulation Techniques for Water Resource Systems* (Cambridge: Harvard University Press, 1966).

It is this method which has been used to calculate the safe yield of almost all watersheds in Massachusetts. In 1914, the New England Water Works Association published the results of an exhaustive empirical study of watershed yields in the northeastern United States derived from the performance records of 22 drainage areas.[9] From these records were developed a series of curves which depicted the amount of storage capacity required to obtain specified yields of runoff in the watersheds studied, with variable amounts of the total watershed area being water surface. The runoff or yield in these curves is expressed in number of gallons per square mile of watershed. Of primary significance to this report was the fact that the lowest recorded flows on Massachusetts streams up to that time, and also the lowest series of low flows, had occurred during the period 1908–11 and were included as examples of the minimum flows "likely" to be experienced in the watersheds studied.

The importance to our study of this method of estimation is that it pegs the level of supply assurance for Massachusetts cities and towns in terms of the hydrologic severity of the 1908–11 drought. This allows us to discuss not only the likelihood of more severe events but also how much more severe such an event would be. Thus, not only can we say that the 1908–11 drought appears to have a 3 percent chance of recurrence and the recent drought about a 1 percent chance,[10] as shown in Chapter 6 below, but we can also associate with each drought a value for one or more variables which may serve as climatic indices.

In carrying out the specification of our model, we will find it convenient to turn to precipitation-based indices for climatic surrogates. A key hypothesis of the study will be that there is a fixed relation between the severity of a drought relative to the design drought (measured in terms of our index) and the level of the demand/supply (demand/safe-yield) ratio at which systems will begin to suffer shortages on account of the drought. This contention puts some analytical content in the general statements made above concerning the likelihood of shortage for towns with differing demand/ supply relations. The complete discussion of this matter will be set out in Chapter 6.

[9] "Report of the Committee on Yield of Drainage Areas," *Journal of the New England Water Works Association*, XXVIII (1914), 416.

[10] Because of the records we use in estimating these recurrence chances, we must say that the chance of recurrence of the 1908–11 drought is 7 out of 100 draws from a sample of 100 overlapping 4-year periods; that is, 1900–1903, 1901–04, 1902–05, 1903–06, etc.

CHAPTER 4

MEASUREMENT OF THE DEMAND FOR WATER

Water system managers tend to view the existing rate structure as given for the future as well as the present and to see their role as the provision of "all the water people want" at present prices.[1] Thus, observed variations in demand over time in the same city will generally be attributable to changes in non-price variables such as per capita income and the water-use characteristics of local industry. Differences between cities in the same year, however, will reflect differences in the level of water rates. Our interest is in the time-series variation for each city, and so we concentrate on non-price variables in examining variations in demand.

For example, the level of average per capita daily demand for water will vary between towns with the composition of demand. In particular, cities where a high proportion of total demand comes from industrial and commercial users will have higher per capita demand rates than cities where the major use of water is domestic. In our survey towns, the upper third of towns in terms of percentage of industrial demand (average industrial demand 60 percent of total) consumed an average of 178 gallons per day (gpd) per person between 1962 and 1966. In contrast, the lower third (average industrial demand 10 percent of total) consumed an average of 89 gpd per person during the same period.

In addition, the variation in use between different industries is very large in terms of gpd per employee or per dollar of value added. For example, in Fitchburg, water use per capita increased dramatically from about 1940

---

[1] This view is supported by the data on managers' attitudes reported below in Chapter 8 and by such examples of extreme historical rate constancy as that of New York City reported in Jack Hirshleifer, James C. DeHaven, and Jerome W. Milliman in *Water Supply: Economics, Technology, and Policy* (Chicago: University of Chicago Press, 1960), p. 263.

on with the growth of the plastics industry and the demise of the textile industry even though population and total employment showed little change.

The growth of demand is, of course, the product of a number of different influences. In particular places, shifts in the composition of the industrial sector can, as just reported, cause significant corresponding shifts in demand. The rate of growth of population will be reflected to some extent in the rate of growth of demand. In general, a high rate of population growth will accentuate the rate of growth of demand which results from a set of influences common to virtually all urban and suburban areas. Particularly important among these latter factors has been the widespread adoption by households of water-using appliances and devices such as home laundries, air-conditioning equipment, dishwashers, and garbage disposals.[2] Another major factor has been suburbanization, with the attendant growth in the acreage of lawn and garden space. The demand for water to irrigate these planted areas has affected virtually all municipal water systems.[3]

The net impact of these several influences will, of course, differ from community to community. But in Massachusetts a common rule of thumb cited by engineers suggests that the long-term average annual increase in per capita daily water use in the past was on the order of 1 to 1.5 gallons per year. For 25 communities from our detailed survey, however, the average annual increase in per capita daily consumption between the years 1950 and 1962 was 3.4 gallons.

MEASUREMENT: RECORDED CONSUMPTION

The measurements of municipal water use, or consumption, used throughout this study are those made by the individual cities and towns in the sample. The figures used for the calculation of demand (i.e., average per capita daily consumption, P), are based on the total water system outputs of the communities studied, as opposed to the amount of water passing through customers' meters. These records are of differing origin, some

[2] See John C. Geyer, Jerome B. Wolff, and F. P. Linaweaver, Jr., "Final and Summary Report on Phase One of the Residential Water Use Research Project," Department of Sanitary Engineering and Water Resources, The Johns Hopkins University, Baltimore, Oct. 1963.

[3] F. P. Linaweaver, Jr., John C. Geyer, and Jerome B. Wolff, "Final and Summary Report on the Residential Water Use Research Project," Department of Environmental Engineering Science, The Johns Hopkins University, Baltimore, June 1966. Linaweaver, et al. reach the conclusion that "for practical use in design, water distribution systems serving metered residential areas with gross densities of about seven homes per acre or less should be designed to supply irrigation water in an amount equivalent to evapotranspiration from a crop of grass covering the entire area served."

being meter readings from source outflows, others estimates based on pump use. Similarly, their quality varies with the accuracy of the equipment involved and the care with which readings were made and recorded. In addition, of course, there will generally be a discrepancy between system output as measured at the source and the total quantity delivered to customer meters. This wastage was determined for 23 of our study cities and, expressed as a percentage of output, averaged about 17 percent over this subsample.[4]

RELATIONSHIP BETWEEN RECORDED CONSUMPTION AND DEMAND

A more fundamental observation for our efforts to measure historic demand is the fact that the recorded consumption for any given year in a particular town, even if accurately measured, need not reflect the average level of demand at the existing price. Leaving aside the imposition of restrictions due to low supplies, any number of other major and minor disturbances could cause differences between the average level of demand and the actual level of consumption. For example, distribution difficulties could lead to the imposition of restrictions on peak period uses such as lawn-sprinkling; strikes on the one hand or overtime work on the other could shift the water use for one or more significant industrial firms.

These considerations suggest that the recorded values for consumption (say, average per capita per day) should be "smoothed," and the resulting trend lines considered as representing the path of demand over time. This approach will be more or less well grounded depending on the extent to which there really are a fairly large number of independent random disturbances acting to make observed consumption different from demand (again abstracting from the pure measurement problems).

Our particular approach to this matter of smoothing the recorded consumption data is to assume, first, that the major influences on the growth of per capita demand can be represented simply by time itself. But, while this might be acceptable as a first approximation, additional reflection suggests that it ignores at least two factors affecting the level of demand which may not be correlated with time. Because we are ultimately interested in projection of demand for individual years and not simply in the identification of trends, it is necessary for us to take account of such additional influences.

The most important such factor surely is weather, particularly through its effect on lawn-sprinkling. A priori we would also expect the pace of

[4] This compares with the average percentage of unaccounted for water in United States waterworks of 15 percent, cited in Gordon M. Fair, John C. Geyer, and Daniel A. Okun, *Water and Waste Water Engineering* (New York: Wiley, 1966), I, 5–15.

economic activity, especially as reflected in the industrial sector, to play a significant part in modifications of water demand from the trend level. (This will be true to the extent that the correlation between economic activity and time is not so close as to obscure the independent impact of the former.)

Accordingly, our method is to estimate the parameters in the regression equation:

$$P_t = a + b_1 t + b_2 W_t + b_3 E_t + e_t \qquad (4\text{-}1)$$

for each of the 47 communities for which we have sufficient data. In the equation:

P_t = the observed consumption in year t in gallons per day per capita.

t = time, running from year 0 (1950) to year 12 (1962), giving 13 observations. (For several towns, one or more observations on P_t were missing.)

W_t = a weather index for year t. It equals the sum of the Palmer Drought Index[5] over the 4 summer months of year t. This index is available for the western, central, and coastal regions of the state; not for any finer division.

E_t = an index of industrial employment in the particular community in year t. 1950 level of employment = 100.[6,7]

e_t = an error term, assumed to have the usual convenient properties.

We use only the years through 1962 in our analysis, because, by 1963, the drought had begun all over the state, and our major purpose is to project demand levels into the drought period when for many systems they could be expected to be greater than actual deliveries. (See the discussion of the time pattern of the onset of drought across the state in Chapter 6.)

[5] The derivation of the Palmer Drought Index is shown in Chapter 6.

[6] This index of the pace of economic activity was chosen because of its availability on a town-by-town basis through the publications of the Massachusetts Department of Labor and Industries, Division of Statistics, particularly their *Employment Newsletter*. It would, of course, have been preferable to have an index of production such as value-added in constant dollars. Such an index could have been developed for some of our towns for some of the years of interest, but not for every year in any town. This was the result of the combination of spatial and temporal gaps in the coverage of the *Census of Manufactures*, published occasionally by the same Massachusetts agency.

[7] Unfortunately, we did not have sufficient information to use either demand composition by sector or industrial sector makeup as explanatory variables.

34   *Water Supply and Demand*

TABLE 5. SUMMARY OF RESULTS OF REGRESSION ANALYSIS

Equation estimated:

$$P_t = a_t + b_1 t + b_2 W_t + b_3 E_t + e_t$$

1. Of 47 trials *33* resulted in significant relationships (as measured by the *F*-ratio test) at the 0.05 level.

    Median r^2 for 33 significant relations   *0.834*

2. Estimated b_1 significant at 0.05 level by *t*-test in *25* cases. (Range of b_1 values: -3.12 to 10.82; mean $= 3.58$)

3. Estimated b_2 values significant at 0.05 level by *t*-test in 9 cases. (Range of b_2 values: -6.88 to -0.24; mean $= -0.76$)

4. Estimated b_3 significant at 0.05 level by *t*-test in 7 cases.

    (Range of b_3 values: -1.19 to 1.90; mean $= 0.55$)

Note: If we apply a significance test to the *numbers of successes* in each "trial" listed above, we find that the first two results could have occurred by chance only with probability less than 0.0010; the last result is significant at the 1 percent level.

Our results are summarized in Table 5.[8] We note from this table that both time and weather behaved rather well as explanatory variables, while the employment index behaved badly. This is primarily the result of the multicollinearity between time and employment in our data. Since we are interested primarily in projection of *P* into the four drought years, however, we need not be particularly concerned over this. It is reasonable to expect that the relation between time and employment which has interfered with our results above will continue over the short projection period and hence that our projection will not suffer.

[8] A similar analysis of the determinants of per capita demand was made for four towns (Fall River, Fitchburg, Pittsfield, and Worcester) for the period 1929–62. Again, time, the summer Palmer Index value, and an employment index were used as explanatory variables. The results achieved do not differ in any significant way from those discussed above. Generally high *r*-squares were obtained (median $= 0.92$), and time was the strongest explanatory variable. The coefficients for employment and weather were each significant in only one town, though *P* was strongly related to employment in three towns. (Collinearity of time and employment was again a problem, even though the distinctive employment pattern of the depression years was reflected in the values used.)

PART II

CLIMATIC VARIATION, THE LEVEL OF SHORTAGE, AND THE NATURE OF SHORT-RUN ADJUSTMENTS

CHAPTER 5

PROJECTION OF DEMAND AND MEASUREMENT OF SHORTAGE

The heart of the impact of drought on a water system is the creation of a discrepancy between the demand for water at the existing prices and weather and the available supply. The losses which arise from a "drought" are the results of decisions as to how to deal with this discrepancy; that is, particularly, decisions to ration the limited supply through restrictions or to augment the normal sources with "emergency supplies." In order that our study might provide us with the information we desired for planning applications, we needed to be able to relate observed shortages to both the measured severity of the drought and the chosen adjustment levels of the systems involved. But just what are "observed shortages" in terms of the measures we have been discussing?

THE DEFINITION OF SHORTAGE

One straightforward and reasonable way of obtaining a measure of system shortages during the several years of the recent drought is to project into this period our estimates of per capita daily demand based on the regression equations of Chapter 4, and values of the weather and employment indices appropriate to each community and year. Multiplication of these projections by 365 and by population produces an estimate of total annual demand which may be compared with observed system output.[1]

If projected demand is found to be greater than observed consumption for a particular city and year, it is reasonable to say that that city suffered a water shortage in that year. We may, in addition, transform the absolute

---

[1] See Chapter 4 for a brief comment on the difference between system output and deliveries to customers.

amount of shortage into a percentage figure by dividing it by the projected demand level.

In order to express this definition symbolically, we use the following notation:

P_{it} = projected per capita daily demand for water from system i in year t for given price, and for known weather and employment conditions (from our regression analysis of the last section).

C_{it} = observed total annual consumption of water from system i in year t.

N_{it} = population served by system i in year t.

S_{it} = water shortage (as a percentage of projected demand) suffered by system i in year t.

Then in per capita per day terms we have:

$$S_{it} = \frac{P_{it} - \dfrac{C_{it}}{N_{it} \cdot 365}}{P_{it}} \times 100. \tag{5-1}$$

If we let $D_{it} \equiv P_{it} \cdot N_{it'} \cdot 365$ (total, annual projected demand), we have in total annual terms:

$$S_{it} = \frac{D_{it} - C_{it}}{D_{it}} \times 100. \tag{5-2}$$

It will not always be correct, however, to use actual consumption alone in our measurement of shortage. As noted earlier, in many instances a community threatened with potential shortage will choose to reduce or eliminate the gap by obtaining emergency supplies, for example, by pumping from a nearby recreational lake into the reservoir system. But, though no consumer may actually lack water, there is still clearly an opportunity cost involved for the community, and indeed for the society as a whole. Thus, if we wish to connect the severity of drought (in shortage terms) with its costs, we will certainly wish to measure the original gap and to include the costs of emergency supplies along with the other losses.

These considerations lead us to define another quantity, Normal System Supply (V_{it}) as the actual consumption (C_{it}) less the amount of emergency supplies (E_{it}) obtained by system i in year t.[2] Thus, symbolically, we have,

---

[2] Some measurement problems arose here in addition to the expected one of doubtful record quality. Some systems which obtained emergency supplies used these not only to meet current demands but also to attempt to refill lowered reservoirs. Whenever we had information that this had been done, we attempted to make appropriate corrections for it.

$$V_{it} \equiv C_{it} - E_{it}.^3 \qquad (5\text{-}3)$$

Shortage, then, is correctly and completely defined as the percentage difference between potential demand and normal system supply; thus, in per capita per day terms:

$$S_{it} = \frac{P_{it} - \dfrac{V_{it}}{N_{it} \cdot 365}}{P_{it}} \times 100 = \frac{P_{it} - \left[\dfrac{C_{it} - E_{it}}{N_{it} \cdot 365}\right]}{P_{it}} \times 100; \qquad (5\text{-}4)$$

and, in total annual terms:

$$S_{it} = \frac{D_{it} - V_{it}}{D_{it}} \times 100 = \frac{D_{it} - (C_{it} - E_{it})}{D_{it}} \times 100. \qquad (5\text{-}5)$$

THE MEASUREMENT OF SHORTAGE

The actual sample of cities for which shortage measurements for the drought years were available was established in the following way. For 33 systems, we had significant regression relations as discussed in Chapter 4. For 5 of these, however, data were not available on actual consumption in one or more of the drought years. The latter five systems were omitted from the sample because we wished to use the same set of systems in each drought year in testing hypotheses about the relation between climatic severity, level of adjustment, and observed shortage. Thus, we began with a set of demand projections for each of 28 systems for the years 1963 through 1966.

As noted in Chapter 4, there are certain difficulties with our projection equations, and it seemed desirable to test them in some way. To do this, we compared our projections of average per capita daily consumption with observed consumption for each of nine cities in the four years 1963–66. These nine cities had neither imposed restrictions nor obtained emergency supplies during the drought, and hence we had reason to hope that any discrepancy between predicted and observed consumption would not, at least, be due to problems of supply. A more complete discussion of the

---

[3] In principle, normal system yield should be defined to exclude net drawdown of overyear storage. In our original work, we viewed a 4-year drought period as a single demand period and hence were able to assume relatively full reservoirs at the beginning of 1963 and at the end of 1966, leaving no net drawdown. Some of the difficulty we find in considering each year separately is undoubtedly traceable to the fact that, particularly in the early drought years, shortages never appear because of net drawdowns. It seems, however, that this means of dealing with the drought proved inadequate as the dry spell stretched into 1964 and reservoir levels fell. Thus, 1965 and 1966 are probably relatively free of the problem since the refilling of reservoirs in 1966 was almost entirely confined to the fall, after the high consumption period had passed.

test and its results is contained in Appendix A. We confine ourselves to noting here that:

For 5 of the 9 cities, our average prediction error over the 4-year period was less than 10 percent; for 7 it was less than 15 percent.

In no year was the average prediction error across the towns greater than 1.2 percent.

Of the total of 36 errors calculated (9 cities over 4 years), 18 were less than 10 percent and 29 were less than 15 percent.

While there is no apparent bias in our predictions when applied to the group of towns, there is a tendency consistently to over- or under-estimate for a particular city over the period. Thus, for only one city does the sign of the prediction error change over the period.

We are now prepared to measure the shortages suffered by various Massachusetts cities during the drought. Two major tasks remain in our effort to extract useful planning information from this study: first, these shortages must be related to chosen levels of adjustment and severity of climatic events; and second, losses must be attached to various levels of shortage suffered. As our next step in the direction of completing these tasks, we consider in Chapter 6 the measurement and perception of climatic variation.

CLIMATIC VARIATION:
MEASUREMENT AND PERCEPTION

Since "climate" is really a multidimensional concept, involving temperature, precipitation, solar radiation, and other factors, variation in the
climate may take any of a large number of forms. All of these are more or
less remotely relevant to drought. For example, it is clear that variations
in the number of cloudless days per summer and in average summer temperatures will affect both the demand for water deliveries—especially
through increased lawn irrigation—and the available supply in a surface
storage system—through surface evaporation. It is, however, the variation
in precipitation that is most closely associated with drought. For example,
the recent drought period was characterized by cooler-than-average temperatures over the Northeast.[1] We will confine our discussion of climatic
variation to that observed in precipitation and related series.

We chose to use precipitation rather than streamflow records as our
basic climatic measures for several reasons. First, precipitation records are
more extensive in areal and temporal coverage, and extended series could
be developed for each of the systems studied in detail.[2] In addition, precipitation records, while subject to the vagaries of change in station location, are not as easily affected as streamflow by the permanent changes
(only partly understood) that accompany urbanization.[3] Finally, we felt it

[1] See Jerome Namias, "Nature and Possible Causes of the Northeastern United
States Drought during 1962–65," *Monthly Weather Review*, XCIV (1966), 543–54.

[2] Streamflow records were not, in general, available for this purpose. Some Massachusetts streams have very long records, but others were not even being recorded during
the 1908–11 period of design drought.

[3] For a discussion of the hydrologic changes attributable to urbanization, see John
Savini and J. C. Kammerer, *Urban Growth and the Water Regimen*, Water Supply Paper
1591a (Washington: U.S. Government Printing Office, 1961); and Luna Leopold,
Hydrology for Urban Land Planning, Circular 554 (Washington: U.S. Geological
Survey, 1968). A review of the runoff process and an explanation of its complexity are
given in *Handbook of Applied Hydrology*, Ven Te Chow, ed. (New York: McGraw-Hill,
1964), 14/4–14/5.

significant that precipitation records were the measures of climate preferred by our respondent managers, 27 percent of whom employed rainfall
measurements or rainfall plus measures of the behavior of the water
storage system to define drought. In contrast, none of the superintendents
interviewed utilized streamflow in this way. (See Table 8 and our later
discussion of managers' perception of climate.)

LONG-TERM ANNUAL PRECIPITATION SERIES: DESCRIPTION

The specific precipitation records which we used in developing measures
of climatic variation were those for stations at Fall River, Fitchburg,
Pittsfield, and Worcester. These sites were chosen in connection with other
studies of engineering reports and additions to system capacity.[4] The stations used in the analysis are shown in Figure 10, and a summary of sources,

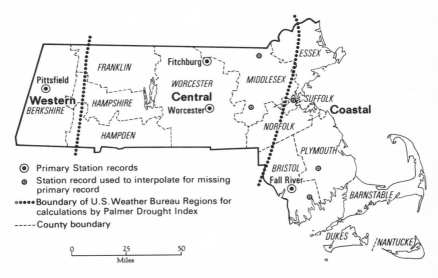

Figure 10. Stations used in rainfall analysis.

record lengths, and relevant statistics is given in Table 6. The most striking
features of this table are the high autocorrelations exhibited by three of the
series; only Fall River's record fails to show first-order autocorrelation at

---

[4] The records were assembled with the interpolation of missing values from a regional
gaging station network. See J. L. H. Paulhus and M. A. Kohler, "Interpolation of
Missing Precipitation Records," *Monthly Weather Review*, LXXX (1952), 129–33. It
has since been suggested to us that regression methods of interpolation might have been
preferable.

the 95 percent confidence level.[5] We note also that we found no evidence of trend for any of the series and that, as we would expect, the series are highly intercorrelated, the degree of this intercorrelation varying inversely with the distance between the sites.

TABLE 6. STATISTICS OF RECORDS FOR STATIONS USED IN ANNUAL PRECIPITATION SERIES

Station	Record length	Mean annual precipitation	Standard deviation of annual precipitation	First-order autocorrelation coefficient	Evidence[a] of trend	Correlations Between Records			
						Fall River	Fitchburg	Worcester	Pittsfield
	(*years*)	(*inches*)	(*inches*)						
Fall River	96	45.0	6.66	0.119[b]	None	1.000	0.606	0.708	0.506[c]
Fitchburg	96	42.4	7.56	0.383	None	0.606	1.000	0.832	0.609[c]
Worcester	96	44.1	6.65	0.250	None	0.708	0.832	1.000	0.554[c]
Pittsfield	66	40.5	5.24	0.428	None	0.506[c]	0.609[c]	0.554[c]	1.000

Sources: U.S. Weather Bureau, *Climatology of the U.S.*, No. 10–23 (1955), 11–23 (1958), and 86–23 (Washington: U.S. Government Printing Office, 1964). U.S. Weather Bureau, *Climatological Data*, Annual Summaries, Volumes 72–77 (Washington: U.S. Government Printing Office, 1960–66). E. K. Knox and R. M. Soule, *Hydrology of Massachusetts*, Part 1, U.S. Geological Survey, Water Supply Paper 1105 (Washington: U.S. Government Printing Office, 1949).

[a] Evidence of trend was taken to exist if the regression of annual rainfall on time was significant (as measured by the F-test) at the 5 percent level.

[b] Not significant at the 5 percent level. Test for significance of autocorrelation coefficient based on R. H. Anderson, "Distribution of the Serial Correlation Coefficient," *Annals of Mathematical Statistics*, XIII (1942), 1–13.

[c] The correlation coefficients involving Pittsfield were computed using 68 years for which all four records are complete, 1899–1966.

TRANSFORMATION OF THE PRECIPITATION SERIES

In order to capture the persistency feature of the drought, we experimented with several moving-sum transformations of the annual data. We chose to use as our basic transformation a 4-year cumulation of deviations from the long-term mean for each series. The choice of period length was made primarily on the grounds that four years seemed to span the critical portions of the two important New England droughts of this century:

[5] This finding was not expected and runs counter to the intuition of experienced hydrologists. There is, however, evidence that while precipitation records in relatively dry climates exhibit serial independence, the degree of serial correlation will increase with increases in the humidity of the climate. See, for example, V. M. Yevdjevich, *Fluctuations of Wet and Dry Years, Part II, Analysis of Serial Correlation*, Hydrology Papers, No. 4 (Fort Collins, Colo.: Colorado State University, 1964), pp. 42–48.

1908–11 (used by engineers as the "design drought") and 1963–66.[6] In symbolic terms, the value of our transformed variable in year t is given by:

$$\Delta_t \equiv \sum_{j=t-3}^{t} (R_j - \overline{R}); \qquad (6\text{-}1)$$

where R_j is the precipitation total for year j, $\overline{R}$ is the long-term mean of annual precipitation, and Δ_t is the cumulated deviation. The relevant statistics for the four series of cumulated deviations are presented in Table 7 and the series are shown graphically in Figure 11.

TABLE 7. STATISTICS FOR CUMULATED PRECIPITATION SERIES

Station	Mean	Standard devia-tion	First-order correlation coefficient	Fall River	Fitch-burg	Worces-ter	Pitts-field[a]
				Correlations Between Series			
	(*inches*)	(*inches*)					
Fall River	+3.40	14.37	0.778	1.000	0.523	0.755	0.519
Fitchburg	+4.55	20.31	0.855	0.523	1.000	0.867	0.512
Worcester	+2.44	16.16	0.833	0.755	0.867	1.000	0.408
Pittsfield	+1.48	14.90	0.826	0.519	0.512	0.408	1.000

[a] See note 3 to Table 6.

The series of cumulative deviations all exhibit, of course, very strong first-order autocorrelation. This has been guaranteed by the moving-sum process itself. We note also that the correlations between the series are roughly as they were before, though in general somewhat higher. The means of the series are all positive, though close to zero.

From the figure we can see that there have been four major periods of precipitation shortfall over the last 100 years in Massachusetts, with the trough years being 1883, 1911, 1943 (or 44), and 1966. The depth of these droughts varies from station to station for each event, but the recent period was clearly the most severe one at Fall River and Pittsfield. In central Massachusetts (represented by Worcester and Fitchburg), the period of the 1880's was an event of even greater intensity. In addition, it appears from the figure that the recent drought "moved" from west to east across the state. If we adopt some arbitrary level of severity for purposes of comparison—for example, a cumulated precipitation deficit of 10 inches—we find that this level was reached in 1962 at Pittsfield, in 1964 at Fitchburg,

[6] Originally, we also felt it would be desirable to maintain comparability with a study conducted by the Massachusetts Water Resources Commission which stressed the cumulated precipitation deficiency over the critical drought period. This did not turn out to be a significant advantage as our study progressed.

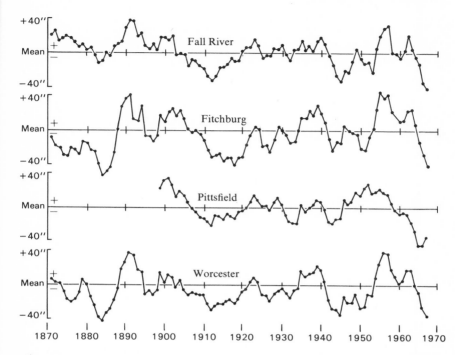

Figure 11. Four-year cumulative deviations from mean of annual precipitation in 4 Massachusetts Communities, 1867–1966.

and in 1965 at Fall River and Worcester. By the beginning of 1967 at Pittsfield the cumulated deviation series had turned up, while at the other sites, the turning point had not yet been reached.[7]

In order to produce a distribution of climatic events roughly typical of the state for later use in the estimation of actual shortages and in the derivation of expected loss functions, we pooled the deviation series for the

[7] Another measure of climatic severity which we may use in assessing the duration and timing of the stress of precipitation shortfall across Massachusetts is the Palmer Index. This is a measure of the moisture stress placed on plants and was developed by W. C. Palmer on the basis of earlier work by C. W. Thornthwaite. In it, "normal" weather produces a value of zero while drought conditions are indicated by negative numbers, with extremely dry conditions giving readings in the neighborhood of −4.0. Through the cooperation of the U.S. Weather Bureau, the Index values for three broad regions of the state (western, central, and coastal), were made available to us for the years 1929 through 1966. By this measure, the period of drought stressful to the natural world began in 1961 in the west, 1962 in the center of the state, and in 1963 along the coast. Its extreme value (−5.00) was reached in the west in 1965. In the same year the central region stress also appeared to reach bottom at −4.14. The index was still falling in 1966 for the coastal area. (Figures based on average of 4 summer months for each year.)

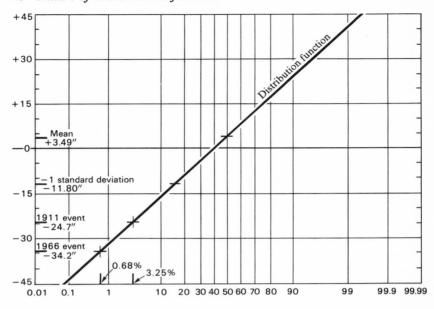

Figure 12. Pooled record distribution function for cumulative precipitation deviations.

three 96-year records (Fitchburg, Worcester, and Fall River). It may be shown that if the three deviation series are considered to be drawn from a trivariate normal distribution, the series of weighted sums of the observations is distributed as the univariate normal distribution with moments given (where each series is weighted equally) by:

$$\mu_s = \sum_{i=1}^{3} 1/3\mu_i$$

and

$$\sigma_s{}^2 = \sum_{i=1}^{3} 1/9\sigma_i{}^2 + 2 \sum_{\substack{i<j \\ i=1}}^{3} 1/9\rho_{ij}\sigma_i\sigma_j,$$

where:

μ_s = the mean of the statewide series;

μ_i = the mean of the series for the ith site;

σ_s = the variance of the statewide series;

σ_i = the standard deviation of the series for the ith site; and

ρ_{ij} = the correlation coefficient between the series for the ith and jth sites,[8] for the pooled series.

[8] See, for example, Alexander M. Mood and Franklin A. Graybill, *Introduction to the Theory of Statistics* (New York: McGraw-Hill, 1963), p. 211. This approach to the

These moments as calculated from the three individual-site series are:

μ_s = 3.49 inches
σ_s = 15.29 inches

On the basis of the moments for the pooled series, we may draw the graph of the cumulative distribution function for 4-year precipitation deviations (Figure 12). On it, we also show the recurrence frequencies for the 1908–11 and 1963–66 droughts. These frequencies are based on the severity of the 4-year cumulative deviations (averaged for the three stations) as of the last year of the generally accepted drought period (1911 and 1966).[9] As shown on the graph, the cumulated precipitation deficiency as of 1911 was an event which could be expected to occur over the long run in about 3.25 percent of the years. The 1966 event, on this same basis, would occur on the average in only 0.68 percent of the years.

This pooled series will be used in Chapter 7, in combination with system inadequacy data, in predicting shortages for a sample of cities for which actual shortage estimates are available.[10] This exercise forms the basis of our assessment of the physical impact of drought.

"pooling" of our records seems adequate for our purposes here, though it is not the most efficient use of the data. The question of an efficient method for pooling non-independent series to estimate recurrence frequencies of extreme events is currently being investigated by the U.S. Geological Survey. For independent series, a pooling method is described in W. J. Conover and M. A. Benson, "Long-Term Flood Frequencies Based on Extremes of Short-Term Records," *Geological Survey Research 1962*, Professional Paper 450-E (Washington: U.S. Government Printing Office, 1962), 159–60.

[9] By a similar set of calculations, we may compute the moments of a probability distribution reflecting all four of our records over their 68 common years. These are:

$$\mu_s = .95'' \text{ and } \sigma_s = 13.23''$$

Using this distribution the recurrence frequencies are:

For 1908–11—3.45 percent
For 1963–66—0.47 percent

[10] As will become clear in the next chapter, one of our interests in working with our indices of climatic variation is to measure the severity of the climatic stress on a water supply system relative to that stress encountered during the design-drought period 1908–11. At one point it seemed desirable to broaden our inquiry to include streamflows and to estimate the relation between rainfall and streamflows for the areas of Massachusetts with which we were working. This led us to compare streamflow and precipitation records in simple regressions. The results of these regressions were not sufficiently good, nor were their subsequent applications in our drought-impact description sufficiently valuable to us, to justify the considerable tedious detail in which reporting them would involve us. Suffice it to say that working with annual precipitation and streamflow figures leaves one with considerable unexplained variation in the latter which we hypothesize is due largely to the differential runoffs from precipitation of the same amount occurring in different seasons. Thus a large storm in March while the ground is still

MANAGERS' PERCEPTION OF CLIMATIC VARIATION

The analysis of climatic variation so far presented in this chapter represents one set of perceptions as to the recurrence of extreme events. The perceptions of the system managers themselves are also important, for a complete understanding of the role of drought in water supply systems requires estimates of duration, recurrence, and intensity as held by the operators of the system as well as the estimates of the actual recurrence. Fortunately there is relatively little divergence between the two sets of estimates, although managers appeared somewhat more pessimistic than we were. However, those differences might occur simply because of the different terms of reference employed in our analysis and in the respondent answers to our questions.

First, we used in the original interview schedule the term "drought" to describe past and current situations of water shortage which are the joint product of climatic variation and system inadequacy. Thus, estimates of the recurrence of "drought" were colored for all managers by estimates of their supply capacity.

Secondly, managers face many of the same problems that we faced in studying drought frequency. What is the best measure of climatic events? What is the appropriate duration unit? Are climatic events independent events? Is there periodicity or persistence in climatic events that contributes to drought?

These questions were not clearly seen as issues at the time we planned the study. Thus, many of them either were not posed at all or were inadequately posed to the sample of respondent managers. It was, however, clear from the answers to our questions that managerial personnel use an operational definition of drought rather than a climatological one. Indication of drought occurrence was derived primarily from measurement data referring to the behavior of community storage systems. This suggests that our definition of drought as a water shortage imposing social costs corresponds with empirical evidence on managerial behavior. As shown in Table 8, fully 58 percent of the superintendents rely solely on system measurements such as reservoir or groundwater levels to indicate drought, while 79 percent use system measures alone or in combination with rainfall data.

frozen will probably have a substantially larger impact on streamflow than a similar storm in August.

For some related work also aiming at using precipitation records to make statements about probabilities of low flows see: F. A. Huff and S. A. Changnan, Jr., "Relation Between Precipitation Deficiency and Low Streamflow," *Journal of Geophysical Research*, LXIX (1964), 605–13.

TABLE 8. TYPES OF DATA USED BY SYSTEM MANAGERS TO INDICATE THAT THE DROUGHT WAS AFFECTING THEIR WATER SUPPLY

	Number of managers	Percentage of total
A. System measures alone		
1. Reservoir level only	16	33.3
2. Groundwater level only	4	8.3
3. Reservoir and groundwater level	8	16.7
Subtotal for A	28	58.3
B. System measures in combination with rainfall data		
1. Rainfall and reservoir level	10	20.8
2. Rainfall and groundwater level	0	0
Subtotal for B	10	20.8
Subtotal for A + B	38	79.1
C. Rainfall data alone	2	4.2
D. Other data		
1. Rainfall and "other" data	1	2.1
2. Safe-yield or water-use data	6	12.5
3. External advice	1	2.1
Subtotal for D	8	16.7
Grand Total	48	100.0

Perception of the Beginning of the Drought

On the average, the water managers who responded to our questions about timing saw the drought as beginning approximately 1½ years after the date suggested by the Palmer Index for their region. This lag time represents, no doubt, the year or more of grace provided by most municipal storage systems.[11] Indeed, this lag may be seen as evidence of the usefulness of our definition of drought; for purely meteorological drought, as defined by the Palmer Index, may or may not have an impact on a particular system, depending on the relative inadequacy of that system. The meteorological conditions required to push the Palmer Index just over the edge into the drought range are still far more favorable than those corresponding to safe-yield flows. Hence even systems with demand much greater than safe yield will not feel a pinch in the first year of a "Palmer" drought.

The lag time in perception varied significantly, however, among the water managers. Of the 27 respondents, eight (30 percent) felt that the

[11] For further evidence on this drawdown-of-storage phenomenon, see the results of testing the model as reported in Chapter 7.

drought began in the same year as indicated by the Palmer Index; eleven (44 percent) perceived the beginning with at least a 2-year lag; four (15 percent) with a 3-year lag (Table 9). There was a tendency for this lag to be shorter for managers whose systems were affected later by meteorological drought. Thus, in 1961, the communities of two of our respondents were affected by "drought" according to the Palmer Index, but it was not until two years later that the water managers in these communities felt that their systems were affected. This lag averaged 1.2 years for managers whose communities were affected in 1962 and only 6 months for those affected in 1963.

TABLE 9. MANAGERS' PERCEPTION OF BEGINNING OF DROUGHT

Manager's region	Actual beginning (Palmer Index)	Manager Perceived Drought as Beginning						
		Earlier	Same year	1-year lag	2-year lag	3-year lag	4-year lag	Total
Western	1961	0	0	0	0	2	0	2
Central	1962	0	4	5	4	2		15
Coastal	1963	0	4	3	3			10
Total		0	8	8	7	4	0	27
Percentage of total[a]		0	30	30	26	15	0	

[a] Percentages do not add to 100.0 because of rounding.

Thus, the managers seem to have been influenced by a "bandwagon" effect. As more communities officially or unofficially recognized the problem, it became easier for other managers to do so also. Indeed, it may very well be that drought was "perceived" because public concern demanded it, rather than because of actual system inadequacy relative to climatic events. This suggestion is supported by such evidence as could be constructed relating time of perception to conditions of shortage or surplus existing at that time.[12] These data are available for 13 communities. In three of these, drought was perceived as a problem when our calculations show an available surplus of water. In the other 10, the range of shortages at time of perception was from 1 to 19 percent.

Perception of the End of the Drought

As for the end of the drought, those managers who were willing to take a stand were about evenly divided between those who thought the drought

[12] Shortage was defined in Chapter 5 as the percentage difference between projected demand and actual deliveries from the normal water system.

had ended and those who believed it had not. (Note that these interviews were conducted in the summer of 1966.) The results on this point are summarized in Table 10. The ambivalence apparent in the responses to the question about the end of the drought may simply represent an expected division of people into groups of optimists, pessimists, and "skeptics," or it may be an indication of lack of dependence on expert advice. At the time of these interviews, no public statements had been made by such agencies as the U.S. Geological Survey, the Massachusetts Water Resources Commission, and the U.S. Weather Bureau either indicating the termination of the drought or its continuation past the summer of 1966. In the absence of expert assessments of the likely course of the future, the managers apparently relied on intuition and the behavior of their own water systems. Such inductive reasoning regarding natural events has been noted in the past.[13]

TABLE 10. MANAGERS' PERCEPTION OF END OF DROUGHT
(QUESTION: HAD DROUGHT ENDED BY THE SUMMER OF 1966?)

	Yes	No	Can't tell	External sources say yes-no	Not ascertained	Total
Number of managers answering	20	17	8	2	1	48

Perception of the end of the drought appears to be unrelated to the emergency status of the community, its location in the state, the severity or progress of the drought as measured by the Palmer Index, or the type of storage system used by the community.

By combining interview information on when the managers believed the drought began and whether or not they thought it had ended, it is possible to determine how long at least some of the managers believed the drought was. Doing this, we find that 10 of the 12 respondents for whom we could define the duration period saw the drought as a 3- or 4-year event (Table 11). This is considerably shorter than the 4- to 6-year period indicated by the Palmer Index. Once again we turn to the main source of the managers' perceptions, system performance, for a likely explanation of this discrepancy between the perceived world and the "objectively" measured world. It is not difficult to imagine that whereas the first year of drought is discounted by the drawdown of storage, the last year (or more) may be

[13] See Ian Burton and Robert Kates, "The Perception of Natural Hazards in Resource Management," *Natural Resources Journal,* III (1964), 434.

TABLE 11. DROUGHT DURATION PERCEIVED BY MANAGERS BELIEVING DROUGHT
HAD ENDED BY SUMMER OF 1966
(QUESTION: HAS THE DROUGHT ENDED?)

Duration when answer was yes	Section			
	Western	Central	Coastal	Total
(years)				
1	0	0	0	0
2	0	1	0	1
3	1	3	1	5
4	0	2	3[a]	5
5	0	1[a]	0	1
6	0[a]	0	0	0
Total ascertained	1	7	4	12
Total not ascertained[b]	1	4	3	8
Total believing drought over in 1966	2	11	7	20
(% of total interviews)	50	44	37	
Total interviews	4	25	19	48

[a] Duration as measured by the Palmer Drought Index.

[b] Managers who believed drought was over but who gave no answer on year of its beginning.

similarly discounted because of successful adjustments to reduce supply through water restrictions or other demand-reducing measures.

Another interesting feature of Table 11 is the variation across the state in the percentage of managers definitely feeling the drought was over in 1966. From 50 percent in the west, this figure shrinks to 37 percent along the coast. In this, our climatic statistics support the perception of the managers, for we find the drought moderating in the western part of the state in 1966, but peaking along the coast in that same year. (See Figure 11 and footnote 7 in this chapter.)

Perception of Severity and Recurrence Frequency. Other perceptual questions related to the comparative severity and recurrence interval of droughts. The drought of the sixties was by far the worst drought within the memory of the system managers. Table 12 shows that only 4 managers cited drought events which they believed to have been more serious.

Two different methods were used in eliciting frequency of recurrence estimates.[14] In response to these questions, managers' modal estimate of

[14] Note that the questions asked in this area did not properly distinguish between "droughts" of one or more years, nor were they entirely explicit on the severity of the event, the recurrence interval of which was to be estimated.

TABLE 12. MANAGERS' PERCEPTION OF RELATIVE SEVERITY OF PAST DROUGHTS

	No.	Percent
Past droughts were:		
All less severe than 1963–66	36	75.0
As severe as 1963–66	4	8.3
More severe than 1963–66	4	8.3
No answer, not ascertained	4	8.3
	48	99.9

the recurrence frequency of a drought similar to the one being experienced was once in 25 years. If we ignore for the moment problems raised by differing perceptions of the *length* of the drought event being discussed, we may compare this estimate with our earlier recurrence estimates based on rainfall data. There we estimated that the recent drought was roughly the 150-year event (in terms of 4-year cumulated precipitation deviations); the 1908–11 drought appeared to be about a 30-year event. Thus, the managers' modal perception is very pessimistic relative to the "objective" estimates of the frequencies of the two most serious droughts of the century.

TABLE 13. MANAGERS' ESTIMATES OF RECURRENCE FREQUENCY OF DROUGHT OF EARLY 1960's

Managers expected drought to recur:	Number	Percent
Once in 5 years	1	2.1
Once in 10 years	9	18.8
Once in 20 years	5	10.4
Once in 25 years	10	20.8
Once in 50 years	5	10.4
Once in 100 years	4	8.3
Once in 500 years	0	
Once in 1,000 years	0	
No answer, not ascertained	14	29.2
	48	100.0

Certainly, the expectation that at some future date there will be another drought as serious as the recent one (as shown in Table 14) represents a willingness of managerial personnel to accept the challenge provided by uncertain nature.

A major divergence between our technical estimates and those of the managers centers on their perception of periodicity, a belief that drought comes in cycles. Only 8 of 43 managers rejected the cyclical notion of

TABLE 14. MANAGERS' PERCEPTION OF RECURRENCE OF DROUGHT

Managers:	Number of Managers	Percent
Believe there will be drought like 1963–66 in the future.	33	68.8
Do not believe there will be drought this bad again.	4	8.3
Do not know or cannot tell whether there will be droughts like this.	11	22.9
	48	100.0

drought occurrence, although 19 of those who accepted a cyclical view were reluctant to cite some specific duration of the cycle. (It seems reasonable to characterize the views of these 19 as quasi-random, since if the duration of the cycle were unknown after 100 years of recording weather variations, they might be expected to act as though it were unknowable.) If one considers, however, how deeply imbedded in scientific thinking is the grail-like search for cycles,[15] then perhaps this managerial opinion is less an irrational conclusion and more a deep reflection of the desire for an ordered universe shared by professional and nonprofessionals alike.

[15] The literature pertaining to cycles in climatological data is extensive, and as Mitchell has pointed out, "If one takes the trouble to amass the prodigious literature on the subject of cycles in climate and to try to collate all the conclusions thereof, he becomes utterly perplexed rather than enlightened." He goes on to say that "with one possible exception (a cycle of 80 to 90 years related to solar activity), if . . . cycles exist at all they must be so small in amplitude and/or so variable in period that their *practical* significance for long-range prediction is vanishingly small." J. Murray Mitchell, Jr., "A Critical Appraisal of Periodicities in Climate," in *Proceedings of a Conference*, May 3–6, 1964 sponsored by the Center for Agriculture and Economic Development (Ames: Iowa State University, 1964), pp. 189–227. Another recent review of the cycle hunt is provided in John T. Carr, "Predicting Droughts," *Symposium on Consideration of Droughts in Water Planning*, Texas Water Commission Bulletin 6512 (Austin: Texas Water Commission, 1965), pp. 7–24.

CHAPTER 7

SHORTAGE IN RELATION TO SYSTEM INADEQUACY: AN A PRIORI MODEL AND THE EMPIRICAL RESULTS

Thus far, in discussing the various components of our index of system inadequacy and in introducing our methods of measuring shortage, we have avoided any but qualitative statements about the relation between the demand-supply balance and the level of shortage suffered under a particular climatic event. We must now, however, proceed with the task of attempting to quantify this relation. It is appropriate to begin by reviewing briefly some of the ground we have covered.

In Chapter 5 we defined the percentage shortage suffered by town i in year t as:

$$S_{it} = \frac{D_{it} - V_{it}}{D_{it}} \times 100 \qquad (7\text{-}1)$$

where D_{it} = projected demand (annual total) in town i for year t; and V_{it} = the amount of water (also annual total) available from the system of town i in year t without emergency augmentation.

If we divide through on the right of Equation 7-1 in both numerator and denominator by Y_{it}, the safe yield of town i's system in year t, we obtain:

$$S_{it} = \frac{D_{it}/Y_{it} - V_{it}/Y_{it}}{D_{it}/Y_{it}} \times 100 \qquad (7\text{-}2)$$

which we may write for convenience as:

$$S_{it} = \frac{\alpha_{it} - \alpha^*_{it}}{\alpha_{it}} \times 100 \qquad (7\text{-}3)$$

55

where, obviously, $\alpha \equiv D/Y$ and $\alpha^* \equiv V/Y$. This expression emphasizes that there are two determinants of the size of shortage: the chosen level of system inadequacy (where we concentrate on choices of safe yield relative to given levels of projected demand); and the percentage of the safe-yield flow available from the normal system (without emergency augmentation). It is the second determinant which reflects climatic variation. We would, for example, expect that if town i experienced in year t an event worse than the safe-yield event (the design drought), the ratio α^*_t would be less than 1. Clearly, the definition of safe yield implies that in a repetition of the design drought, α^*_t would equal 1. On the other hand, any stress less severe than the design drought, from a slightly less severe drought to the largest imaginable annual rainfall, will result in some α^*_t more than 1. For a particular α^*, shortages will be greater, the greater the relative inadequacy of the system.

Now, it is our aim to construct a model of the impact of drought which can be applied to planning for future supply increments. We need, then, in essence, a probability distribution of α^*_t events. But direct evidence on this point is lacking, so we are forced to turn to other measures of climatic variation. Specifically, we wish to use available information from the record of some climatic variable to develop a surrogate distribution of α^*_t events. Hence our concern in the last chapter with various indicators of climatic variation.[1]

It is clear that the "actual" distribution of α^*_t events would reflect the nature of the particular watershed being looked at, the intrayear and over-year storage provided by the system, and the distribution of precipitation events, not only on an annual but also on a seasonal basis. We have already mentioned the implications of ignoring, as we do, the intrayear variations in precipitation. We are, of course, also abstracting from differences in watershed types, for we are attempting to construct a single, relatively simple model of drought impact applicable across a climatic region. As a final simplification, we ignore storage effects.

This may seem too drastic a bit of model-building sleight of hand, but several comments may help to put it in perspective. First, because we are not dealing with seasonal rainfall variations, overseason storage would not, in any case, be of concern. Second, as the genesis of this study demonstrates, "drought" becomes a phenomenon of general interest when several dry years follow consecutively. A single dry year, or the first of

---

[1] We emphasize that our work is directly applicable only to surface supply systems. While the same principles probably apply to groundwater systems, the practical matter of estimating the frequency of occurrence of various α^*_t events, the fraction of the maximum dependable draft available in year t, seems extremely difficult.

several dry years, creates the situation which overyear storage is designed to handle. But it seems reasonable to suppose that for most systems the cushion of overyear storage will be eliminated in the first year of a drought period. In subsequent years, the system will be more directly dependent on streamflow levels. The bias introduced by ignoring storage effects will be in the direction of overstating the expected shortages and losses over the long run. This will be so because some fraction of the α^*_t events giving rise in the model to shortages will, in fact, represent isolated dry years in which no shortages (or only very small shortages) need occur as overyear storage is drawn down.[2]

In the absence of storage effects, α^*_t will be approximated by the ratio of the year t streamflow to the streamflow associated with the safe-yield event, for the stream serving as the source of the system's supply. We may think of Equation 7-3, with streamflows used to predict α^*_t, as the most satisfactory version, a priori, of our model of drought impact. Unfortunately, however, there are not sufficient streamflow data available to permit us to test this model using the appropriate record for each system in estimating α^*_{it}. Because the characters of the streams used for water supply vary so much across the state, it seemed particularly dangerous to choose one or two long records as the basis of a streamflow variable to be applied to every system. Accordingly, the model described by Equation 7-3 was actually tested with variously transformed versions of our rainfall series,[3] based either on the individual sites or on the pooled record. These attempts to show that we could explain the observed shortages on the basis of Equation 7-3 were uniformly unsuccessful. In particular, significant shortages were observed in several cities for which the model predicted no shortage; and relatively small shortages (on the order of 20 to 30 percent) were observed in cities for which the model predicted very large ones (on the order of 50 percent).[4]

Although we cannot show that our a priori model is an accurate guide to the world, we can suggest two considerations which tend to explain the significant departures from it in the data. First, while it is true that if the available amount of water for delivery is smaller than that demanded,

[2] This bias originally seemed particularly harmless because our work with the implications of the empirical results, presented below, indicated that drought losses were a very much less serious problem than generally believed. The a priori model developed here, however, casts these losses in a far more serious light and suggests that a more intensive research effort, one including storage effects and intrayear precipitation patterns, would be of benefit in more accurately diagnosing the degree of danger.

[3] One of these versions was based on our attempts to relate rainfall and streamflows and thus was intended to be a good surrogate for streamflow. This version did not perform significantly better than any of the others tested.

[4] See Appendix B for a description of the data and sample used.

shortage (by our definition) *must* occur, it is not true that if the amount of water is adequate, shortage must *not* occur. Interposed between the supply system and the consumer is the judgment of the system manager. Thus, in the midst of worsening drought the system manager may act to conserve water—perhaps, intially, by refusing to use his overyear storage cushion, later, by cutting back demands he could satisfy from current watershed yields—and, by so acting, create shortages where the model would predict none. There is no check except local political pressure on such a conservative policy, on forcing a famine in the midst of plenty. And, of course, except in retrospect, one can never be at all sure that there is "plenty." The system manager who tried, through demand restriction, to build an overyear storage cushion between 1965 and 1966, would have been a hero in the summer of 1966. Trying to repeat his coup in 1966, he would have wound up a scapegoat in those areas for which the drought ended in late 1966.

Second, a complementary explanation of the failure of our first model is the possibility that most, if not all, municipal supply systems may have significant safety factors built into their estimates of safe yield. For example, standard engineering texts recommend that water systems be designed with a "25 percent reserve for the drought that occurs once every 20 years."[5] Another source of a safe-yield cushion may be the bank storage capability of the reservoir system. In the proper soils such storage may be large, and as reservoir levels drop, the system would tap more and more of it. The rate of inflow of stored water would increase with the fall in the surface of the reservoir.[6]

If we tentatively accept the argument that there are, for one reason or another, safe-yield reserves built into most systems, why do *any* systems suffer as large shortages as those predicted by the model? We note that if such reserves are the result of the factors we have discussed, their purpose would be compromised if town officials were made aware of them. We may guess that some towns become aware of them of political necessity. If, for example, a town with a relatively inadequate system is faced with what appears to be a steadily worsening drought, it will be apparent that very large shortages might be in store. (For example, if $\alpha_{it} = 2$ and $\alpha^*_t = 1$,

[5] Gordon M. Fair, John C. Geyer, and Daniel A. Okun, *Water and Waste Water Engineering* (New York: Wiley, 1966), I, Chap. 8, p. 6.

[6] The motives of consulting engineers, conscious or unconscious, probably work in the direction of inclusion of cushions in safe-yield estimates. First, particularly given the state of public and managerial attitudes towards water shortage, the reputations of firms and specific engineers might be endangered by the occurrence of shortage in a client system which had built the recommended improvements. Second, consulting fees are tied to the size of the project undertaken; such projects might be significantly smaller if, for example, bank storage were taken into account in determining safe yield.

then the potential shortage is 50 percent. We observed no shortages larger than 30 percent in any town in any year of the drought.) It may, indeed, seem that there is a limit of political feasibility to the stringency of restrictive measures which may be enacted and to the emergency purchases which can be funded. The response to this situation may often be for the officials, after some point, to shut their eyes and keep pumping, hoping that the weather will break. Towns with lower potential shortages may, on the other hand, feel the necessary measures feasible. If this argument is accurate, the larger the potential shortage, the more likely the town would be to use some of its safe-yield reserve. Hence our model would tend to overestimate the shortages to be observed in relatively inadequate systems.

EMPIRICAL RELATIONS AMONG SHORTAGES, INADEQUACIES, AND CLIMATIC VARIATIONS

Having attempted to explain why our a priori model does not fit the available data well, we now seek some relation which does. We intend in subsequent chapters to follow-up the implications for the expected costs of system inadequacy of both the a priori model and the relation fitted to the actual data. At this point we include a scatter diagram of shortage against system adequacy for 1964 for 15 towns (Figure 13). On this diagram we show the function relating shortage to adequacy under 1964 conditions as implied by the a priori model.

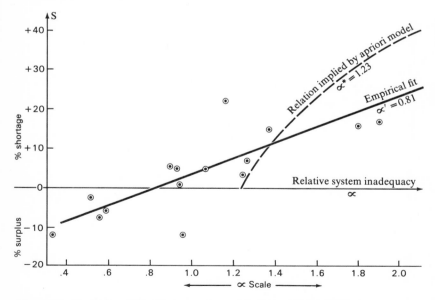

Figure 13. Scatter for 1964: 15 observations of shortage and system inadequacy.

We may, however, experiment by fitting to the data the regression:

$$S_{it} = k_t + \beta(\alpha_{it}) + \epsilon_{it} \tag{7-4}$$

for each year (so that climatic conditions will be invariant for regression). We hypothesize that k_t will be different for each year, reflecting climatic variation, but that β will be the same for every year. The results of this experiment indicate that for 1964–66, β is approximately equal to 20, and that k_t varies in the proper direction to be reflecting the worsening of the drought.

We next consider an equation of the form:

$$S_{it} = \zeta + \beta(\alpha_{it} - \alpha_t') \tag{7-5}$$

where α_t' represents the adequacy ratio at which shortages would be zero in the empirical formulation of Equation 7-4, that is, the α-axis intercept. We use the cumulated rainfall deviation information discussed in the last section to obtain estimates of α_t' for use in the regressions.[7] Specifically, we estimate α_t' from the relation:

$$\alpha_t' = \frac{\Delta_{(o)}}{\Delta_{(t)}} = \frac{\text{cumulative rainfall deviation } (1908-11)}{\text{cumulative rainfall deviation } (t-3 \text{ to } t)} \tag{7-6}$$

The null hypotheses are:

$$\zeta = 0 \text{ and } \beta = 20.$$

The results of this analysis are summarized in Table 15. The following observations are relevant to the propositions being tested:

1. Based on r^2's (mean for the 4 years = 0.60) and on the F-ratio tests (all highly significant, well over the requirements for significance at the 1 percent level), we may conclude that a simple linear relation of the form we have postulated is a good description of the empirical connection between degree of shortage and the existing D/Y ratio for a town experiencing a given climatic event.

2. We note that the estimates of β ($\hat{\beta}$) are quite close for the years 1964–66 and that the null hypothesis that $\beta = 20$ cannot be rejected in those years. The estimate for 1963 is, on the other hand, significantly different from 20. The mean $\hat{\beta}$ for the years 1964–66 is 18.78, and the value of $\hat{\beta}$ from a pooled regression for 1964–66 is 19.37.[8] It is probably the

---

[8] For a discussion of pooled cross-section regressions, see E. Kuh, *Capital Stock Growth: A Microeconometric Approach* (Amsterdam: North-Holland, 1963), Chs. 5 and 6.

[7] A confusion developed because, by looking originally only at the role of α_t' when shortages were zero, we came to identify it with the fraction of safe-yield flow available, or α_t^* in the a priori model. If this were true, then β would have to equal $1/\alpha_{it}$ and could not be constant.

TABLE 15. RESULTS OF TEST OF EMPIRICAL MODEL HYPOTHESES

Regression Equation:

$$S_i = \zeta + \beta(\alpha_{it} - \alpha_t') + \epsilon_i \qquad i = 1, \ldots, 15$$

For each of the years (t), 1963–66.

Null Hypotheses:

$\zeta = 0 \qquad\qquad \beta = 20$

1963 (Let $[\alpha - \alpha'] = x$) $\qquad\qquad \alpha_{63}' = 2.77$

$$S = 23.66 + 13.00\,(x)$$
$$(5.25)\quad(2.98)$$

F-test sig. at 1 percent; $r^2 = 0.59$

t-tests ζ—significantly different from 0 at 1 percent
β—significantly different from 20 at 5 percent

1964 $\qquad\qquad \alpha_{64}' = 0.81$

$$S = -0.0192 + 18.79\,(x)$$
$$(2.01)\qquad(4.13)$$

F-test sig. at 1 percent; $r^2 = 0.61$

t-tests ζ—*not* significantly different from 0 at 90 percent
β—*not* significantly different from 20 at 70 percent

1965 $\qquad\qquad \alpha_{65}' = 0.76$

$$S = 3.895 + 17.88\,(x)$$
$$(2.24)\quad(4.07)$$

F-test sig. at 1 percent; $r^2 = 0.60$

t-tests ζ—*not* significantly different from 0 at 20 percent
β—*not* significantly different from 20 at 70 percent

1966 $\qquad\qquad \alpha_{66}' = 0.70$

$$S = 3.594 + 19.68\,(x)$$
$$(2.73)\quad(4.39)$$

F-test sig. at 1 percent; $r^2 = 0.61$

t-tests ζ—*not* significantly different from 0 at 30 percent
β—*not* significantly different from 20 at 90 percent

Pooled—1964–66

$$S = 2.33 + 19.37\,(x)$$
$$(1.31)\quad(2.36)$$

F-test sig. at 1 percent; $r^2 = 0.61$

t-tests ζ—*not* significantly different from 0 at 5 percent
β—*not* significantly different from 20 at 70 percent

previously mentioned opportunities for reservoir drawdown in the first of a series of dry years which explain the 1963 slope estimate. The lower β for 1963 than for later years indicates that shortages increased less rapidly in that year with increases in system inadequacy.

3. The null hypothesis that $\zeta = 0$ must be rejected for the 1963 regression. For 1964 it may be accepted with a high degree of confidence. For 1965 and 1966 we are only able to say that it cannot be rejected with any assurance.

In summary, our empirical model seems to be fundamentally valid for the *later* years of a series of dry years. This limitation does not seem too great a handicap for the reasons already discussed. We must, however, note that there are real dangers in extrapolating purely empirical relations into the future.[9]

[9] It may have occurred to the reader to question these regression results because of the underlying link between both the dependent and independent variable and the level of projected demand. Thus, expressing S_{it} in terms of its components, we may write Equation 7–7 as:

$$\frac{D_{it} - V_{it}}{D_{it}} = \zeta + \beta(\alpha_{it} - \alpha'_t) + \epsilon_i$$

Both sides of this equation vary directly with the size of D_{it} for given values of the other variables. There is, then, certainly at least initial reason to suspect the presence of a spurious correlation bias.

To test for the presence of such spurious correlation, we calculated correlation coefficients between D_{it} and S_{it} and between D_{it} and $(\alpha_{it} - \alpha'_t)$. These were insignificant even at the 50 percent confidence level for every year between 1963 and 1966. In addition, we calculated the partial correlation coefficient of S and $(\alpha_{it} - \alpha'_t)$ (netting out the influence of D explicitly), and found that it is virtually equal in each year to the simple correlation coefficient for S and $(\alpha_{it} - \alpha'_t)$.

The evidence thus indicates that in fact the correlation between S_{it} and $(\alpha - \alpha'_t)$ attributable to their common link with D_{it} is negligible.

CHAPTER 8

DROUGHT ADJUSTMENT:
THE RESPONSE TO SHORTAGE

Before moving on to the business of measuring the economic impact of water shortages, we should pause to consider some of the ways in which a community may react to impending trouble. In addition, it will be useful to see how the study communities actually did react during the 1962–66 drought.

We concentrate in this chapter entirely on active responses to potential shortage. It is, of course, possible (if not politically feasible) for a community to react passively; that is, to do nothing out of the ordinary, supplying all customary uses at customary prices and suffering the relatively spectacular consequences when there is no water left for anyone. This type of behavior is, understandably, not often observed; and we feel safe in assuming for the sake of exposition that a town with reasonably accurate knowledge of its position will make some active response or set of responses. In general, such responses may be chosen from two alternative groups: those adjustments to the normal state of affairs which aim at increasing (even if only temporarily) the available supply of water; and those adjustments which aim at restricting the level of withdrawals from that supply.

ADJUSTMENTS THAT REDUCE CONSUMPTION

Adjustments that reduce water withdrawals are directed toward a more efficient utilization of the present water supply. Such adjustments include changes from flat-rate to commodity charges through metering, changes in the price where meters exist, restrictions on the use of water, and reuse of water.

Changes From Flat-Rate to Metered Supply

One of the major factors affecting the consumption of residential water is whether or not the distribution system is metered. As Table 16 shows, water use in metered areas is significantly lower than in flat-rate areas, primarily because of the impact of metering on lawn-sprinkling. Note also that peak demands, hourly and daily, tend to be very much lower in the metered areas, a fact that is not directly relevant to this study but is obviously of great importance for the planning of water systems. Household use (inside uses such as flushing and cooking) is relatively constant as between metered and flat-rate areas.[1]

TABLE 16. WATER USE IN METERED AND FLAT-RATE AREAS
(OCTOBER 1963–SEPTEMBER 1965)

(gallons per day per dwelling unit)

	Metered areas	Flat-rate areas
Annual average		
Leakage and waste	25	36
Household	247	236
Sprinkling	186	420
Total	458	692
Maximum day	979	2,354
Peak hour	2,481	5,170

Source: Charles W. Howe and F. P. Linaweaver, Jr., "The Impact of Price on Residential Water Demand and Its Relation to System Design and Price Structure," *Water Resources Research*, I (1965), 14.

The literature is replete with examples of the impact of universal metering on the use of water. In Kingston, N.Y., a universal meter installation program was initiated in 1958. By 1963, with 98 percent of the system metered, average water use had decreased from 5.47 to 4.0 million gallons per day (mgd) even though the number of services had increased from 7,800 to 7,935.[2] When Philadelphia completed universal metering between 1955 and 1960, demand for water declined from 370 to 327.8 mgd (11 percent). In 1955, approximately 73 percent of the water services were metered; hence, metering was estimated to have reduced demand among the unmetered users by at least 28 percent.[3] Another example is Elizabeth City,

[1] See also, F. P. Linaweaver, Jr., John C. Geyer, and Jerome B. Wolff, "Final and Summary Report on the Residential Water Use Research Project" (The Johns Hopkins University, Department of Environmental Science, June 1966), pp. 48–49.

[2] E. T. Cloonan, "Meters Save Water," in *Modern Water Rates* (New York: Buttenheim Publishing Co., 1965), pp. 12–13.

[3] Ibid., p. 14.

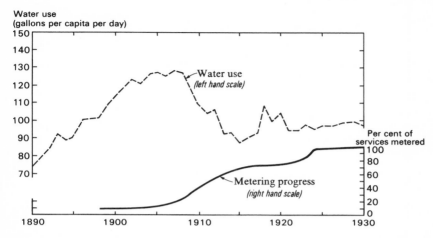

Figure 14. Effect of introduction of metering on water consumption by Metropolitan District Commission customers.

N.C., where, in 1931, universal metering of an originally flat-rate system reduced average consumption from 1.8 to 0.3 mgd. Although demand later increased slightly, per capita consumption as of 1946 was still lower than for the period prior to 1931.[4] Figure 14 shows how average per capita daily consumption of water by customers of Metropolitan District Commission reacted to metering.

The scope for this particular form of adjustment is somewhat limited, however, in that most municipalities in the United States have already installed individual water meters.[5] There are some notable exceptions. For example, only 25 percent of the water users in New York City are metered, though in a recent report, the former Water Commissioner of the city estimated that complete metering would reduce consumption by 125 mgd, or approximately 10 percent of average daily use in the early sixties.[6]

Increases in Price of Metered Supply

Where systems are already metered, it is, of course, possible to reduce the level of water withdrawals by increasing the charge per gallon. In principle, the economist would look in this direction for a method of

[4] "What Water Meters Did for Elizabeth City, North Carolina," *American City*, 61 (1946), 9.

[5] Jack Hirshleifer, James C. DeHaven, and Jerome W. Milliman, *Water Supply: Economics, Technology and Policy* (Chicago: University of Chicago Press, 1960), p. 44; and American Water Works Association, *Water Rates Manual* (New York: The Association, 1957).

[6] *Report on Universal Metering* by Armand D'Angelo submitted to Hon. Robert F. Wagner, Mayor of New York City, October 7, 1964 (mimeo.), p. 6.

rationing the available water so as to minimize the welfare loss from the shortage. However, in practice, the pricing policies of most systems are so widely at variance with even roughly optimal policies,[7] and so little is known of the shapes of the existing demand functions, that it is not clear that even a second-, third-, or *n*-th best solution could be found. Virtually the only solid evidence available on water demand functions concerns residential use and suggests that the demand for sprinkling water is relatively elastic, that for other domestic uses relatively inelastic.[8] As a drought adjustment, the use of a temporary surcharge equal to several multiples of the normal price might be applied to all water used above some minimum. Since sprinkling use is the more elastic, and since a drastic temporary increase is envisioned, such a plan could result in a sharp decrease in use during summer months. There are, however, significant administrative problems: in particular, the infrequency of meter readings might make it difficult to devise a fair base use and would tend to destroy the immediacy of the price increase for customers. Perhaps even more important are the practical political difficulties involved.

In addition to reducing the use of water directly, the introduction of metering and increases in prices may indirectly have the same tendency by increasing customers' sensitivity to leaks and by making leaks in the distribution mains easier to find.[9] This may be quite important, for as noted earlier, as much as 15 percent of water withdrawn from the source may be lost in distribution. To this must be added an unknown, but probably fairly large, leakage after water is delivered to the customers' meters.

Restrictions on Water Use

Restrictions on water use can be very effective in reducing a community's withdrawals, and it is to restrictions that system managers very frequently turn when confronted with a potential shortage.[10] One of the great ad-

[7] See American Water Works Association, "Determination of Water Rate Schedules," *Journal of the American Water Works Association*, 44 (1954), 188; and Gordon M. Fair, John C. Geyer, and Daniel A. Okun, *Water and Waste Water Engineering* (New York: Wiley, 1966), I, Ch. 13, p. 14, which states that ". . . rates are obtained by dividing the system costs by the volume of water delivered. . . ."

[8] Charles W. Howe and F. P. Linaweaver, Jr., "The Impact of Price on Residential Water Demand and Its Relation to System Design," *Water Resources Research*, I (1965), 13–32, and certain other studies cited therein.

[9] John Simmons, "Economic Significance of Unaccounted for Water," *Journal of the American Water Works Association*, LVIII (1966), 639–41.

[10] Glen D. Heggie, "Effects of Sprinkling Restrictions," *Journal of the American Water Works Association*, XLIX (1957), 275; and Dwight F. Metzler, "Recommended Action Against Effects of Severe Droughts in Kansas," *Journal of the American Water Works Association*, XLVIII (1956), 1003.

vantages of this strategy is its flexibility. Restrictions may be voluntary or legally imposed; they may be based on hours of use or types of activity; they may be confined to peak demand periods or be more general. Indeed, in some communities, restrictions have been imposed on *all* uses, the water being shut off for all except a few hours each day.[11]

Certainly, from a review of the literature, it appears that communities, when faced with a potential shortage, are quick to formulate and impose programs of water-use restrictions. For example, at least 64 of the 75 communities in Illinois that suffered shortage at some time during the drought of 1952–55 enacted restrictions on use.[12]

One drawback, however, to reliance on restrictions is that their effectiveness appears to be severely limited unless the people of the town are convinced that there is, indeed, a crisis situation.[13] It might be that publicity for the cost implications of system failure would increase public tolerance for and cooperation with restrictions.[14]

Reuse of Water

Although the reuse of water for domestic purposes has recently become more attractive and viable, few communities in the United States have recycled effluent from sewage treatment plants subsequent to filtration,

[11] Symposium, "Eastern Water Shortage and Drought Problems," *Journal of the American Water Works Association*, LXVII (1955), 203–29.

[12] The other 11 communities may also have had water-use restrictions, but the data on restrictions were reported for 1953 only. A community was considered to have a shortage if restrictions on water use were imposed or if less than 6 months' supply was available for systems with surface-water supplies. H. E. Hudson, Jr., and W. J. Roberts, *1952–55 Illinois Drought with Special Reference to Impounding Reservoir Design*, Illinois State Water Survey Bulletin No. 43 (Urbana: Illinois Department of Registration and Education, 1955), p. 1.

[13] "Publicity in Water-Waste Prevention Work," *Journal of the American Water Works Association*, VI (1919), 8.

[14] It has been suggested that one rational and effective way of dealing with the problem of customer acceptance both of restrictions and of the idea of a planned failure rate for a municipal water supply would be to publish, in advance, lists of planned restrictions to be applied under various threatened levels of shortage. Thus, for example, the system's customers would know that in the face of a 10 percent potential shortage, all outside use of water (sprinkling, car-washing, etc.) would be forbidden during July and August, no non-recirculating air conditioners would be permitted to operate, and no water could be served in restaurants. If the potential shortage were 15 percent, swimming pools could not be refilled. A shortage as large as 30 percent might involve slowdowns or shutdowns of local water-using industries. This suggestion deserves a practical test in one or more cities, perhaps in combination with the temporary surcharge scheme outlined above.

purification, and dilution.[15] Because of a serious drought, Chanute, Kans., reused its water an average of 8 to 15 times from October 1956 to February 1957.[16] Although the taste and odor of the drinking water became esthetically disturbing to many consumers, the U.S. Public Health Service minimum standards for drinking water were never violated during the 5-month period. In a study concerning the feasibility of a 100-mgd waste-water purification plant utilizing secondary-treatment sewage, it was estimated that potable water could be produced at approximately 16¢ per 1,000 gallons.[17] Frankel and others have demonstrated that groundwater recharge of treated sewage is economically superior to conventional methods of providing water and sanitary services which use a stream both as source and as receiver of effluent, with treatment at both ends of the municipal "pipe."[18]

The obstacles to reuse appear to lie primarily in the minds of system managers and customers for whom the reuse of water is esthetically unacceptable.[19] Our study indicated that this was certainly true of Massachusetts: system managers uniformly avoided this alternative in discussing steps they could take in the face of potential shortage; and in a small public opinion poll only 46 percent of those interviewed indicated a willingness to drink recycled domestic water. (Over 70 percent indicated such a willingness in Kansas and Illinois.)[20] These attitudes could probably be significantly changed by an educational campaign.

[15] Recirculation of water within a single water-using activity such as an industrial plant or even a city is clearly a means of reducing withdrawals by that activity. Recirculation which involves use of natural mechanisms, as in artificial recharge of groundwater aquifers with treated waste waters, might be characterized under methods of increasing the available supply. The appropriate definition would depend on our view of the physical system of water resources being considered as potential supply. For our purposes, all types of recirculation are classified as means of reducing withdrawals.

[16] Bernard Berger, "Public Health Aspects of Water Reuse for Potable Supply," *Journal of the American Water Works Association*, LII (1960), 599–606.

[17] Leon W. Weinberger, David G. Stephan, and Francis M. Middleton, "Solving our Water Problems—Water Renovation and Reuse," *Annals of the New York Academy of Sciences*, 136 (1966), 143. "The suggested plant employs aeration, chemical coagulation and sedimentation, carbon absorption and chlorination to purify the effluent from a secondary sewage treatment plant. If the product water is mixed with water from other sources in a large system no further treatment is necessary."

[18] See, for example, Richard J. Frankel, "Water Quality Management: Engineering-Economic Factors in Municipal Waste Disposal," *Water Resources Research*, I (1965), 185, 186. See also Frankel, "Water Quality Management: An Engineering-Economic Model for Domestic Waste Disposal," Ph.D. thesis, University of California, Berkeley, January 1965.

[19] Dwight F. Metzler and Heinz B. Russelmann, "Wastewater Reclamation as a Water Resource," *Journal of the American Water Works Association*, LX (1968), 101: "The challenge of acceptance is greatest with water utility managers."

[20] The Massachusetts poll involved 177 respondents in 6 towns. In Kansas and Illinois 271 persons were interviewed.

ADJUSTMENTS THAT INCREASE SUPPLY

In contrast to the above strategies, which attain their goals by impinging more or less directly on consumer choice and behavior, a second set of adjustments relies primarily on technology and aims to increase the available supply through construction of new sources of supply, use of emergency sources, weather modification, evaporation and seepage control, and desalination of salt or brackish water. Observation of past behavior suggests that communities faced with persistent long-term shortages of water have looked more often to the development of new or improved sources of supply than to such relatively new alternatives as weather modification and desalination. In cases of short-run shortages, we have very little evidence on the choices among adjustments other than the development of an emergency source of supply.

Provision of Emergency Supplies

Emergency sources of water supply have alleviated shortages in many drought-stricken communities. Simple chlorination of nearby ponds, quarries, and polluted streams, and utilization of abandoned wells have enabled communities to withstand serious droughts. During the Illinois drought of 1952–55, of the 75 communities that experienced shortages, 8 hauled in emergency water, 8 supplemented existing supplies with groundwater sources, and 13 laid pipelines to reach emergency sources of surface water. Except for specific accounts in the more popular journals, little is known concerning the frequency with which communities rely upon emergency supplies or about the nature of those supplies.

Weather Modification

Twenty years have elapsed since the Langmuir and Schaeffer cloud-seeding experiments. Since that time, the study of weather modification has emerged as a scientific discipline; the social and economic consequences of modifying the weather are being studied; and federal recognition has been translated into research funds.[21] Cloud-seeding techniques have been observed to increase average precipitation by 10 to 15 percent under appropriate weather conditions.[22] And it is predicted by some that

[21] Thomas Malone, "Weather Modification: Implications of the New Horizons in Research," *Science*, 156 (1967), 897.

[22] National Academy of Sciences—National Research Council, *Weather and Climate Modification: Problems and Prospects*, Final Report of the Panel on Weather and Climate Modification (Washington: U.S. Government Printing Office, 1966), p. 23; Peter H. Wycoff, "Evaluation of the State of the Art," in *Human Dimensions of Weather Modification*, W. R. D. Sewell, ed., Department of Geography Research Paper No. 105 (Chicago: University of Chicago Press, 1966), p. 31; and U.S. Department of the In-

with continued research "weather modification as a means of increasing the water supply will be possible" by 1975.[23]

Protecting Supply Sources

In conjunction with plans to increase public water supplies, techniques to reduce evaporation and seepage in reservoirs have been implemented, without great success, especially in the Southwest where evaporative losses are nearly three times greater than in the Northeast. Monomolecular film has been successful on small ponds, although the cost is rather high.[24] The construction of deep reservoirs (relative to volume) has also aided in the reduction of losses to the atmosphere by reducing the water surface area from which evaporation can occur.

Desalination

A final and rather dramatic alternative, one mentioned frequently during the recent Northeast drought, is the desalination of salt or brackish water. But, because of the time required for construction of facilities, desalting is not a realistic alternative for a community faced with a shortage and in need of an immediate boost in supply. Even over a longer time horizon, desalting is not yet competitive with conventional sources. For a large (300 mgd), dual-purpose seawater desalting plant for New York City, the average annual costs were estimated to be approximately $77,000 per mgd of safe yield. In contrast, it was calculated that use of Hudson River water would cost about $37,000 per mgd of safe yield.[25]

DROUGHT ADJUSTMENT IN MASSACHUSETTS

Among these possible alternatives, what were the choices of the communities in Massachusetts during the recent drought? In particular, did the town tend to take on the burden of reducing shortages by obtaining

---

terior, Bureau of Reclamation, Office of Atmospheric Water Resources, *Plan to Develop Technology for Increasing Water Yield from Atmospheric Sources* (Washington: U.S. Government Printing Office, 1966), p. 27.

[23] U.S. Senate Select Committee on National Water Resources, *Water Resources Activities in the United States: Weather Modification*, Committee Print No. 22, 86th Congress, 2nd Sess. (Washington: U.S. Government Printing Office, 1962), p. 45.

[24] For a review of the state of the art see C. W. Lauritzen, "Water Storage-Seepage, Evaporation, and Management," paper presented at Symposium on Water Supplies for Arid Regions, Committee on Desert and Arid Zones Research, Tucson, May 1967.

[25] U.S. Department of Commerce, Northeast Desalting Team, *Potentialities and Possibilities of Desalting for Northern New Jersey and New York City* (Washington: The Department, 1966).

emergency supplies, or was the impact primarily felt by customers through the instrument of restrictions on use?

Of the 48 communities in which interviews were conducted in the course of our study, 39 adopted one or more drought-related adjustments at some time during the 1963–66 period. The most common response to the drought was the imposition of restrictions on water use. But other measures to reduce the level of demand were rarely taken. Efforts to obtain new sources, to improve existing sources, and to provide emergency supplies were, on the other hand, all quite popular strategies. (See Figure 15.)

For the towns included in the mail survey, the water superintendents were asked to rate their system as adequate or inadequate during the drought period. In over 50 percent (82 of 150) of the mail-survey communities, the existing water supply was considered inadequate at some time during the drought. Restrictions on water use were imposed in all but 2 of these places, with more than 50 percent of the restrictions being compulsory. Emergency water sources were used by 50 of the systems classified by their managers as inadequate. (The mail-survey data on adequacy and adjustments are summarized in Table 17.)

It should also be noted that, of the 68 communities served by systems classified as *adequate* by their managers, 8 enacted restrictions and 4

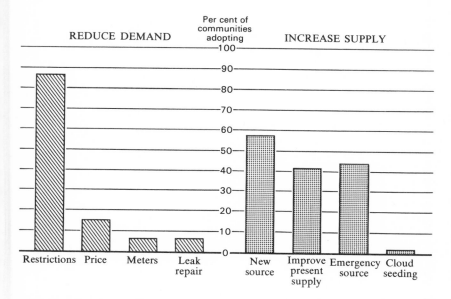

Figure 15. Nature of adjustments made by 39 Massachusetts communities during 1963–66 drought.

TABLE 17. MAIL-SURVEY COMMUNITIES: ADJUSTMENTS TO DROUGHT[a]

Characteristics of systems — Status and adjustments	Groundwater systems			Surface-water systems			Combination systems			Total systems		
	Number of systems	Percentage of groundwater systems	Mean index of inadequacy[b]	Number of systems	Percentage of surface water systems	Mean index of inadequacy[b]	Number of systems	Percentage of combination systems	Mean index of inadequacy[b]	Number of systems	Percentage of total systems	Mean index of inadequacy[b]
Total adequate	52	54%	0.48	13	45%	0.56	3	12%	0.61	68	45%	0.50
Restrictions	6	6	0.39	2	7	0.49	—	—	—	8	5	0.41
Voluntary	4	4	0.42	2	7	0.49	—	—	—	6	4	0.45
Compulsory	2	2	0.34	0	0	—	—	—	—	2	1	0.34
Emergency supply	3	3	0.54	1	3	0.54	—	—	—	4	3	0.54
Planning	21	22	0.47	5	17	0.62	—	—	—	26	17	0.48
Total inadequate	44	46%	0.52	16	55%	0.72	22	88%	0.77	82	55%	0.63
Restrictions	43	45	0.51	15	52	0.65	22	88	0.77	80	53	0.60
Voluntary	31	32	0.51	5	17	0.51	14	56	0.70	50	33	0.62
Compulsory	20	21	0.54	11	38	0.66	15	60	0.67	46	31	0.62
Emergency supply	29	30	0.52	13	45	0.70	8	32	0.68	50	33	0.59
Planning	37	39	0.53	14	48	0.78	18	72	0.78	69	46	0.62
Survey totals	96	64.0	0.50	29	19.3	0.65	25	16.7	0.75	150	100	0.57
	Percentage of total sample			Percentage of total sample			Percentage of total sample					

[a] System "adequacy" was determined by system managers. Systems were listed under both voluntary and compulsory restrictions if both types were imposed.

[b] The index of inadequacy of a system was calculated from U.S. Department of Health, Education, and Welfare, *1963 Inventory of Municipal Water Facilities,* Public Health Service Publication No. 755 (Washington: U.S. Government Printing Office, 1964) as average plant output over safe yield or maximum dependable draft as appropriate. We give the means for the systems listed to the left in the particular category.

utilized emergency supplies. This observation points up the difficulties of relating a measure of inadequacy based on managerial perception with measures based on physical capability. Thus, it is quite reasonable to suppose that managers would seek to bolster or save apparently adequate supplies when surrounded by the din of crisis publicity. It is also true that in the absence of accurate measures of potential demand and available supplies, adequacy is, like beauty, in the eye of the beholder.[26]

One of the most interesting features of Table 17, however, is the extent to which even in this context, with only imperfect measures available, our concept of relative system adequacy shows up as important. We calculated a surrogate measure of relative inadequacy from the information in the 1963 USPHS Inventory,[27] using the "average plant output" as a measure of the level of demand in combination with the given features for safe yield or maximum dependable draft as appropriate. The table shows the mean of these ratios for the systems in the particular category. Examining the table, then, we can see that within each system type (by source) the "mean inadequacy" ratio for the "adequate" systems is invariably lower than is that for the "inadequate" systems. This comparison is least pronounced for groundwater systems, to which our model is not expected to apply. For surface and combined-source systems, the contrast is much sharper. The ratio of the mean inadequacy index for "inadequate" systems to that for "adequate" systems is, for each category, equal to about 1.25. Since the higher the mean inadequency ratio, the *lower* the level of relative system adequacy, we find the satisfactory result that "inadequacy" in the perception of managers (and the performance of the system as it affects that perception) corresponds to relative inadequacy, in our sense, for a given climatic event.

Adjustments to Decrease Withdrawals

Returning now to the 48 interviewed communities, in the 39 systems which adopted some type of adjustment during the drought period, the choices ranged from appeals for voluntary reduction in use to a weather modification project. (See Table 18.) Aside from the widespread community adoption of water use restrictions, very few attempts to reduce consumption were made. The emphasis was on augmenting supply through technology, while strategies requiring water use behavior modification were narrowly perceived and adopted. (See Figure 15 for a graphic summary.)

[26] See comments in Chapter 7, on the possibility of "created" shortages attributable to conservative water-management policy.

[27] U.S. Department of Health, Education, and Welfare, *1963 Inventory of Municipal Water Facilities*, Public Health Service Publication No. 775 (Washington: U.S. Government Printing Office, 1964).

TABLE 18. ADJUSTMENT TO DROUGHT MADE BY 39 COMMUNITIES

Adjustments that decrease withdrawals			Adjustments that increase supply		
Type	Number report-ing	Per-centage of inter-view sample adopting	Type	Number report-ing	Per-centage of inter-view sample adopting
I. Restrictions	34	87	I. New sources	23	59
Domestic	34	87	Reservoirs	5	13
Industrial	23	59	Groundwater	19	49
Public use	19	49			
			II. Improve existing supply	16	41
II. Price adjustment	6	15	Reservoir	10	26
			Groundwater	6	16
III. Meter adjustment	3	8	III. Emergency supplies	17	44
			Surface	10	26
IV. Leak survey/repairs	3	8	Ground	9	23
			Purchase	7	18
			IV. Weather modification	1	2

Note: Subtotals do not add because some communities used more than one.

In Table 19, we summarize the choices made among a variety of types of restrictions by the 34 cities and towns which turned to this general type of drought adjustment. We note that *every* system that used restrictions imposed lawn-watering restrictions on the domestic sector. This finding supports our expectations based on casual observation (and on exposure to irate lawnowners). The next most popular single type of restriction was that on home car-washing adopted by 76 percent of the restriction towns. Refilling of private swimming pools was restricted by 50 percent of the towns, but all outside use was restricted by only 29 percent of those introducing any restrictions.

Restrictions on the industrial (or commercial) sector were introduced by 13 of the 34 towns (38 percent). In 9 of these 13 places, the restrictions applied to the cooling water for large air conditioners; industries and commercial establishments were required to recirculate cooling water for all machines over a specified size, such as 5 tons. (Of the 9 communities, 2 extended this requirement to all cooling water. Only 1 community acted to require industries to recirculate process water where feasible.)

Other restrictions imposed on the industrial and commercial sectors took a variety of forms. Five communities took action to affect the use of water by commercial car-washes, including such measures as required recirculation and limits on hours or days of operation. One community

TABLE 19. NATURE OF RESTRICTIONS ADOPTED BY 34 COMMUNITIES

Sector applied to and description	Number of towns adopting	Percentage of all towns imposing any restrictions	Percentage of those towns imposing restrictions on particular sector
Domestic sector:	34	100	100
Lawn-sprinkling	34	100	100
Car-washing	26	76	76
Swimming pool (re)fill	17	50	50
All outside use	10	29	29
Industrial sector:	13[a]	38[a]	100
Cooling water recirculation	9	26	69
Air conditioning	9	26	69
General cooling	2	6	15
Process water recirculation	1	3	8
Restrictions on air-conditioning use (hours, temperature)	2	6	15
Car and truck washing (including commercial establishments)	5	15	38
Public sector:	19	56	100
Ponds, fountains	13	38	68
Hydrant flushing	12	25	63
Swimming pool (re)filling	6	18	32

[a] Several towns took measures with reference to the industrial sector which did not seem to qualify as voluntary restrictions for the purposes of this table. Specifically, 7 towns "requested" industries to recirculate one or more streams (generally air conditioning). Two other towns "recommended" such recirculation. If these are included, 22 towns, or 65 percent of the restricting towns, took some action with respect to industry.

imposed a restriction on the hours during which industrial and commercial establishments could operate air-conditioning equipment, allowing only 5 hours operation at mid-day. Another community prohibited operators of air-conditioning equipment from reducing the temperature inside their buildings more than 10° F. below the outside temperature. It would be interesting to know why this last, rather ingenious limitation came to be adopted and to find out how, and how strenuously, it was enforced. For while the idea of a "temperature patrol" is mildly amusing, the enforcement of this restriction seems perhaps more practical in the short run than the more common restriction requiring investment in recirculation equipment.

Nineteen of the interview communities adopted restrictions on public-sector uses of water. Most common here were rules shutting down or requiring recirculation for decorative ponds and fountains. Twelve communities altered or abandoned normal schedules of hydrant flushing and testing. Six communities curtailed operation of municipal swimming pools.

Restrictions and the Level of Shortage. We felt that it would be interesting to investigate the relationship between the restrictive actions taken by communities and the levels of shortage they faced; in particular, to see whether certain restrictions tended to be adopted only under the pressure of relatively great potential shortage. Are some sectors favored over others when it becomes necessary to distribute a potential shortage; that is, to ration a limited supply of water?

We chose to measure the severity of the drought's impact on a town by the estimated potential shortage faced by the town during the depth of the drought.[28] We used this in preference to a measure of shortage faced at the time of initial imposition of restrictions because almost half of the communities we dealt with in this comparison instituted restrictions in 1963, and, as we have seen, our model does not appear to perform particularly well in explaining the size of shortages in 1963. This did not seem to be a dangerous strategy; we were interested in comparisons of relative shortage levels; and, for the communities we were able to survey, no important changes in relative adequacy took place during the drought. Thus, measures of relative severity for the last years of the drought should not differ significantly from what we would find had we a good measure of relative severity for the first year.[29]

Accordingly, in Table 20 we show, for the sample of 17 communities for which we had sufficient data, the average shortages faced by communities taking a number of different restrictive measures.[30] We also include data showing how prevalent each type of restriction was within the group of 34 communities imposing any restrictions, and how prevalent within the narrower sample of 17. The agreement between these two measures is generally good, indicating that our sample of 17 is at least not

[28] For the central and coastal regions of the state, we used the average shortage faced in 1965 and 1966; for the western region, the 1965 shortage alone.

[29] One test of the validity of this claim is to compare the pattern of shortage and restriction found below in Table 20 with that computed using the shortage estimate for the first year of restrictions for towns initiating restrictions in 1965 or 1966. (No towns in the sample we were able to work with initiated restrictions in 1964.) This was done, and the two are essentially the same. The small number of such towns, however, means that for several types of restrictions, no representatives were available in the group.

[30] The earlier discussions concerning our narrowing down of the list of towns with which we could work are applicable here. We are able to include here certain towns which could not be included in the regression testing of the shortage model presented in the last chapter. This is true, for example, for towns for which we lacked safe-yield estimates, since the D/Y ratio need not be measured here.

obviously biased with respect to any particular type of restriction. The restrictions for which the comparisons are presented are those which were relatively rare in our original sample and those which seem a priori to have a relatively greater psychological impact on the public. As a base for comparisons we use the average percentage shortage associated with the towns imposing lawn-sprinkling restrictions; that is, with the entire sample of 17.

TABLE 20. AVERAGE SHORTAGE FACING COMMUNITIES ADOPTING
VARIOUS RESTRICTIONS

Type of restriction	Total communities adopting this restriction of 34 adopting any	Per-centage of 34	Number of communities adopting this restriction of 17 in shortage-restriction sample	Per-centage of 17	Average shortage faced by those adopting
					(*percent*)
Lawn-sprinkling	34	100	17	100	8.5
Restrictions on public swimming pools	6	18	4	24	9.5
Restrictions on private pools	17	50	10	59	13.6
Ban on all outside domestic use	10	29	3	18	25.9
Compulsory restrictions on commercial/industrial sector	13	38	8	47	14.5
Compulsory industrial cooling-water re-circulation	9	26	5	30	14.6
Compulsory industrial process water re-circulation	1	3	1	6	22.3

Some of the conclusions suggested by the table are mildly surprising. In particular, it seems odd that use of private pools was restricted only at a higher level of shortage than was required to trigger restrictions on public pools. This, however, may simply be a manifestation of where the effective power lies. In addition, since almost every community banned car-washing and every community did restrict sprinkling, it seems odd that "all outside use" would be restricted only at such a very high average shortage. The explanation here seems to be that, in fact, water managers mentioned "all outside use" only when they had *banned* such use. This represents, then, a considerably more serious step than the mere institution of permitted hours of use, etc., for sprinkling or car-washing.

From the point of view of some of our later findings concerning the apparent differential economic impact on sectors of shortages of different sizes, the most interesting findings in Table 20 concern the levels at which restrictions are imposed on the industrial and commercial sectors. We note from item 5 that the broad range of compulsory restrictions on the water-use activities of these sectors were instituted by systems facing an average shortage of 14.5 percent, considerably higher than the 8.5 percent shortage found for domestic restrictions. The one community which attempted to force industrial recirculation of process water faced a shortage of 22.3 percent, while the level for the 5 communities confining their recirculation edicts to cooling water was 14.6 percent. This all suggests that if the potential shortage does not exceed about 10 percent, the community will probably attempt to meet it by restricting domestic (and perhaps public) use, probably supplementing these restrictions with emergency supplies, either purchased or obtained from nearby ponds and similar sources. Only when the potential shortage is significantly larger than 10 percent do the communities attempt to clamp down on industrial use, and then they attempt to avoid the more sensitive areas. This phenomenon too is presumably tied to the relatively great power wielded by industrial customers, at least in Massachusetts. It is interesting to see this finding emerge from a direct look at the types of restrictions imposed. Later, in Chapter 9, a very similar conclusion is shown to be implied by the indirect evidence of the sectoral economic impact of the drought in three Massachusetts towns.

Enforcement of Restrictions. The extent to which a community may enforce restrictions is governed by law. Massachusetts law provides for declaration of a water emergency with the approval of the State Department of Public Health (DPH). If the emergency is approved by the DPH, the community may impose restrictions on water use, with authority to suspend service for noncompliance. The emergency declaration also allows the use of DPH-approved emergency water sources to augment supplies. If a water emergency is not declared, a community may still enact local restrictions on water use without the approval of the DPH; however, punishment for noncompliance may not include actual suspension of supply. A third strategy a community may select, a step less severe than the two outlined above (and therefore likely to precede them), is to appeal to consumers to reduce their water use voluntarily.

The degree of enforcement of restrictions on water use varied among the 34 communities, but in none was service discontinued because of consumer noncompliance. Most (65 percent) of the communities relied on consumer cooperation and did not undertake active enforcement, thus in effect making ostensibly compulsory restrictions voluntary. Only 35 percent of the communities instituting restrictions, then, actually felt it necessary (or were willing) to back up their rules with a strict enforcement policy, including police vigilance.

Introduction or Expansion of Metering. In only three communities were any changes in the metering system instituted during the drought: Fitchburg, Marlboro, and Woburn. But only in Woburn was metering increased (from 50 to 85 percent). In Marlboro, metering of the entire system was completed in 1963, the product of a decision made *prior* to drought. And in Fitchburg a meter-repair program was formulated. In 5 other towns the introduction or expansion of metering would probably have been very helpful in reducing demand. All of these towns had little or no metering[31] at the beginning of the drought but found it necessary to make some adjustment during the drought.

Price Changes. In light of the extensive meter coverage in the sample communities, it might be thought that increases in water rates would have been effective in reducing the quantity of water demanded, particularly if applied during the critical summer sprinkling months. Not one community, however, raised the price of water in an effort specifically to reduce the quantity demanded. In 6 towns, the price of water was raised, but in each case the decision was based on considerations other than the level of demand. In 3 of the communities, water rates were raised because of cost increases resulting from purchases of water from the Metropolitan District Commission. In the other places, the decision to raise the price of water had been made prior to the drought in response to rising costs of operation and maintenance.

Efforts to Reduce Losses from Leaks. Although, as we have indicated, the potential loss of water as a result of leaks may be substantial, only 3 communities endeavored to reduce unaccounted-for water. Of the 39 systems that made some type of drought adjustment, only 1 community hired a leak-detecting firm, and only in two other places was a greater-than-normal effort made with regular personnel to detect leaks in the distribution system.

Other Measures. Neither the reuse of domestic water nor the application of film to cut down on reservoir evaporation were even mentioned by water managers as possible adjustment alternatives.

[31] In three of these towns, domestic water use was not metered though industrial use was, and in the other two systems, less than 50 percent of total water use was metered.

Adjustments to Increase Supply

Permanent new additional sources of water supply were developed by 23 of the communities. (See Table 18.) The drilling of a well, the most common type of new source, was completed in 19 communities; and, in 5 places a new reservoir was added to the existing supply. One or more emergency sources of water supplemented the existing supply in 17 places. Emergency sources of supply included groundwater, surface sources which were not normally used, and the Metropolitan District Commission which had in its giant Quabbin Reservoir a substantial safe-yield cushion.

Even though not a single community raised the price of water to curb demand or discussed the feasibility of water reuse, one city elected to try a cloud-seeding project. With the aid of industry, 3 adjoining communities raised a total of $9,000 for a 35-day silver iodide experiment.[32] The success of the project is debatable, as is true in many weather-modification trials.

Another widespread response to the drought was the heightened interest in planning for future public water supplies. In the mail survey, 63 percent of all the responding systems indicated that they had begun, expanded, or accelerated planning activity because of the drought. Of the 48 interviewed communities, 15 indicated some drought-related planning effort. None of the water managers, however, mentioned any future plans with respect to periodic or seasonal restrictions, increases in water rates, or complete installation of meters to reduce the level, or at least dampen the rate, of increase in the demand for water. It may be possible that prior publication of planned sequences of restrictions and their probable duration would sell communities on planned failure rates and condition the consumer to a more positive reaction to restrictions, but none of our system managers appeared prepared to embark on such a course. This was the traditional response: engineering plans were formulated with emphasis on increases in safe yield. In 8 of the communities that had an adequate supply during the drought period, engineering plans called for construction of new reservoirs. Groundwater development was planned in an additional 7 communities. Data from the mail survey confirms this stress on new supplies. Seventeen percent of the surveyed systems were "adequate" and yet were planning expansion. Forty-six percent were "inadequate" and were planning increases in supply facilities.

To water system managers, the most attractive answer to the adequacy problem, then, is an increase in safe yield. When asked what their systems needed most, 34 of the interviewed managers (71 percent) stated they be-

[32] The towns were Fitchburg, Leominster, and Gardner. J. Andre Provencial, "Emergency Measures Due to the Drought—The Fitchburg, Massachusetts Story," *Journal of the New England Water Works Association*, 79 (1965), 234.

lieved new supplies to be essential either through the construction of new reservoirs or the digging of additional wells. Significantly, not one manager mentioned an improved price structure or the implementation of pre-planned restrictions to curb demand. Opportunities to reduce the level of use by the introduction of metering, changes in prices, etc., will undoubtedly tend to disappear as the drought recedes in memory, and it is likely that not until serious shortages again appear imminent will such measures again receive serious consideration.

TIMING OF DROUGHT ADJUSTMENTS

Prior to 1963, very few water managers experienced an actual water shortage or foresaw an impending one. This was reflected in the absence of drought adjustments. Short-run adjustment to meet a shortage threat was undertaken in only 1 community: Northampton, which enacted restrictions in 1961. Randolph and Lenox developed new additions to their sources of water supply, but these actions were the consequence of decisions made prior to the drought.

In 1963, however, 16 communities initiated action in response to actual or expected shortages. During 1963, more communities adopted some type of adjustment to drought than during any other drought year (Figure 16). During the following year, 1964, 10 communities implemented their first adjustment to drought.

Shortly after a water manager perceived the beginning of drought, action was taken to meet the expected shortage of water. Although the data do not

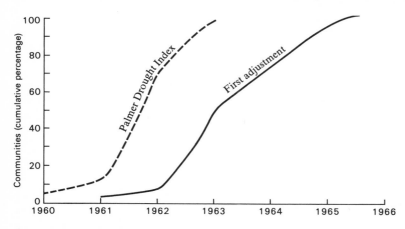

Based on the 39 communities making some type of adjustment to drought.

Figure 16. Community adjustment to drought: time of first adjustment.

allow a more precise statement, analysis of the 25 communities with more complete data suggest that the average time between drought perception and employment of the first adjustment was about 6 months. In 17 communities, the water managers adopted some type of drought adjustment within 1 year. In 2 of the remaining 8 communities, adjustments were not implemented for 2 years *after* recognition of the drought.

There was a tendency for the water managers who perceived drought beginning in 1964 or 1965 to initiate action more rapidly than the managers who viewed drought as beginning 1963 or earlier. Among the former group of managers, the average time of adjustment was about 7 months; whereas, those who recognized drought in 1964–65 were able to initiate action in only 3 months. (This phenomenon may also be related to the publicity generated by that time and the consequent public pressure, as we have already noted in connection with perception itself.)

SEQUENCE OF DROUGHT ADJUSTMENTS

The first response to drought in most communities was the enactment of restrictions on water use. In 25 water supply systems, the first choice among alternatives was the implementation of voluntary or involuntary restrictions (Figure 17). Reliance on emergency water supplies or the

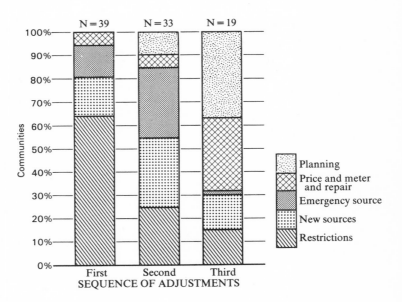

Figure 17. Sequence of community adoption of adjustments.

development of an additional permanent source of water supply constituted the response in 12 of the remaining 14 communities. In none of the communities was the emphasis upon new engineering plans a first adjustment.

Not all communities adopted more than one adjustment to the drought. Of the 39 communities that made some type of adjustment to drought, 33 tried two or more alternatives. Only 19 communities implemented three or more drought adjustments.

In the second type of adjustment adopted by the water managers, a greater emphasis was placed upon emergency and new sources of supply. These two alternatives constituted 60 percent of all second choices. Restrictions on water use were chosen in only 24 percent of the 33 communities as the second adjustment.

In the third group, the emphasis shifted to changes in price, metering, leak surveys, and planning for increases in the existing supply. These alternatives constituted the third choice of adjustment in 62 percent of the communities.

In review, a typical sequence of community adjustment to drought is: (1) enactment of restrictions on water use; (2) emergency and/or new permanent sources of supply; and, finally (3) new engineering plans and modification of consumption. As either a first or second choice, nearly every community adopted restrictions and an emergency or new source of supply. Other types of adjustment to drought were relegated to a third or fourth choice, if considered at all.

In the light of water managers' present solid preference for a few traditional strategies, it appears that some efforts to increase knowledge of alternatives in municipal water supply management and to change attitudes toward the alternatives might be exceedingly useful.

PART III

THE ECONOMIC IMPACT OF WATER SHORTAGE

CHAPTER 9

THE COST OF THE DROUGHT: DEFINITION AND INITIAL ESTIMATES

The essence of drought is the potential shortage of water engendered by interaction between a climatic event and the adequacy of the safe yield of a system in relation to the level of demand. There are, as we have noted, a variety of courses open to the system manager in the face of such a potential shortage: Broadly, he may move to restrict demand or to increase available supplies; or he may choose to combine measures from both areas. Whatever course he selects will imply some cost to the community at large. This section and the next two attempt to appraise the cost of drought in relation to the size of the potential shortage faced by the town. They are based on data collected in Braintree, Fitchburg, and Pittsfield as part of the overall study.[1] It is obvious that, as our results rest essentially on data from only three towns, they should be viewed as indicators of orders of magnitude rather than as "hard" bases for actual planning.

Two interesting questions have, of necessity, been ignored in this study. First, one would like to know more about the relation between the mix of adjustments to shortage chosen by the manager and the resulting size and distribution of drought losses. That the distribution of losses between sectors will be affected by the choice of adjustments is clear enough. It

---

[1] In what follows, "costs" and "losses" and "costs and losses" will often be used interchangeably in referring to the economic penalties paid in connection with the drought. It is realized that the two words have some definite differences in meaning and even more pronounced differences in connotation. We shall attempt to use "costs" where business expenses, equipment purchases, etc., are at stake, and "losses" where physical destruction, production cutbacks, or administrative prohibitions are involved. The reader should, however, be prepared to read both words where one appears and the general study is being discussed; this might be thought of as the price of tedium avoided.

seems that the size of losses will, in general, also be sensitive to this choice because of differences between the sectors in the ability to react. Second, it would be interesting to know if the distribution of losses between sectors varied with the size of shortages in a regular way. (Some comments on this matter are included below, but we have assumed in making use of our data in a planning model that this variation may be ignored.) Neither of these questions could be explored owing to lack of money and manpower for data collection, for a large increase in the number of towns studied intensively would have been necessary to produce enough independent variation in the variables of interest.

The bulk of our data is drawn from interviews with water system managers and executives of individual firms in the industrial and commercial sectors. These were supplemented by interviews with other municipal officials and miscellaneous private-sector persons with special knowledge. (Losses from domestic sprinkling restrictions were estimated quite outside the data-gathering framework, using published demand function estimates.[2]) The largest part of the information gathered in the interviews is considered to be of high quality, but with the commercial sector results being distinctly weaker than those for the industrial and municipal sectors. Data on specific industrial actions and their costs are particularly strong; those on water use before and after the drought somewhat weaker. The remainder of this chapter, then, is devoted to defining, producing, and correcting the estimates of economic losses attributable to the drought.[3] First, we set out to clear up some fundamental conceptual questions concerning the existence and definition of drought losses. Next, we produce gross estimates of total losses for the 3 towns differing from the raw data essentially only by corrections for double counting. These figures may be thought of as slightly modified measures of drought impact as it is perceived by local economic actors. These results are presented as the industrial, commercial, municipal, and domestic sector totals, and also as the costs of adjustments designed either to increase supply or to restrict use.[4]

[2] Charles W. Howe and F. P. Linaweaver, Jr., "The Impact of Price on Residential Water Demand and Its Relation to System Design and Price Structure," *Water Resources Research*, I (1965), 13–32 and Appendix E.

[3] The methods used in this study are related to the previous work of Kates, particularly that reported in *Industrial Flood Losses: Damage Estimation in the Lehigh Valley*, Department of Geography Research Paper No. 98 (Chicago: University of Chicago, 1965). That discussion of the nature and measurement of losses from interrupted production seems applicable to drought as well. The use of value added as a surrogate in the measurement of production losses is shown in Appendix A to be not only the most readily available but also the proper conceptual measure.

[4] The losses and costs turned up in our interviews were incurred, virtually without exception, during the period summer 1965 through summer 1966. We assume that these losses may, in fact, be identified with a single period of 12 months. We admit that other

Such gross figures are, however, economically misleading since they fail to take account of several potentially important aspects of the problem. Most important, the gross estimates do not reflect the investment aspect of many of the actions taken by businessmen. That is, inclusion of simply the capital cost of a water-use adjustment with a long life (for example, a cooling-water recirculation tower expected to last 30 years) ignores the implied future stream of benefits, positive or negative, resulting from the project's impact on future water costs. In addition, in order to make use of loss estimates in discussion of policy, it is necessary to be clear about which group is suffering. That is, we must adopt explicitly an accounting stance which proclaims that we are looking at things from a local, regional, or national point of view. Closely related to the stance we choose is the extent to which interrupted sales and production can be assumed to be eliminated from losses by deferral in time or transfer in space. For example, lost production at a local paper mill may be made up through use of otherwise slack facilities in another region. From the national point of view only a nominal loss is involved, though the local and regional accounts still record the full loss. Again, a local store may claim large sales losses on account of the drought, but these may represent only postponed sales and thus should not count in full as losses even in the local accounts. Both these matters are taken up in Chapter 10. There also are presented the fully corrected accounts for four combinations of discount rate, stance, and deferral assumptions, representing, we believe, the points of view of decision makers at various levels. Finally, Chapter 10 deals with adjustment of the several sets of data to eliminate self-supplied water users.

DROUGHT COSTS AND LOSSES: PRINCIPLES AND PROBLEMS

Before we become involved with estimation techniques and actual numbers, it will be worth while to discuss some of the difficulties lurking behind the innocent question, "How much did the drought cost?" First, of course, we must specify the question more carefully by asking how much the drought cost *whom*? Clearly the resort owner on Cape Cod who had record business during the dry summers has a different view of the cost of the drought than does the lumber company in Pittsfield which believes it lost

losses were almost certainly incurred in the early drought years, but we assume that these were not measured in our detailed study.

At certain points, as in the measurement of lost municipal revenues, we depart from our study data and have sufficient alternative information to estimate drought costs for any year in the 1963–66 period. In these instances we single out for inclusion the results for 1965 in Pittsfield and 1966 in Braintree and Fitchburg to reflect the earlier beginning and peaking of the drought in the West. We thus aim to maintain the figures on as close to an annual basis as possible.

a significant volume of timber growth on its woodlands. Similarly, the business in Fitchburg which lost orders because of a forced shutdown during the lowest river flows reckons a loss where the company in another state which picked up those orders sees a gain. If we agree, for example, that we are interested in how much the drought cost the people of Massachusetts, we would certainly have to net out the gains of the resort owner, but we would ignore the gains accruing to the out-of-state firm which benefited from the shutdown of production activity in Fitchburg.

However, even given a choice of "whom," not all our questions would be so easy to answer. Consider the possibility that production orders lost by one Massachusetts firm are made up by another within the state. What is the loss attributable to the drought? As we show below in Chapter 10, the answer to this question depends on the extent to which idle resources are available at the second firm; if otherwise idle resources are put to work making up the "lost" production, the loss from the state's point of view is very small. Another difficulty arises because some of the costs of the drought take the form of payments to specialized firms (such as well-drillers) for services rendered. Again, if reasonable resource mobility and full employment may be assumed, the increased activity (employment and production) of these firms can be said to represent a reduction in other forms of activity which society would, in the absence of the drought, have preferred to purchase. This activity then is a loss for society. If, on the other hand, the resources devoted to these activities would otherwise have been idle (e.g., the capital and labor inputs specialized to well-drilling), the extent of loss will be significantly smaller than the amount of activity called out by the drought.

Returning to the original question, we may note another difficulty: the reference point against which the costs are to be measured is not well specified. Thus, for example, do we mean to compare the drought period with a period of average precipitation or with one in which precipitation was slightly above or slightly below average. Surely our estimates of cost will be sensitive to this choice of zero point, but just as surely there is no particular reason for choosing one of these alternatives over the others. The information that the drought represented a loss for the people of Massachusetts of X million dollars compared with a similar period in which the long-term mean precipitation fell in each year would be of no particular use to anybody.[5] It is simply not now an alternative to replace drought periods with periods of average rainfall; though such a possibility may, in the future, exist. The choice of a reference point is, then, related

---

[5] It might serve as a talking point in state efforts to obtain federal relief funds.

to the alternatives being considered for improving the situation (the contemplated "adjustments"). In our example, it might be reasonable to ask about the losses compared with a situation in which 10 percent more precipitation had fallen each year.[6] But we are interested in municipal water systems, and hence our reference point becomes one of zero shortage for each system being studied. In other words, we ask, in effect, how much the drought cost the people of Massachusetts compared with a situation in which no municipal water system suffered shortage.[7] In this context, of course, the losses and gains of farmers, lumbermen, and resort owners are irrelevant except as they trace to municipal water-system performance.[8]

DESCRIPTION AND MEASUREMENT OF LOSSES FROM WATER SHORTAGE

In the evaluation of investment projects, a widely accepted criterion involves the present value of the stream of annual net efficiency benefits each project is expected to produce.[9] Net annual benefits are defined as gross efficiency benefits (e.g., total willingness to pay for project output) less the costs incurred in producing the annual output. It seems, therefore, reasonable to define water-shortage losses in broadest terms as gross annual benefits lost by disappointed users less costs avoided by the supplier. (Note that the user may also be the supplier, in which case, clearly, he loses gross benefits *and* avoids some costs.) In order that our measure of loss may have social significance, we must be careful to look at matters from a social rather than only a firm or household point of view.

An example of the application of this rule should make matters clearer. Consider first the problem of measuring the losses from lawn-sprinkling restrictions. Assume for simplicity that in normal periods only price is used to ration sprinkling water, but that as the result of drought, no sprinkling at all is permitted. If the system's (annual) demand curve for sprinkling water is DD in Figure 18, then at price P_o (domestic block rate), w_o gallons per year will be demanded for lawn watering. Now, the total annual

[6] A 10 percent increase in precipitation is the figure most often quoted in discussing the possible payoffs from weather modification. See, for example, National Academy of Sciences—National Research Council, *Scientific Problems of Weather Modification* (Washington: National Academy of Sciences, 1964).

[7] Our concern is actually with our 3 cities individually, though we compare different accounting points of view. We do not aggregate our estimates to the state level.

[8] For example, no municipal water system could take credit for the months of sunny weather which brought crowds to the beaches, but the failure of a system in a shore community could cost resort owners dearly if they had to shut down or truck in water.

[9] See, for example, Arthur Maass et al., *The Design of Water Resource Systems* (Cambridge: Harvard University Press, 1962), Ch. 2.

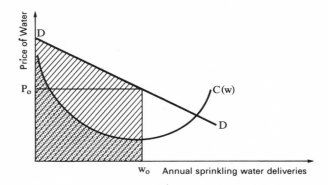

Figure 18. Losses from a total ban on lawn-sprinkling.

willingness to pay (*WTP*) for sprinkling water is the shaded area under *DD* up to w_o or:

$$WTP = \int_0^{w_o} D(w)dw \qquad (9\text{-}1)$$

If $C(w)$ is the marginal cost of supplying sprinkling water, then the quantity:

$$C_A = \int_0^{w_o} C(w)dw, \qquad (9\text{-}2)$$

(the *cross-hatched area*) represents costs avoided by the supplier when sprinkling is forbidden. Total social loss from the prohibition of sprinkling is:

$$\text{Social Loss (net)} = WTP - C_A. \qquad (9\text{-}3)$$

It may be convenient to express this aggregate social loss in terms of its impact on various economic sectors. In this case, lawnowners lose $WTP - P_o w_o$, or consumer surplus, since they don't pay for water they don't use; and the water system loses $P_o w_o - C_A$, or lost revenue less costs avoided.[10] Our accounts are generally set up in a manner to reflect this sectoral impact of shortage.[11]

It is, of course, quite possible that the water system, if it is an arm of government, will attempt to make up the $P_o w_o$ loss through taxation. In that case the full burden of the loss will be shifted to the citizens, though

[10] We assume here that the costs avoided are measured from the social viewpoint. We also assume that the simple concept of consumer surplus is applicable. This seems reasonable in view of the small fraction of the household budget devoted to the purchase of water.

[11] A second example of loss calculation, that of business losses resulting from shutdown, is discussed in Appendix D.

there may be some redistribution of it from lawnowners to other tax-payers. It should be clear, however, that whether or not the community regains the lost revenue in taxes has no bearing on the size of loss, only on its distribution between sectors and citizens. Our tables reflect the initial impact, and no account has been taken of any later redistribution of burden. Note, finally, that in practice we ignore the costs avoided by the municipal systems; it seems reasonable to assume that they are very small, particularly in Massachusetts where the emphasis is on upland sources requiring little or no filtration or treatment.[12]

Other reported costs involve successful attempts temporarily to restrict use, as with save-water campaigns and temporary installation of water-saving equipment, or to augment supplies, as with emergency supply efforts. In connection with these efforts, society may avoid certain costs which reduce the net social opportunity cost of the actions taken.

The concept of "opportunity cost" itself tends, however, to become more cloudy when we discuss these successful efforts temporarily to restrict use or augment supply. We may very well look on the related expenditures as part of the cost of having created a concentration of population greater than naturally occurring climatic conditions will support, much as Kuznets and others have suggested that the national accounts of a devel-oped country contain a number of items more properly thought of as costs of supporting an urbanized industrial society.[13] In the national accounts, then, the drought might very well appear as a stimulant to economic activity as numerous manufacturing and service firms answer the demand for equipment and talent aimed at relieving the situation. Are we, in effect, giving the drought a bad name by insisting that expenditures for temporary relief be counted as opportunity costs when other similar costs of urbani-zation, etc., are accorded the status of chosen "goods"? We generally as-sume that employment is full and that the turning of resources to the meeting of the drought crisis represents a social "evil."

We may summarize, then, our responses to the general problems posed above under the following points:

1. In assessing the costs and losses attributable to the drought we shall use as our zero point the situation in which the municipal system had

---

[12] By the same token the costs avoided may be substantial if extensive treatment is involved at the intake. They may also be larger, the deeper the drought, as the concen-tration of undesirable substances in the source increases with lower flows. Fuchs has estimated that the drought caused the Passaic Valley Water Commission to incur extra treatment costs of $399,000. See H. W. Fuchs, "The Economic Impact of Drought on Water Supply Systems in the Passaic River Basin, New Jersey," Master's thesis, College of Agriculture and Environmental Science, Rutgers, The State University, New Bruns-wick, N.J., May 1968.

[13] See Simon Kuznets, *Economic Change* (New York: Norton, 1953), pp. 161–62, 195–97.

enough water available in its normal system to meet demand at existing prices. (We shall, however, begin by listing all the losses found in our interviews, only later removing those incurred by self-supplied water users.)

2. The fundamental principle of measurement is that the losses equal gross benefits not enjoyed less any costs avoided.

3. We assume that resources used in countering the drought's effect, as in the drilling of domestic wells, would otherwise have been employed in the production of goods and services which society would have preferred in the absence of the drought. (We do take account of the possibility that production "losses" may be shifted to areas or time periods in which unemployed resources are available.)

4. An attempt is made to show drought losses and costs as their impact is initially felt by the various sectors. Thus, for domestic sprinkling losses we include consumer surplus lost in the domestic sector and revenue lost (less costs avoided) in the municipal sector. This approach makes double counting a danger and we have been concerned to insure that our estimates of revenue lost by the water system do not include losses already counted in other sectors.

ESTIMATES OF COSTS AND LOSSES: UNCORRECTED EXCEPT FOR DOUBLE COUNTING

In presenting results such as these loss estimates, we clearly have two primary responsibilities. First, we must explain in more or less detail how they were derived. And second, we must call to the reader's attention the particular results and patterns we feel are of greatest interest or of greatest relevance to our general argument. The latter duty is relatively the easier of the two, for the former involes us in difficult trade-offs between reader boredom and scientific correctness.

The problem of the appropriate degree of detail in discussing estimation procedures is particularly troubling where, as in this study, sources and methods vary widely across the sectors covered. The solution we propose is as follows: first, in the body of the text we discuss in a general way the different sectoral estimates, indicating especially those areas in which the methods involved significant departures from the compilation of survey interview results; second, accompanying the summary table will be a set of notes covering details of more limited interest; and third, certain matters will be the subjects of technical appendices which may be ignored by those not interested.

GENERAL METHODOLOGY

The first set of estimates of costs and losses corrected only for double counting is summarized in Table 22 below. In the discussion following we adopt the same sectoral order as that in the table.

1. *The Industrial Sector.* Here, we have broken down our estimates into three subclasses: Business Losses, Investments and Other. Business Losses, the losses resulting from forced slowdowns or shutdowns in production due to the drought, were claimed very infrequently. Where claimed, they were estimated on the basis of value added (generally from *Census of Manufactures* data) that was lost during the interruption, corrected for water costs avoided. (See Appendix D.)

Investment includes the claimed capital costs of all permanent water-use adjustments. Examples of such adjustments are cooling towers for the recirculation of cooling water; wells drilled to increase the plant's independent supply capability; process-water recirculation systems; additions to existing dams; new dams; installation of air-cooled window air conditioners; and others. This category produced the largest single gross cost figure and was generally estimated directly from the interview results.

The Other category includes such disparate costs as those of dry-hole wells, attempted rain-making, and save-water campaigns. Again, most data were taken directly from the interviews. Save-water campaign costs were corrected for water costs avoided as required to justify our inclusion of lost revenue totals in the municipal sector.

2. *The Municipal Sector.* Three subclasses were distinguished here: Lost Revenue, Emergency Supply Costs, and the ubiquitous Other. In all three areas, the reliance on direct interview results was somewhat less than for the Industrial Sector.

Lost Revenue was estimated for each town on the basis of the projections of water demand for the drought years. (These projections were discussed in Chapter 5.)

The total loss of revenue to the town involved only the water which could have been sold had it been available. Any emergency supplies which were provided by the system were sold at the going rates. Thus, the applicable quantity of water for use in the calculation of lost revenue is simply the difference between observed consumption and projected demand. Thus,

$$\text{Lost Revenue}^{14} = (C_{it} - D_{it})P_w. \qquad (9\text{-}4)$$

[14] The lost revenue reported is for 1965 in Pittsfield and for 1966 in Braintree and Fitchburg. This reflects our attempt to maintain losses on an annual basis.

In our estimates, P_w was taken to be a weighted average of the domestic and industrial marginal block rates (see Table 21). The weights used were the approximate percentages of total demand accounted for by domestic and industrial use. This approach involves an implicit assumption that shortages were shared about equally, in terms of volume, between the industrial and domestic sectors. There seems to be no way to improve on this approach short of separate measures of projected demand and actual consumption for the two sectors, and we did not gather these data in the original study.[15]

TABLE 21. WEIGHTED AVERAGE WATER RATES FOR LOST REVENUE CALCULATION

	Braintree	Fitchburg	Pittsfield
Percentage of domestic demand	70	30	50
Percentage of industrial demand	30	70	50
Domestic block rate (*per thousand gallons*)	$.47	$.334	$.00[a]
Industrial block rate	$.29	$.134	$.107
Weighted average rate	$.42	$.194	$.054

[a] Flat rate.

Emergency supply costs were estimated from the data obtained in the interviews with system managers, and from such other bits and pieces as could be gleaned from newspaper search. These costs are restricted to costs for equipment (or its operation) directly related to attempts to increase the town's available water supply in the short run. Not included are costs of redistributing water in a desired pattern, as in hiring spray trucks to cart river water to thirsty shrubs and trees in town parks.

"Other" costs and losses include those redistribution costs mentioned directly above, as well as costs of investments intended for specific uses, such as a well for a town swimming pool. Town efforts to find new ground-water sources are included here since they seem somewhat longer-run in intent than truly emergency supply measures.

3. *Commercial Sector.* The Commercial Sector estimates are based entirely on data developed in interviews with managers of firms. The costs and losses are broken down into two categories: Business Losses and Investment. Business losses are again broken down into those claimed by nurseries and those claimed by all other interviewed firms. The figures given represent estimates of value-added lost, based on the businessmen's statements of their lost sales. The percentage of sales accounted for by

[15] It would require a large investment of time and effort to do so, since no separate records are kept on a sectoral basis, and it would be necessary to sum the consumption figures for all industrial-sector customers for quarterly billing periods.

value-added was estimated on the basis of *1958 Census of Business* data on payrolls and sales in retail trades claiming losses (New England and Massachusetts regional figures). This was supplemented by assumptions about the percentage of sales represented by rent, profit, and interest.[16]

4. *Domestic Sector.* Two categories of drought costs are presented here.

First, an estimate of the total capital costs of drought-related domestic well investment is provided, based on telephone interviews with well-drillers all over the state. Each well reported drilled and drought-related in our three towns is valued at $1,200. This includes $900 for drilling (our contacts were virtually unanimous in quoting this as the average cost of drilling a domestic well in Massachusetts) and $300 for pump and installation, connection, etc. This figure represents an attempt to average the high costs of the few wells probably drilled for total domestic use and the many drilled to provide an independent source of sprinkling water.

Second, sprinkling losses, the losses of consumer surplus resulting from a complete or partial ban on lawn-sprinkling, were estimated using the demand equation for sprinkling water estimated by Howe and Lina-weaver for eastern, metered, public sewer areas.[17] Information on housing valuation for use with this equation was taken from the *1960 Census of Housing.*

5. *The Miscellaneous Sector.* Three subclasses are included in this final category: Farm Losses, Golf Club Costs, and Tree Losses. The first covers losses claimed for farms within the Pittsfield city limits by the Berkshire County Extension Agent. These seem primarily to be costs of feed purchases necessitated by hay crop failure. (This item is, of course, related to self-supply problems, and we eliminate it along with all other such items in Chapter 10.) Golf Club Costs were obtained in interviews with club officials and greenskeepers. Over 99 percent of the total here is made up of the capital costs of schemes designed to provide the clubs with self-supplied water for maintenance of greens and fairways. These costs include pumps, wells, ponds, piping, and isolation of inside and outside systems.

Tree Losses reflects city officials' claims of the value of city-owned trees destroyed by the drought. The accuracy of these estimates was impossible to check, both because of questions of valuation and of actual numbers of trees lost. It is not inconceivable that such losses could have been very high (e.g., the Pittsfield estimate is $100,000!) if many old and essentially irre-

---

[16] For our purposes, the assumption that the relation between sales and payrolls was constant between 1958 and 1965–66 did not seem particularly dangerous.

[17] See Howe and Linaweaver, "Impact of Price on Residential Water Demand," p. 13, and Appendix E.

placeable trees had been lost. Such trees would be, however, the least likely to suffer severe damage because of their highly developed, deep root structures. At a later stage, the Pittsfield figure is altered to bring it more nearly in line with the indicated total tree costs (costs of special watering plus losses) per capita in the other 2 towns.

RESULTS

The estimates developed by the methods described above are summarized in Table 22, where we present an all-in picture of gross drought costs and losses corrected essentially only for double counting.

The most striking features of this table are noted below.[18]

1. Fitchburg, where the potential shortage was greatest, accounts for about two-thirds of the total losses measured. Braintree, with the smallest system deficiency, accounts for only about one-tenth.

2. The combined industrial sectors accounted for the greatest sectoral share of total losses (47.0 percent), while the combined municipal sectors accounted for another 30.2 percent. The commercial, domestic, and miscellaneous sectors were relatively much less important as 3-town totals.

3. Between the towns the pattern of sectoral importance varied. Consider, for example, the identity of the sector with the largest losses. For Braintree, which has little industry, municipal sector losses were 72.2 percent of the town total. For Fitchburg, industrial sector losses were 64.0 percent of the total. Indeed, Fitchburg's industrial losses alone were about 40 percent of the total losses for the 3 towns. In Pittsfield, the miscellaneous sector losses (including the heavy tree loss) accounted for 45.2 percent of the total. These figures suggest that for smaller losses the municipal sector can and does bear a large part of the burden of meeting the potential shortage, largely through the purchase of emergency supplies (91 percent of the Braintree municipal sector total is accounted for by emergency supply costs) but also through the sacrifice in revenue implied in the imposition of restrictions on uses such as sprinkling. These alternatives are, of course, substitutes for one another; the purchase of emergency supplies in sufficient quantity will eliminate the necessity for losing revenue through restricting use.

4. The items most closely and dramatically connected with drought in the public mind—especially losses due to lawn-sprinkling bans—are relatively unimportant in the overall picture. On the other hand, emergency

[18] We identify these losses with the percentage shortage for 1966 for Fitchburg (22.8 percent) and Braintree (9.7 percent), and with the 1965 shortage for Pittsfield (14.1 percent), since, as noted already, the drought impact occurred earlier in the western part of the state.

supply costs, also well publicized, are fairly important as a single source of costs (16 percent of the grand total).

One of the most interesting features of the corrections applied below will be their effect on the relative importance of the various towns and sectors in contributing to total losses. As the totals become in general smaller, it will also be true that shifts will occur in the identity of the "big losers."

TYPES OF ADJUSTMENT TO SHORTAGE: MAGNITUDE OF RESULTING LOSSES

One interesting way of looking at the raw-loss data summarized above is to ask to what extent they resulted from one or the other of the two broad types of adjustment open to system managers—restriction of demand or augmentation of supply. Tables 23 through 25 supply the answer to this question.

Table 23 summarizes the cost and loss totals related to measures to increase supply. Table 24 deals with measures to restrict use. Table 25 is reserved for items unclassified under the other two headings.[19] The very few items which could not be so classified (only 3.5 percent of the Table 22 total) are dominated by farm losses. These seemed to involve only passive response to the precipitation shortfall and hence to be unrelated to either form of active response.

The most interesting results obtained by separating costs on this basis include the following:

1. Costs of measures to restrict use, and losses resulting therefrom, are quantitatively more important than those related to attempts to increase supplies (57.4 percent of the Table 22 grand total as opposed to 39.1 percent). This is primarily the result of the inclusion under the former category of both the many industrial-sector recirculation projects in Fitchburg and the municipal-sector lost revenue estimates there. These two items together account for 62 percent of the use-restriction costs and 41 percent of the all-in grand total (Table 22) of costs and losses.

[19] Specific cost and loss items were classified under one of the headings if they represented either the direct cost of a measure designed to achieve that end or if they represented the losses or costs created by such measures taken by the same or another agent. Thus, losses from sprinkling restrictions belong under "Restrict Use" as they result from measures to that end taken by the city.

Emergency supply costs, for obvious reasons, belong in the "Increase-Supply" category. Since "use" must be seen as withdrawals, the installation of recirculation equipment restricts use. The drilling of a well by any agent is seen as a measure to increase supply since we are interested here in the total capacity of the local region to support withdrawals, not only in the public system. Later we shall eliminate from consideration all items relating to self-supplied firms, though not actions to provide some self-supply taken by customers of the municipal system.

TABLE 22. ALL-IN GROSS LOSSES,[a] CORRECTED FOR DOUBLE COUNTING

Sector	Braintree			Fitchburg			Pittsfield			Sector totals	
	Corrected costs ($)	Percentage of town total	Percentage of sector total	Corrected costs ($)	Percentage of town total	Percentage of sector total	Corrected costs ($)	Percentage of town total	Percentage of sector total	Corrected costs ($)	Percentage of grand total
Industrial											
Business losses[b]	—			171,400			—			171,400	
Investments	2,500			549,000			70,200			622,500	
Other	2,500			30,000			17,800			50,300	
Subtotal	5,000	2.6	0.6	751,200	64.0	89.0	88,000	20.5	10.4	844,200	47.0
Municipal											
Lost revenue	—			173,100			54,900			228,000	
Emergency supply	125,000			144,200			12,000			281,200	
Other	12,900			5,200			15,000			33,100	
Subtotal	137,900	72.2	25.4	322,500	27.5	59.5	81,900	19.1	15.1	542,300	30.2
Commercial[c]											
Business losses nurseries	8,600			—			—			8,600	
Business losses—other	—			3,000			3,000			6,000	
Investments	—			6,100			12,000			18,100	
Subtotal	8,600	4.5	26.3	9,100	0.8	27.8	15,000	3.5	45.9	32,700	1.8

		Percentage of GT^f			Percentage of GT			Percentage of GT	Grand Total	Percentage of GT
Domestic											
Wells reported	24,000			31,200			50,400			105,600	
Sprinkling loss^d	14,200			29,400			—			43,600	
Subtotal	38,200	20.0	25.6	60,600	5.2	40.5	50,400	11.7	33.8	149,200	8.3
Miscellaneous											
Farm losses^e	—			—			45,000			45,000	
Golf club costs	—			25,000			48,700			73,700	
Tree losses	1,200			6,000			100,000			107,200	
Subtotal	1,200	0.6	0.5	31,000	2.6	13.7	193,700	45.2	85.7	225,900	12.6
Town: totals	190,900	10.6		1,174,400	65.4		429,000	23.9		1,794,300	

ᵃ In several cases, original calculations (or even original information) included a range of possible values. These ranges depend in most cases on the nature of the assumptions made about the seasonal pattern of demand and the like. In all such cases, the figure in Table 22 is the simple average of the extremes of the range.

ᵇ Industrial business losses were estimated differently, depending on the nature of the information contained in the claim. In some cases, value-added per day per man was projected ahead from the *1963 Census of Manufactures*. This was used where shutdowns were estimated in days. In other cases, value-added unit prices were estimated and used to value estimated lost production in physical terms. Both sorts of calculations were corrected for savings on water purchases and withdrawals.

ᶜ Commercial business losses were estimated on the basis of claims of lost sales made in interviews. These figures were corrected to value-added by using an estimate of value-added as a percentage of sales. This, in turn, was derived from figures on wages as a percentage of sales in various affected areas of retailing from the *1958 Survey of Business* and from assumptions about the size of profits (36 percent), rent (10 percent), and interest (4 percent) relative to sales.

ᵈ Domestic sprinkling loss calculations are explained in detail in Appendix E.

ᵉ Farm losses were estimated by the Berkshire County Extension Agent as $1,500 per farm for 30 commercial farms within the city limits.

ᶠ GT = grand total.

TABLE 23. LOSSES RELATED TO MEASURES TO INCREASE SUPPLY[a]

Sector	Braintree			Fitchburg			Pittsfield			Sector totals	
	Corrected costs ($)	Percentage of town total	Percentage of sector total	Corrected costs ($)	Percentage of town total	Percentage of sector total	Corrected costs ($)	Percentage of town total	Percentage of sector total	Corrected costs ($)	Percentage of grand total
Industrial											
Business losses	—			—			—			—	
Investments	2,500			92,300			70,000			164,800	
Other	2,500			24,000			4,600			31,100	
Subtotal	5,000	3.0 (2.6)	2.6 (0.6)	116,300	36.1 (9.9)	59.4 (13.8)	74,600	35.1 (17.4)	38.1 (8.8)	195,900	27.9 (10.9)
Municipal											
Lost revenue	—			—			—			—	
Emergency supply	125,000			144,200			12,000			281,200	
Other	12,900			5,200			15,000			33,100	
Subtotal	137,900	82.6 (72.2)	43.9 (25.4)	149,400	46.4 (12.7)	47.5 (27.5)	27,000	12.7 (6.3)	8.6 (5.0)	314,300	44.8 (17.5)
Commercial											
Business losses nurseries	—			—			—			—	
Business losses—other	—			—			—			—	
Investments	—			—			12,000			12,000	
Subtotal	—			—			12,000	5.6 (2.8)	100 (36.7)	12,000	1.8 (0.7)

	Value		Percentage of GT	Value		Percentage of GT	Value		Percentage of GT	Value	Percentage of GT
Domestic										**Grand Total**	
Wells reported	24,000			31,200			50,400			105,600	
Sprinkling loss	—			—			—			—	
Subtotal	24,000	14.4 (12.6)	22.7 (16.1)	31,200	9.7 (2.6)	29.5 (20.9)	50,400	23.7 (11.7)	47.7 (33.8)	105,600	15.0 (5.9)
Miscellaneous											
Farm losses	—			—			—			—	
Golf club costs	—			25,000			48,400			73,400	
Tree losses	—			—			—			—	
Subtotal	—			25,000	7.8 (2.1)	34.1 (11.1)	48,400	22.8 (11.3)	65.9 (21.4)	73,400	10.5 (4.1)
Town totals	166,900		23.8 (9.3)	321,900		45.9 (17.9)	212,400		30.3 (11.8)	701,200	(39.1)

ᵃ Two sets of percentage figures are given for each subtotal. The set *not* enclosed in parentheses represents the percentage calculated, wholly within that table. For example, in Table 23, Fitchburg's industrial sector subtotal ($116,300) is 36.1 percent of the town total of increase-supply measures ($321,900) and 59.4 percent of the total for the industrial sector over the three towns ($195,900). The percentage figures *in* parentheses relate the sector and town subtotals to the all-in totals of Table 22. Thus, the $116,300 figure is 9.9 percent of the all-in Fitchburg total ($1,174,400) and 13.8 percent of the all-in industrial sector subtotal ($844,200).

TABLE 24. Losses Related to Measures to Restrict Use[a]

Sector	Braintree			Fitchburg			Pittsfield			Sector totals	
	Corrected costs ($)	Percentage of town total	Percentage of sector total	Corrected costs ($)	Percentage of town total	Percentage of sector total	Corrected costs ($)	Percentage of town total	Percentage of sector total	Corrected costs ($)	Percentage of grand total
Industrial											
Business losses	—			171,400			—			171,400	
Investments	—			457,500			200			457,700	
Other	—			—			13,200			13,200	
Subtotal	—			628,900	74.6 (53.6)	97.9 (74.5)	13,400	7.8 (3.1)	2.1 (1.6)	642,300	62.3 (35.8)
Municipal											
Lost revenue	—			173,100			54,900			228,000	
Emergency supply	—			—			—			—	
Other	—			—			—			—	
Subtotal	—			173,100	20.5 (14.7)	75.9 (31.9)	54,900	32.0 (12.8)	24.1 (10.1)	228,000	22.1 (12.7)

		Percentage of GT		Percentage of GT		Percentage of GT	Grand Total	Percentage of GT
Commercial								
Business losses nurseries	—		—		—		—	
Business losses—other	—		6,100	0.7 (0.5)	—		6,100	
Investments	—		—		3,000	1.8 (0.7)	3,000	
Subtotal	—		6,100	67.0 (18.7)	3,000	33.0 (9.2)	9,100	0.9 (0.5)
Domestic								
Wells reported	—		—		—		—	
Sprinkling loss	14,200	92.2 (7.4)	29,400	3.5 (2.5)	—		43,600	
Subtotal	14,200	32.6 (9.5)	29,400	67.4 (19.7)	—		43,600	4.2 (2.4)
Miscellaneous								
Farm losses	—		—		—		—	
Golf club costs	—		—		—		—	
Tree losses	1,200	7.8 (0.6)	6,000	0.7 (0.5)	100,000	58.4 (23.3)	107,200	10.4
Subtotal	1,200	1.1 (0.3)	6,000	5.6 (2.6)	100,000	93.3 (44.3)	107,200	(6.0)
Town totals	15,400	1.5 (0.8)	843,500	81.9 (47.0)	171,300	16.6 (9.5)	1,030,200	(57.4)

a See note to Table 23.

TABLE 25. LOSSES UNCLASSIFIED WITH RESPECT TO CAUSE[a]

Sector	Braintree			Fichburg			Pittsfield			Sector totals	
	Corrected costs ($)	Percentage of town total	Percentage of sector total	Corrected costs ($)	Percentage of town total	Percentage of sector total	Corrected costs ($)	Percentage of town total	Percentage of sector total	Corrected costs ($)	Percentage of grand total
Industrial											
Business losses	—			—			—			—	
Investments	—			—			—			—	
Other	—			6,000			—			6,000	
Subtotal	—			6,000	66.7 (0.5)	100 (0.7)	—			6,000	9.5 (0.3)
Municipal											
Lost revenue	—			—			—			—	
Emergency supply	—			—			—			—	
Other	—			—			—			—	
Subtotal	—			—			—			—	
Commercial											
Business losses nurseries	8,600			—			—			8,600	

		Percentage of GT		Percentage of GT		Percentage of GT	Grand Total	
Business losses—other	—		3,000		—		3,000	
Investments	—		—		—		—	
Subtotal	8,600	100 74.1 (4.5) (26.3)	3,000	33.3 25.9 (0.2) (9.2)	—		11,600	18.4 (0.6)
Domestic								
Wells reported	—		—		—		—	
Sprinkling loss	—		—		—		—	
Subtotal	—		—		—		—	
Miscellaneous								
Farm losses	—		—		45,000		45,000	
Golf club costs	—		—		300		300	
Tree losses	—		—		—		—	
Subtotal	—		—		45,300	100 100 (10.6) (20.0)	45,300	72.0 (2.5)
Town totals	8,600	13.7 (0.5)	9,000	14.3 (0.5)	45,300	72.0 (2.5)	62,900	(3.5)

[a] See note to Table 23.

2. Within the increase-supply table, municipal emergency supply costs are the single most important item, followed by industrial investments and domestic wells. The three together account for 78.5 percent of the total attributable to measures to increase supply.

3. The costs and losses from measures to restrict use (Table 24) are, as mentioned above, dominated by business investments and lost revenue. These two items account for 62 percent of the costs and losses recorded in this table. Even within the set of losses from restrictions, sprinkling losses still show up as relatively unimportant (4.2 percent of the reduced total).

It is, however, necessary to consider certain important adjustments to these raw cost data. First, we look at the investment aspect of certain of the reported costs. Then, corrections are made for considerations of accounting stance and assumptions about the extent of deferral or transferral of "lost" production. Finally, because this study focuses on the municipal system, we eliminate from the final accounts losses and gains accruing to self-supplied water users. These matters are taken up in Chapter 10.

THE COST OF THE DROUGHT: CORRECTION OF INITIAL ESTIMATES FOR VARIOUS ECONOMIC CONSIDERATIONS

It is now necessary to correct for the fact that not all out-of-pocket expenses connected with the drought are necessarily net losses even for the firm whose pocket is involved. In addition, it may be that some losses which are quite real to local economic actors may be cancelled out when the drought is viewed from a larger regional or national stance. Finally, after these considerations have been allowed for, the concern of this study with the municipal system will dictate the elimination from our accounts of losses (and gains) accruing to firms, individuals, and organizations supplying themselves with water.

DROUGHT ADJUSTMENTS AS INVESTMENTS

Certain of the claimed drought costs represented investments in facilities which promise to have some effect on the water costs of their owners over a number of years in the future. In order to assess the economic impact of the drought we must take note of the future streams of annual net benefits (positive or negative) implied by these investments.

Table 26 shows the types of investments reported within each sector and indicates the relative importance of these general types. The industrial sector demonstrates, as we might expect, the greatest variety of adjustments. Recirculation of process and cooling water clearly were the most important of these, though industrial spending on wells was still greater than the total investment of any other sector. The amounts spent by industry on dams and miscellaneous projects were relatively insignificant. In all, investment spending accounted for almost 74 percent of the sector's claimed costs, and for 35 percent of the grand total. For the municipal sector, investments were a very small part of total gross costs, if spending on emergency supply facilities is ruled out. This is almost certainly due to a combination of inflexibility in the planning and execution of "lumpy" projects and the existence of a smaller range of available alternatives than is open to industry, particularly the absence of a common and publicly accepted recirculation technology for municipal sewage.

TABLE 26. SUMMARY OF INVESTMENT PROJECTS

Sector/Description	Reported cost ($)	Percentage of sector total	Percentage of grand total
Industrial			
Cooling-water recirculation	277,000		
Process-water recirculation	175,000		
Wells	162,300		
Dams	2,500		
Miscellaneous	5,700		
Subtotal	622,500	73.7	34.7
Municipal			
Wells	2,600		
Miscellaneous	600		
Subtotal	3,200	0.5	0.2
Commercial			
Air-conditioning recirculation	6,100		
Wells	12,000		
Subtotal	18,100	55.3	1.0
Domestic			
Wells	105,600	70.7	5.9
Miscellaneous			
Golf club sprinkling systems	73,300	32.4	4.1
Total	822,700		45.9

All together, investment in adjustment projects accounted for 45.9 percent of the $1,794,300 total loss. Clearly, it is important to know what part, if any, of this investment represented projects whose future returns will offset the claimed cost.

Appendix F contains a discussion of the conceptual framework for dealing with water-use adjustments. Here, it may be said briefly that these corrections involve comparison of total annual water costs to the firm (or household) before and after the adjustment. Clearly, lower future water bills represent benefits to the firm. Comparison of water costs requires, in turn, knowledge of withdrawals from various sources before and after the investment; the costs to the firm of water from each source and the extent of recirculation introduced (if any); the makeup fraction required by this recirculation system; and the variable cost of recirculation. Given sufficient information about these quantities, our investment corrections would be completely straightforward. The problem, of course, was that our information was far less than complete, and a considerable part of the work involved construction of estimates from available rules of thumb, observed relations, and the incomplete information furnished in the interviews. The major reason for our difficulties in this respect was that the interviewed managers did not, in general, know the impact of the investments on water withdrawals.

The Discount Rate

A major consideration in the evaluation of time streams of costs and benefits is the choice of an appropriate discount rate. We chose to use two rates—8 and 20 percent—intending that the higher one represent the business sector's evaluation of alternative investment opportunities. The lower one, intended as a discount rate appropriate to the public sector, falls within the range of rates recommended for the evaluation of public investments by several economists in testimony before the Joint Economic Committee of the Congress.[1]

Investment in Wells and Recirculation

The challenge in evaluating these investments was in supplying missing information. For wells, this was done by estimating a cost-yield curve for Massachusetts wells based on the experiences of several firms recorded in our interviews. This curve gave us an approximation of yield for projects for which we had only costs, and vice versa. For cooling towers, we relied heavily on the work of Berg et al. and of Cootner and Löf.[2] In the one reported case of installation of process-water recirculation, we used the cost and volume figures supplied us by the firm in question.

---

[1] For example, Otto Eckstein recommended 7–7.5 percent; Arnold Harberger, 10.8 percent. See U.S. Congress, Joint Economic Committee, *Economic Analysis of Public Investment Decisions: Interest Rate Policy and Discounting Analysis*, Hearings of July 30, 31, and August 1, 1968 (Washington, U.S. Government Printing Office, 1968).

[2] See Brian Berg, Russell W. Lane, and Thurston E. Larson, "Water Use and Related Costs with Cooling Towers," *Journal of the American Water Works Association*, 56 (1964), 311–29; and Paul Cootner and George O. G. Löf, *Water Demand for Steam Electric Generation* (Washington: Resources for the Future, 1965).

Slightly different procedures were employed for domestic-sector wells and commercial-sector recirculation of air-conditioning cooling water. In the former case, discount rates of 4 and 8 percent were used to reflect the lower opportunity cost of investable funds to the average homeowner. In the latter, we had first to estimate hours of air conditioning required per year and to combine this with our cost data to estimate volume of use.[3]

For a small number of investments, our information was insufficient to permit any but the crudest estimates of possible present values. These represent about 7.5 percent of total reported investments in terms of original cost. In all but one of these cases, we simply used the capital cost of the project as its present value to the investor, assuming no net benefits over the life of the project.

Finally, in Table 27, we summarize the results of the various calculations discussed above. The pattern of results shown in this table is not surprising, though the absolute size of the corrections involved may well be. That is, we should not be surprised to find that the industrial-sector investments in wells and recirculation equipment generally result in the largest net present values (the greatest future savings net of capital costs). The scale on which these projects were carried out and the relatively high number of hours of use per year combined to produce this effect. In general, air-conditioning cooling water recirculation projects showed up as less profitable; this was because of the low number of gallons recirculated per year in these seasonal operations. It did, however, appear that the commercial-sector projects involving such recirculation were profitable at both discount rates. These were the only projects outside of the industrial sector which showed up as profitable under *either* rate. Most other cases for which calculations were possible exhibited streams of future savings with present values very close to zero; here, the savings per gallon was often significant, but the number of gallons involved in each future year was so small that total annual savings was not significant.

The observation that the total positive present value calculated under the 8 percent discount rate is almost as large in absolute value as the original total of costs and losses (Table 22) may startle the reader. As we shall see when we combine these results with the other items corrected for various stances, under the 8 percent discount rate for certain accounting stances, the drought is no longer a producer of costs but of benefits in the aggregate. Abstracting from distributional questions, then, under certain sets of assumptions the drought appears as a boon to society. But distributional questions are clearly important here, for the benefits accrue to firms as returns on investments, while the costs are borne by households and municipal governments.

[3] See Berg et al., "Water Use and Related Costs."

TABLE 27. SUMMARY OF CORRECTIONS FOR FUTURE RETURNS TO INVESTMENTS[a]

Sector /description	Reported cost	Present value at 8 percent	Present value at 20 percent
Industrial			
Cooling	−277,000	+999,500	+77,600
Process	−175,000	+438,000	+190,000
Wells	−162,300	+161,200	−46,700
Dams	−2,500	−2,500	−2,500
Miscellaneous	−5,700	−1,700	−1,700
Subtotal	−622,500	+1,594,500	+216,700
Municipal			
Wells	−2,600	−2,600	−2,600
Miscellaneous	−600	−600	−600
Subtotal	−3,200	−3,200	−3,200
Commercial			
Air conditioning	−6,100	+8,700	+400
Wells	−12,000	−10,600	−11,600
Subtotal	−18,100	−1,900	−11,200
Domestic			
Wells (40-year life)	−105,600	−99,900[b]	−102,300[c]
Miscellaneous			
Golf club sprinkling	−73,300	−73,300	−73,300
Totals	−822,700	+1,416,200	+26,700

[a] — figures are costs, gross or net as appropriate; + figures are net benefits.

[b] Evaluated at 4 percent.

[c] Evaluated at 8 percent.

Even at the 20 percent (private opportunity cost) discount rate a small, positive present value results for the aggregate of all investments, and a larger one results for the industrial sector alone. This is particularly striking, since informal contact with businessmen *outside* our study area suggests that they feel that most water-use adjustments are at best breakeven propositions when evaluated in relation to alternative investment opportunities.[4]

Now, it is certainly not true that the results of these investments were always positive. As mentioned earlier, smaller and less intensively used installations tended to produce negative present values, and the aggregates for each important subclass are very much the reflections of the large returns accruing to one or a few firms. This accentuates the distributional

[4] This dim view of water-use investments was *not* common among those interviewed who had made such investments. See the discussion on this point below.

questions raised by aggregation of these results with those from other sources and sectors.

There remain two interesting questions to be discussed in connection with the investment corrections. First, to what extent do the perceptions of the firm managers involved agree with our results where project profitability is concerned? There were 16 firms in the industrial and commercial sectors for which we had both a reasonable basis for the estimation of returns and an answer to our question concerning the perceived profitability of water-use investments.[5] The results of a comparison of our present value calculations and the managers' responses to the question on perceived profitability are shown in Table 28.

TABLE 28. COMPARISON OF CALCULATED AND PERCEIVED PROJECT
PROFITABILITY, 16 PROJECTS

	Projects firm managers perceived as profitable	Projects firm managers perceived as unprofitable
Positive present value at both discount rates	6	1
Negative present value at both discount rates	3	2
Positive present value at 8 percent; negative present value at 20 percent	1	3

Note that in only one case did a manager find unprofitable a project which our calculations found profitable at both discount rates. In three cases, projects profitable at 8 percent but not at 20 percent by our estimates were perceived as unprofitable by the managers involved. In general, Table 28 indicates that our results accord with the perceptions of managers when we use the 20 percent discount rate reflecting the assumed opportunity cost of private capital.

We have thus found two striking results in our study of water-use investments undertaken because of the drought. First, some of these investments have been extremely profitable for those who undertook them. But, second, managers do not seem to have been aware of these opportunities until the crisis atmosphere of the drought drew their attention to them. This second

[5] These 16 firms represented 17 separate projects; but the 1 firm with 2 projects made only one overall answer to the profitability question, and we were forced to treat these two investments as a single project.

conclusion seems implicit in managers' statements that all these adjustments were forced on them by the drought.

To what extent are the results above likely to be applicable to future droughts or to droughts in other climatic regions? Can we expect it always to be the case that the industrial sector will be able to avoid loss by investment in recirculation, etc., and not realize it beforehand? Our answer to these questions also amounts to an explanation of the existence of such enormously profitable opportunities within so mundane an area as the firm's water-use pattern.

We feel that there exists, at least in the humid Northeast, a large degree of slack in the adoption of existing industrial water-use technology by firms.[6] This slack is explained not by a lack of profit incentive—our results tend to show that many such adjustments are highly profitable—but by a lack of interest in and knowledge of water use on the part of management. This, in turn, may be attributed to the relatively small part of total costs accounted for by water inputs; to the general lack of training in water-use technology in industrial engineering curricula; and, most importantly, to the existence of an inherited attitude which emphasizes the availability of water without reference to its price and encourages vague notions of water as somehow "special" and not subject to the same market calculations as other inputs. It seems to be true that in this situation a relatively severe drought, with attendant public pressures and real or imagined dangers of low flows and falling water tables, serves to bring the firm's water-use pattern under the scrutiny of management.

One implication of this view is that it is difficult to predict the impact of future droughts, for this will depend on the rate at which existing technology is adopted relative to the rate at which new technology is developed, and on the comparative rates of change of water withdrawals and safe yield. However, if the slack in adoption of technology is gradually taken out of the system and the aggregate water withdrawals do not fall relative to safe yield, one could expect that droughts, as defined in our model, will have an increasingly severe impact on the industrial sector. On the other hand, large-scale adoption of withdrawal-reducing adjustments on the part of industry, particularly that segment served by public systems, would tend to lower the projected-demand safe-yield ratios of the affected towns and decrease their vulnerability to long periods of rainfall shortage and consequent low runoffs and streamflows.

[6] For some evidence on the relatively greater use of water per unit of value added in humid regions as opposed to drier regions, see L. M. Falkson, "Regional Variations in Industrial Water Use Technology," in *Proceedings of the Second Annual Water Resources Conference* (Urbana, Ill.: American Water Resources Association, 1967).

ACCOUNTING ASSUMPTIONS AND THE CHANGING PICTURE
OF DROUGHT LOSSES

A final question in the correction of raw losses is that of the effect on our estimates of costs and losses of various choices of accounting stance. By "accounting stance" we mean the geographical or political area from whose point of view we choose to measure the level of economic activity and hence the size of the economic impact of the drought. For example, if we choose a local stance—defining "local" in terms of the geographic area served by the public water supply system—we shall wish to count as losses the full gross business losses suffered by all firms located in this area (assuming away for the moment the question of deferral of lost production to future days). If, on the other hand, we adopt a regional stance—say the state or all of New England—we shall have to take into account the possibility that production lost by one firm because of the water shortage may be made up during the same period by increased production at another firm in another part of the region. (For a multiplant firm, this transfer may be from one plant to another.) This would be the case, for example, if orders which could not be filled were shifted by buyers to other firms. Clearly, however, the deferral of production cannot, in fact, be assumed away, and it is likely that production lost during short shutdowns will be made up by the same firm at a later date.[7] Thus, for any accounting stance we must consider the possible transfers in time or space of "lost" production. When, however, production is deferred or transferred—and we take account of this under the particular stance we are using—it is still true that, in general, costs will have been incurred by the accounting unit.

The transfer of production presumably means that the real cost of obtaining the given amount of goods goes up by at least the increase in transport costs required to get the goods to their point of use.[8] Similarly, deferral of production has a real cost. This will include at least the cost of waiting (the social rate of time discount) and possibly that of the more intensive

[7] The possibility of deferral of production exists where the goods are, in a sense, storable; for example, an electric utility cannot make up lost production of energy at a later date (except to the extent that the activities depending on the energy are themselves postponable). On the other hand, the production of energy would probably be easily transferred to some other utility.

[8] We do not assume that transport costs decrease or remain the same, since this contradicts the normal economic assumptions about the behavior of firms. For consistency, this position is maintained even though in an imperfect world it may very well be incorrect in many cases. This assumption is conservative in the light of our conclusions above regarding firms' nonefficient behavior with respect to their water inputs, and in the sense that it tends to increase the recorded level of losses where our findings generally (and most controversially) point to the conclusion that drought losses are small relative to those resulting from other "disasters."

use of factors of production in making up the production later. For example, overtime use of facilities will involve costs of accelerated depreciation of equipment and of sacrificed leisure on the part of labor. Similar extra costs may attach to transferred production if the facilities to which it is transferred are otherwise fully employed. As these last two statements imply, it is necessary to make explicit assumptions about the degree of unemployment in the area or at the time to which production is shifted.

Now, of course, business losses need not be the only item in our cost/loss totals which will be affected by choice of an accounting stance. It may be that certain claimed costs are, from a regional accounting view, really only income transfers, though from the town's point of view they may be legitimate costs. And perhaps some of the gains we have just calculated as accruing to certain investing firms should not appear in the local and regional accounts because certain national firms will remit profits to headquarters to be distributed to other investment projects (retained earnings) and to stockholders, only a small fraction of whom will live in the locality or region of interest.

Appendix G describes in somewhat more detail our approach to corrections for accounting stance and deferral or transferral of production and sales. It also describes how we dealt with the problem of net earnings remittals from divisions of national firms. Originally, we considered 12 different combinations of discount rate, accounting stance, defer/transfer percentages, and degree of factor unemployment. As expected, the extremes of the resulting range of total losses were marked by the following accounts:

1. highest loss—local stance, 20 percent discount rate, no deferral or transferral;
2. smallest loss (highest net gain)—national stance, 8 percent discount rate, 100 percent deferral or transferral, high unemployment.

It also seems reasonable to contend that these accounts represent the proper information sources for two important levels of decision-makers. The local/20 percent figures are probably the best source of loss information for the local government officials who wish to take account of private sector investment opportunities. The national/8 percent account, on the other hand, represents the overview required of the economist and policy-maker working for federal agencies.

It may be that local officials prefer to work with something approximating the public's conception of drought loss, i.e., with figures uncorrected for investment returns or anything else. It is, of course, the burden of this section that such an approach would be conceptually incorrect and dangerously misleading in that it seriously overstates the economic impact of drought.

In addition to the two basic accounts mentioned above, we have included their discount-rate twins for contrast. That is, we show the local/8 percent/ zero deferral and the national/20 percent/100 percent deferral account results as well as our decision-maker accounts. This serves to emphasize the dramatic effects produced by varying the discount rate used in evaluating investment projects. (See Tables 29 through 32.)

These results, then, represent the corrected versions of the original aggregate annual community losses as estimated from our survey data (Table 22). They include, however, the losses (gains) incurred by self-supplied water-users as well as those related directly to the performance of the municipal system. Because we are interested in the impact of drought on the municipal system, it is necessary for us to remove this influence of self-supply.

LOSSES INCURRED BY SYSTEM CUSTOMERS

In our survey, virtually the only self-supplied users were industrial firms. Outside of this sector, only the farms included in the Pittsfield miscellaneous sector were not system customers.

The methods adopted to remove losses related to self-supply problems were straightforward. In the industrial sector, all the recorded business losses due to shutdowns resulted from low flows in the streams serving self-suppliers. Investment projects were allocated between municipal and self-supply categories, depending on the pre-adjustment withdrawal source. For example, a well dug by a system customer to escape municipal use restrictions was charged to the municipal system since it reflects system inadequacy.

Farm losses were attributed entirely to problems with self-supply.

The results of this separation of costs by supply source are presented in Table 33. Here, the results are not broken down more finely than the sectoral totals by town and are presented only for the two key accounts: local/20 percent/zero deferral; and national/8 percent/100 percent deferral.

COMMENTS AND CONCLUSIONS: LOSSES TO ALL WATER USERS

While our principal interest will be in the per capita losses discussed in Chapter 11, certain features of the estimates presented so far require comment.

First, as might be expected, total losses for each town decrease in passing from the raw data of Table 22 to the corrected figures in Tables 29 through 32. Of the several corrections made to the initial loss estimates, the most significant are clearly those for the investment aspects of various adjustments made by water-users. These corrections are most important for the industrial sector where some very large and very profitable adjustments were undertaken. Unfortunately, our data do not allow us to separate the effects of demand composition and size of shortage, but evidence we present in the next chapter suggests strongly that the two factors are interdependent. As shortages increase above some threshold level, apparently about 10 percent, the industrial sector begins to suffer from restrictions. Up to that threshold, it appears that every effort is made to place the burden on the domestic sector through restrictions on outside use or to bear it at the municipal level by obtaining emergency supplies. The involvement of the industrial sector seems to trigger the plant managers' awareness of water problems and available technology discussed in connection with the investment corrections themselves.

COMMENTS AND CONCLUSIONS: LOSSES TO SYSTEM CUSTOMERS

The most striking result of eliminating from consideration losses and gains not related to the performance of the municipal system is that some of the widest swings in town losses disappear. Under no combination of accounting stance and interest rate do the gains accruing to those *system customers* investing in profitable water-use adjustments fully offset the losses suffered by other customers. Thus, the Fitchburg total, which showed a net gain of about $1,130,000 under the national/8 percent combination, is changed by the elimination of returns to self-suppliers, to a net *loss* of about $64,000. As could be expected from the great importance of industrial-sector investments in the Fitchburg totals, this change comes about because a large part of the total investment gain recorded in Table 32 (national/8 percent combination) accrued to self-suppliers.

It is not surprising to discover that the greatest positive impact of water-use adjustments spurred by the drought was on self-supplied users, for these tend to be the heaviest users, and the most profitable investments were those involving the largest quantities of water. Municipal users, on the other hand, were often in the position of having to install air-conditioning recirculation equipment by virtue of town ordinance, and such installations generally involved a small amount of water and relatively few hours of operation, making for small annual water-cost savings or, indeed, in several cases, for higher annual costs.

The other 2 cities display considerably less sensitivity to our inclusion or exclusion of drought impact on self-suppliers. This is partly because Braintree and Pittsfield have fewer large self-supplied industrial users.

TABLE 29. THE EFFECT OF CHANGING ASSUMPTIONS ON ESTIMATED DROUGHT LOSSES: LOCAL STANCE/20 PERCENT DISCOUNT RATE/ZERO DEFERRAL OR TRANSFER (LOCAL DECISION-MAKER)

Sector	Braintree			Fitchburg			Pittsfield			Sector totals	
	Corrected costs ($)	Percentage of town total	Percentage of sector total	Corrected costs ($)	Percentage of town total	Percentage of sector total	Corrected costs ($)	Percentage of town total	Percentage of sector total	Corrected costs ($)	Percentage of grand total
Industrial											
Business losses	—			171,400			—			171,400	
Investments	2,500			(53,800)			27,300			(24,000)	
Other	2,500			30,000			17,700			50,200	
Subtotal	5,000	2.6	2.5	147,600	26.0	74.7	45,000	15.0	22.8	197,600	18.7
Municipal											
Lost revenue	—			173,100			54,900			228,000	
Emergency supply	125,000			144,200			12,000			281,200	
Other	12,900			5,200			15,000			33,100	
Subtotal	137,900	72.6	25.4	322,500	57.0	59.5	81,900	27.2	15.1	542,300	51.4
Commercial											
Business losses nurseries	8,600			—			—			8,600	
Business losses—other	—			3,000			3,000			6,000	
Investments	—			(400)			11,600			11,200	
Subtotal	8,600	4.5	33.3	2,600	0.5	10.1	14,600	4.8	56.6	25,800	2.4
Domestic											
Wells reported	23,000			30,200			49,100			102,300	
Sprinkling losses	14,200			29,400			—			43,600	
Subtotal	37,200	19.6	25.5	59,600	10.6	40.8	49,100	16.3	33.6	145,900	13.8
Miscellaneous											
Farm losses	—			—			45,000			45,000	

	Value	Percentage of GT	Value	Percentage of GT	Value	Percentage of GT	Grand total	Percentage of GT
Golf club costs	—		25,000		48,700		73,700	
Tree losses	1,200		6,000		16,500		23,700	
Subtotal	1,200	0.6 / 0.8	31,000	5.5 / 21.8	110,200	36.6 / 77.4	142,400	13.5
Town totals	189,900	18.0	563,300	53.4	300,800	28.5	1,054,000	—

Notes:

1. Business-loss corrections were calculated using the following two general formulae.

(a) Full Employment

Corrected Loss $= (1 - d)$ (original net value-added lost) $+ d$(wages lost $+$ transfer/defer charge),

where "wages lost" are the estimated portion of original value-added lost, and the transfer/defer charge is 2 percent of lost gross production as discussed in the text; d is the percent deferral assumed.

(b) Unemployment

Corrected Loss $= (1 - d)$ (original net value-added lost) $+ d$(transfer/defer charge)

The same procedure is used for both the industrial and commercial sectors. In the former, information was drawn from the *1963 Census of Manufactures* and the Federal Power Commission, *Annual Statistical Series.* For the latter, the primary source of information was the *1958 Census of Business,* Vol. I, *Retail Trade Statistics.*

2. Corrections for remitted net returns are made as discussed in the text. The assumption is 95 percent drain from local area; no drain on national level.

3. One small item on the Pittsfield industrial/other total was eliminated. It involved an increase of about $100 in a firm's water costs due to its shift to city water under low-flow conditions in the brook it normally tapped. It was assumed that this was a cost only to the firm because there was sufficient slack in the municipal system to take on this load without any net social cost. It would, in any case, be eliminated later as purely the result of self-supply deficiencies.

4. Tree losses in Pittsfield were given a "credibility" correction. This consisted of calculating the per capita "tree expenditures" for Braintree and Fitchburg (tree losses and expenses of measures to save trees and shrubs). These followed the expected pattern being high for heavily residential Braintree (about $.40) and low for Fitchburg (about $.18). As Pittsfield's demand composition was midway between the other two, a simple average of these figures (about $.295) was used as a per capita tree loss estimate. (Pittsfield did not report any spray-truck or similar measures to save trees.)

5. Farm losses in Pittsfield were reduced to a 3.5 percent transfer charge in the national accounts to reflect the large degree of slack existing in the nation's farm sector.

6. Lost-revenue estimates have not been corrected to reflect the impact of deferral (or of transferral in the wider stances). This problem seemed too complex to tackle with the information available—particularly as our original lost-revenue estimates were derived independently of business losses.

TABLE 30. THE EFFECT OF CHANGING ASSUMPTIONS ON ESTIMATED DROUGHT LOSSES: LOCAL STANCE/8 PERCENT DISCOUNT RATE/ZERO DEFERRAL OR TRANSFER

Sector	Braintree			Fitchburg			Pittsfield			Sector totals	
	Corrected costs ($)	Percentage of town total	Percentage of sector total	Corrected costs ($)	Percentage of town total	Percentage of sector total	Corrected costs ($)	Percentage of town total	Percentage of sector total	Corrected costs ($)	Percentage of grand total
Industrial											
Business losses	—			171,400			—			171,400	
Investments	2,500			(1,113,800)			(1,200)			(1,112,000)	
Other	2,500			30,000			17,700			50,200	
Subtotal	5,000	2.6	—	(912,400)	—	—	16,500	6.1	—	(89,000)	—
Municipal											
Lost revenue	125,000			173,100			54,900			228,000	
Emergency supply	12,900			144,200			12,000			281,200	
Other				5,200			15,000			33,100	
Subtotal	137,900	73.0	25.4	322,500	—	59.5	81,900	30.3	15.1	542,300	—
Commercial											
Business losses nurseries	8,600			—			—			8,600	

		Percentage of GT		Percentage of GT		Percentage of GT	Grand total	Percentage of GT
Business losses—other	—		3,000		3,000		6,000	—
Investments	—		(8,700)		10,600		1,900	
Subtotal	8,600	4.6	(5,700)	—	13,600	5.0	16,500	—
Domestic								
Wells reported	22,000		29,600		48,300		99,900	
Sprinkling loss	14,200		29,400		—		43,600	
Subtotal	36,200	19.2 25.2	59,000	41.1	48,300	17.8 33.6	143,500	—
Miscellaneous								
Farm losses	—		—		45,000		45,000	
Golf club costs	—		25,000		48,700		73,700	
Tree losses	1,200		6,000		16,500		23,700	
Subtotal	1,200	0.6 0.8	31,000	21.8	110,200	40.7 77.4	142,400	—
Town totals	188,900	—	(505,600)	—	270,500	—	(46,200)	—

Note: See notes to Table 29.

TABLE 31. THE EFFECT OF CHANGING ASSUMPTIONS ON ESTIMATED DROUGHT LOSSES: NATIONAL STANCE/20 PERCENT RATE/100 PERCENT DEFERRAL OR TRANSFER WITH UNEMPLOYMENT (NATIONAL DECISION-MAKER)

Sector	Braintree			Fitchburg			Pittsfield			Sector totals	
	Corrected costs ($)	Percentage of town total	Percentage of sector total	Corrected costs ($)	Percentage of town total	Percentage of sector total	Corrected costs ($)	Percentage of town total	Percentage of sector total	Corrected costs ($)	Percentage of grand total
Industrial											
Business losses	—			6,200			—			6,200	
Investments	2,500			(246,500)			27,300			(216,700)	
Other	2,500			30,000			17,700			50,200	
Subtotal	5,000	2.8	—	(210,300)	—	—	45,000	17.7	—	(160,300)	—
Municipal											
Lost revenue	125,000			173,100			54,900			228,000	
Emergency supply	12,900			144,200			12,000			281,200	
Other				5,200			15,000			33,100	
Subtotal	137,900	75.9	25.4	322,500	—	59.5	81,900	32.2	15.1	542,300	—

		Percentage of GT		Percentage of GT		Percentage of GT	Grand total	
Commercial								
Business losses nurseries	300		—		—		300	
Business losses—other	—		100		100		200	
Investments	—		(400)		11,600		11,200	
Subtotal	300	0.2	(300)	—	11,700	4.6	11,700	—
Domestic								
Wells reported	23,000		30,200		49,100		102,300	
Sprinkling loss	14,200		29,400		—		43,600	
Subtotal	37,200	20.5 25.5	59,600	40.8	49,100	17.3 33.6	145,900	—
Miscellaneous								
Farm losses	—		—		1,800		1,800	
Golf club costs	—		25,000		48,700		73,700	
Tree losses	1,200		6,000		16,500		23,700	
Subtotal	1,200	0.7 1.2	31,000	31.2	67,500	26.3 67.5	99,200	—
		Percentage of GT		Percentage of GT		Percentage of GT		Percentage of GT
Town totals	181,600	28.4	202,500	31.7	254,700	39.9	638,800	—

Note: See notes to Table 29.

TABLE 32. The Effect of Changing Assumptions on Estimated Drought Losses: National Stance/8 Percent Discount Rate/100 Percent Deferral or Transfer with Unemployment (National Decision-Maker)

Sector	Braintree			Fitchburg			Pittsfield			Sector totals	
	Corrected costs ($)	Percent-age of town total	Percent-age of sector total	Corrected costs ($)	Percent-age of town total	Percent-age of sector total	Corrected costs ($)	Percent-age of town total	Percent-age of sector total	Corrected costs ($)	Percent-age of grand total
Industrial											
Business losses	—			6,200			—			6,200	
Investments	2,500			(1,567,900)			(29,100)			(1,594,500)	
Other	2,500			30,000			17,700			50,200	
Subtotal	5,000	2.8	—	(1,531,700)	—	—	(11,400)	—	—	(1,538,100)	—
Municipal											
Lost revenue	125,000			173,100			54,900			228,000	
Emergency supply	12,900			144,200			12,000			281,200	
Other				5,200			15,000			33,100	
Subtotal	137,900	76.4	25.4	322,500	—	59.5	81,900	—	15.1	542,300	—

		Percentage of GT	Percentage of GT		Percentage of GT		Percentage of GT	Grand total
Commercial								
Business losses nurseries	300		—	—		—		300
Business losses—other	—		100	100		100		200
Investments	—		(8,700)	10,600		10,600		1,900
Subtotal	300	0.2	—	(8,600)	—	10,700	—	2,400
Domestic								
Wells reported	22,000		25.2	29,600		48,300		99,900
Sprinkling loss	14,200			29,400		—		43,600
Subtotal	36,200	20.0	25.2	59,000	41.1	48,300	33.6	143,500
Miscellaneous								
Farm losses	—			—		1,800		1,800
Golf club costs	—		1.2	25,000		48,700		73,700
Tree losses	1,200			6,000		16,500		23,700
Subtotal	1,200	0.7	1.2	31,000	31.2	67,000	67.5	99,200
Town totals	180,600	—	—	(1,127,800)	—	196,500	—	(750,700)

Note: See notes to Table 29.

TABLE 33. SEPARATION OF LOSSES BY USERS' WATER SUPPLY SOURCE
Raw data (Table 22)

(dollars)

Sector	Braintree		Fitchburg		Pittsfield	
	Municipal customer	Self-supplier	Municipal customer	Self-supplier	Municipal customer	Self-supplier
Industrial	2,500	2,500	241,300	509,900	87,700	300
Municipal	137,900		322,500		81,900	
Commercial	8,600		9,100		15,000	
Domestic	38,200		60,600		50,400	
Miscellaneous	1,200		31,000		148,700	45,000
Total	188,400	2,500	664,500	509,900	383,700	45,300
Combined total	190,900		1,174,400		429,000	

Local/20 percent data (Table 29)

(dollars)

Sector	Municipal customer	Self-supplier	Municipal customer	Self-supplier	Municipal customer	Self-supplier
Industrial	2,500	2,500	61,400	86,200	45,000	
Municipal	137,900		322,500		81,900	
Commercial	8,600		2,600		14,600	
Domestic	37,200		59,600		49,100	
Miscellaneous	1,200		31,000		65,200	45,000
Total	187,400	2,500	477,100	86,200	255,800	45,000
Combined total	189,900		563,300		300,800	

National/8 percent data (Table 32)

(dollars)

Sector	Municipal customer	Self-supplier	Municipal customer	Self-supplier	Municipal customer	Self-supplier
Industrial	2,500	2,500	(339,600)	(1,192,100)	(11,400)	
Municipal	137,900		322,500		81,900	
Commercial	300		(8,600)		10,700	
Domestic	36,200		59,000		48,300	
Miscellaneous	1,200		31,000		65,200	1,800
Total	180,600	2,500	64,300	(1,192,100)	194,700	1,800
Combined total	180,600		(1,127,800)		196,500	

Note: Figures in parentheses are net benefits or gains reflecting investment returns.

Thus the scope for the kinds of investments found profitable in Fitchburg was considerably smaller. In addition, as noted above, it appears that the industrial sector is not generally involved in drought problems until the level of potential shortage climbs to something above 10 percent. Thus, in Braintree with a shortage somewhat less than 10 percent, the largest part of the loss was borne (at least initially) by the municipal system itself through the provision of emergency supplies. Pittsfield had a somewhat larger shortage, but the town's one really large industrial concern is a system customer which accounts for almost one-quarter of total system demand.

In the next chapter we take these losses related to the performance of the municipal system as our basic data in calculating per capita annual losses for the 3 towns and the several sectors. We also discuss the relation of these per capita losses to the level of system shortage faced by each town.

CHAPTER 11

PER CAPITA LOSSES AND
THEIR RELATION TO SHORTAGE

In order to make comparisons among our sample communities and later to construct a function relating expected losses to the chosen level of system adjustment, we must standardize our loss estimates at least for the obvious variation due to city size. The familiar deflator for this purpose is population, although one could certainly conceive of other meaningful size indicators relevant to variations in water use, such as the size of the city's industrial sector as measured by floor space, employment, or value added. No single deflator can be expected to remove all the variation not in fact due to size of shortage suffered. But since we do not have a large enough sample to permit regression analysis, we cannot explore the possibility of removing several extraneous influences.

In Table 34, the loss estimates from Chapters 9 and 10 are presented in per capita terms.[1] Only the results for the local/20 percent and national/ 8 percent combinations are shown because they are most relevant for decision-makers at the respective levels. They also represent the extremes in the variation of losses under our different assumptions.

SECTORAL PATTERNS

The sectoral patterns of loss found in Table 34 appear quite irregular when compared with the variations in shortage, from Braintree (9.7 percent) through Pittsfield (14 percent) to Fitchburg (22 percent). Of the "raw" (uncorrected) sectoral per capita losses, only the industrial sector increases in step with shortages. The losses of the other sectors either vary

[1] Population data are from the U.S. Census of 1960 and the Massachusetts Census of 1965. For 1966, the trend between 1960 and 1965 was simply extrapolated. The 1965 Pittsfield population is used to maintain consistency with the decision to identify the losses there with the peak year of the drought in the western part of the state.

irregularly with shortage (as for the municipal, domestic, and miscellaneous sectors) or are essentially constant (the commercial sector). The differences in the municipal and domestic figures seem to be attributable to the nature of the city government's choice in each case concerning the way in which the burden of potential shortage would be borne. In Pittsfield, for example, domestic restrictions do not deprive the government of revenue, since domestic water is sold at a flat annual rate. The constancy of the commercial sector losses may, on the other hand, be due to the varying completeness of our coverage of this sector in each of the cities.

Under the local/20 percent/zero deferral or transferral combination, the pattern of sectoral losses is substantially like that just discussed. The industrial sector still exhibits an increase from Braintree to Fitchburg, though its size has been considerably reduced.

TABLE 34. PER CAPITA LOSSES
Raw data (Table 22)

(dollars)

Sector	Braintree	Fitchburg	Pittsfield
Industrial	0.07	5.60	1.55
Municipal	3.99	7.48	1.45
Commercial	0.25	0.21	0.26
Domestic	1.10	1.41	0.89
Miscellaneous	0.03	0.72	2.63
Total	5.44	15.42	6.79

Local/20 percent data (Table 29)

(dollars)

Industrial	0.07	1.42	0.80
Municipal	3.99	7.48	1.45
Commercial	0.25	0.06	0.26
Domestic	1.08	1.38	0.87
Miscellaneous	0.03	0.72	1.15
Total	5.42	11.07	4.53

National/8 percent data (Table 32)

(dollars)

Industrial	0.07	(7.89)	(0.20)
Municipal	3.99	7.48	1.45
Commercial	0.01	(0.20)	0.19
Domestic	1.05	1.37	0.85
Miscellaneous	0.03	0.72	1.15
Total	5.15	1.49	3.45

Sources: See footnote 1 of this chapter.
Note: Figures in parentheses represent gains.

When we alter our assumptions to those of a national accounting stance, an 8 percent discount rate, and complete deferral or transferral of lost production (to areas or periods of less than full employment), the original sector patterns in the industrial and commercial sectors disappear completely. Now, reflecting the lower discount rate and the importance of investments in Fitchburg's (and, to some extent in Pittsfield's) industrial sector, the sectoral "losses" become larger gains as we move from Braintree to Fitchburg. We obtain a similar result in the commercial sector, and again it reflects the impact of the changing discount rate on investment evaluation. The other sectoral patterns do not change, though again we subtract a few cents from the domestic losses in reevaluating well investments.

COMMUNITY PER CAPITA LOSSES

The net results of these changing sectoral patterns are the community per capita annual losses, which are graphed against shortages in Figure 19. To illustrate the great sensitivity of our estimate of the loss-shortage relation to the discount rate, we have fitted by eye a curve to each set of points. In addition, because it seems unlikely that present investment opportunities will continue unexploited in the face of rising costs and pressures on sources, we have provided an alternative version of the national/8 percent curve which does not fall off with increasing shortage.

The general shape of the local/20 percent curve is similar to that for the uncorrected data, though for the former the total increase in loss with level of shortage is less than for the latter. In addition, under the local/20 percent assumptions, the per capita loss for Pittsfield was estimated to be less than that for Braintree, though, of course, Pittsfield's shortage was larger. This may reflect an overly conservative view of the tree-loss estimate provided to us for Pittsfield. Our credibility correction to this estimate had the effect of reducing the city's total per capita loss under each accounting stance by $1.47. If this were added back in to the accounts, the Pittsfield loss in the local/20 percent account would be $6.00 per capita, more than that recorded for Braintree ($5.42). In addition, applying this same adjustment to the national/8 percent accounts would give us a total town loss of $4.92 for Pittsfield, essentially equal to the $5.15 figure calculated for Braintree under this combination. These adjusted points are plotted in Figure 19 and were taken into account in fitting the suggested relations.

We now concentrate on the results obtained using the local/20 percent combination, but we also include results reflecting the national/8 percent relation we suggest in Figure 19. Our major reason for choosing to con-

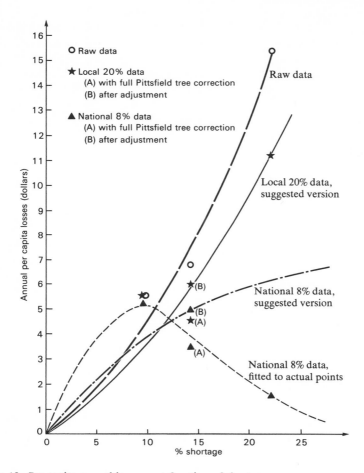

Figure 19. Per capita annual losses as a function of shortage.

centrate on this account is our belief that water supply is likely to continue to be an area of local investment neither receiving much outside financial help nor subject to much outside control. The local/20 percent account results seem to us the appropriate ones to use in evaluating water supply capacity expansion from the purely local point of view.

Before moving on to further calculations, we suggest as a conclusion based on our estimates of the cost of the recent drought, that as we consider larger accounting frameworks and as we allow the discount rate to move toward a level probably more closely reflecting the rate of time preference, the drought tends to lose its image as a crisis, a creator of huge losses. At least in humid areas under present conditions of technological "slack," we may rather view the drought as a fortuitous spur to large-scale industrial rationalization of water use. We may still feel that distributional considerations prohibit us from viewing droughts as social "goods," but certainly realism demands at least a tacit moderation of official preoccupation with drought protection and explicit tempering of official public statements about the fantastic costs being generated by this natural "calamity."

PART IV

A PLANNING MODEL FOR MUNICIPAL WATER SUPPLY SYSTEMS

CHAPTER 12

EXPECTED ANNUAL LOSSES FROM DROUGHT

Our aim now is to put together a planning model designed to answer questions about the optimal size and timing of increments to the supply capability of municipal systems, a model drawing together the separate threads represented by the study of the physical and economic impact of the 1963–66 drought as reported in Parts I and II. To this end we first demonstrate how we may use probability distributions of climatic events to produce functions relating chosen levels of system inadequacy to expected levels of per capita annual losses from water shortage (drought). If we think in terms of the inventory-control or capacity-expansion models used by other authors,[1] the expected annual loss functions we develop are seen as the penalties attached to "undercapacity," although in our model there is no line between under- and over-capacity as such but only degrees of relative inadequacy as represented by the chosen level of the projected-demand/safe-yield ratio.

In order to make rational decisions about avoiding losses, we need to know the cost of doing so. In our model, this cost will be that of adding increments of safe yield to the water system. In Chapter 13, we describe two independent derivations of such a function. Then, in Chapter 14, we set out the planning model constructed from these building blocks. We discuss the form the model takes when expressed as a nonlinear programming problem and then go on to explain briefly the method used in finding

[1] See for example, H. B. Chenery, "Overcapacity and the Acceleration Principle," *Econometrica*, 20 (1952), 1–28; A. S. Manne, "Capacity Expansion and Probabilistic Growth," *Econometrica*, 29 (1961), 632–49; A. S. Manne, *Investment for Capacity Expansion* (Cambridge: Massachusetts Institute of Technology Press, 1967); and H. A. Thomas, "Capacity Expansion of Public Works," Division of Engineering and Applied Science, Harvard University (mimeo.), 1967.

the solutions. We also summarize the results of applying the planning model to hypothetical water systems under various assumptions about the relevant parameters. First, we assume away, temporarily, the important question of uncertainty in the projections of demand, being initially concerned with exploring the sensitivity of our model to changes in such parameters as the rate of discount, the scaling factor in the safe-yield cost function, and the exponent in the expected-loss function.[2] Finally, we take account of the uncertainty inherent in projections of the rates of growth of population and per capita daily demand averaged over the year. Essentially we ask how much the town can expect to lose by building according to a plan optimal for the "best" estimates of these growth rates, when in fact other growth rates may actually occur.

One final general comment is in order. In constructing a planning model which minimizes the sum of capacity costs and shortage losses in determining optimal patterns of size and timing of additions to safe yield, we must assume that all alternative paths seek to provide the same streams of gross benefits.[3] Specifically, we assume that no price changes are to take place over the planning horizon, and that the demand functions for system water supply are to be independent of the decisions made by the planners. (This neglects any influence that uncertainty of supply itself might have on demand.)[4] Then the benefits which result from meeting demand under any plan are the same. The differences between the plans lie in their capital costs and in the extent to which they may be expected to provide for demand in the face of a variable climate (drought losses). Minimizing the sum of capital costs and expected drought losses gives us the optimal plan under the given demand conditions.

ESTIMATING EXPECTED-LOSS FUNCTION

We are interested in two sets of expected-loss functions: one corresponding to the a priori model of drought impact; and the other based on the empirical relation between shortage and inadequacy estimated from the actual drought data. (Both relations were discussed in Chapter 7.) It will be seen that the functions implied by these two different views are

[2] This function, as we shall see, is of the form:
$$E(L) = U(D/Y)^z$$
where $E(L)$ is expected annual loss, D is average daily system demand, Y is system safe yield in daily draft terms, and U and z are parameters. We are interested in the model's sensitivity to changes in our estimate of z.

[3] Peter O. Steiner, "The Role of Alternative Cost in Project Design and Selection," *Quarterly Journal of Economics*, 79 (1965), 415–30.

[4] See Stephen Turnovsky, "The Responses of Economic Factors to Uncertainty in Supply," in *Models for Regional Water Management*, R. Dorfman, H. Jacoby, and H. Thomas, eds., to be published by Harvard University Press.

themselves dramatically different. Specifically, expected losses rise very much more rapidly with declining system adequacy (rising demand/supply ratio) under the hypothesis that the a priori model is, in fact, an accurate description of the world.[5]

The Relation Between Shortage and System Adequacy: A Reminder

We pause to remind the reader of the two alternative forms of the shortage-adequacy relation growing out of our work in Chapter 7.

The A Priori Model.

$$S_{it} = 100[1 - (\alpha_t^*/\alpha_{it})]$$ (12-1)

where $\alpha_{it} = D_{it}/Y_{it}$ and α_t^* is the fraction of safe-yield flows available in year t.[6]

The Empirical Model.

$$S_{it} = \beta[\alpha_{it} - \alpha_t']$$ (12-2)

where $\beta = 20$ and

$$\alpha_t' = \frac{\Delta_o}{\Delta_t} = \frac{\text{Cumulative Precipitation Deviation 1908–11}}{\text{Cumulative Precipitation Deviation (years } t\text{-3 through } t)}$$

and α_t' is the level of α_{it} at which shortages begin to occur.

PROBABILITY OF SHORTAGES

We wish to find the probability of a shortage of size $\underline{S} \leq S \leq \bar{S}$ occurring in a city served by a system having inadequacy level $\alpha_{it} = I$. This probability clearly will depend on the distribution of climatic events for

[5] It is unfortunate that the full implications of a priori models designed to determine percentage of safe-yield flows available were not realized earlier. Work based on the empirically determined relation between shortage and adequacy consistently suggests that public and managerial concern over drought is exaggerated. The a priori model, however, tends to lend support to high level of this concern, and in the context of the planning model, leads to capacity expansion programs which look very much like patterns which have been criticized as "overbuilding" when they have appeared in the real world. (See Part V.)

[6] Based on the experimentation, referred to earlier, with streamflow and rainfall records, α_t^* has been estimated from the relation:

$$\alpha_t^* \equiv \frac{(\text{cumulated total precipitation years } t\text{-3 to } t)^2}{(\text{cumulated total precipitation years 1908–11})^2}$$

As noted in Chapters 6 and 7, the actual results of this experimentation and of our attempts to test the a priori model were basically disappointing. It still seems, however, to be worth while to present the loss functions based on the a priori model.

that town. The latter distribution will define the probability of an event $A_* \leq \alpha_t^* \leq A^*$ (or $A_1 \leq \alpha_t' \leq A^1$); that is, the probability of a natural event sufficiently severe to cause a shortage in the size interval of interest. For a given α_{it}, the larger shortage, S, will correspond to the more severe climatic event A_*, i.e., the lower percentage of system safe yield available for delivery.[7]

APPROXIMATION OF EXPECTED LOSSES

Repeated application of the above methods will provide us with the probabilities of shortages in the range S to $S + \Delta S$ percent, for $S = 0, \ldots$ 50, $\ldots$, for any given level of α. We chose to calculate these probabilities for $\alpha = 0.35, 0.45, \ldots, 1.45, \ldots$ and to let $\Delta S = 2$ percent. We may then approximate the expected loss corresponding to a particular chosen α by identifying with the interval S to $S + 2$ percent, the per capita annual losses associated with $(S + 1)$ percent. The appropriate loss data may be read from the functions in Figure 19 for the interval up to about 25 percent shortage. For higher shortages, we approximated the per capita annual losses by functions roughly fitted to the lower interval points for each of the curves, local/20 percent and national/8 percent. The expected loss associated with a particular inadequacy ratio, I, is then approximated by:

$$E(L) = \sum_{S'=0}^{98} \text{Prob} \ (S' \leq S \leq S' + 2|\alpha = I) \cdot L(S' + 1) \quad (12\text{-}3)$$

where $L(S' + 1)$ is the per capita annual loss associated with a shortage of size $(S' + 1)$.[8]

---

[7] For the a priori model, the expression Prob $(\underline{S} \leq S \leq \overline{S}/\alpha = I)$ may be translated into:

$$\text{Prob} \left[100 \left(1 - \frac{A^*}{I} \right) \leq S \leq 100 \left(1 - \frac{A_*}{I} \right) \right];$$

which is equal to

$$\text{Prob} \left[\frac{I(100 - \overline{S})}{100} \leq \alpha_t^* \leq \frac{I(100 - \underline{S})}{100} \right].$$

This last expression may be evaluated in terms of the relevant distribution of climatic events.
For the empirical relation, the corresponding probability expression is

$$\text{Prob} \left[\left(I - \frac{\overline{S}}{20} \right) \leq \alpha_t' \leq \left(I - \frac{S}{20} \right) \right]$$

[8] This expected-loss level is, strictly speaking, a long-run concept; the loss which would, on the average, occur annually in a town which maintained a particular level of the D/Y ratio over a long period. As we use it here, the concept may be considered as a best estimate of the loss likely to occur in a town with a particular D/Y ratio in a particular year.
Concentration on expected value, which seems entirely adequate with respect to the results from the empirical model, may be questioned when dealing with the a priori model because of the rather large losses encountered there.

The results of these calculations are summarized graphically in Figure 20, where we present the expected annual loss functions under both the local/ 20 percent and the national/8 percent accounting combinations and for both the a priori and empirical models. The expected-loss functions associated with the a priori model rise much more rapidly than those associated with the empirical model. The former are, indeed, almost vertical in the interval above about $\alpha = 1.10$. We shall see that the use of this sort of function has some significant implications for the planning of system expansion.

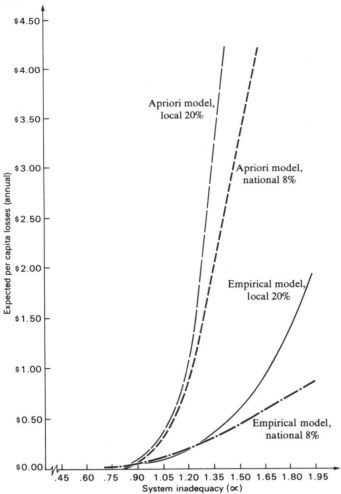

Figure 20. Expected-loss functions.

ESTIMATION OF THE PARAMETERS OF EXPECTED-LOSS FUNCTIONS

In order to retain the simplest possible loss-function form for use in the planning model, and because it seemed conceptually correct, we fitted to our estimates of expected losses for given α, functions of the form:

$$E(L) = U(\alpha)^z \text{ (dollars per capita per year).}$$

The results of this operation are summarized below in Table 35.

TABLE 35. PARAMETERS OF THE EXPECTED-LOSS FUNCTIONS

($ *per capita per year*)

I. A priori model:
    Local/20 percent account $E_1(L) = 0.1(\alpha)^{12.0}$
    National/8 percent account $E_2(L) = 0.1(\alpha)^{11.7}$

II. Empirical model: (fitting to points above 0.35)
    Local/20 percent account $E_3(L) = 0.1(\alpha)^{5.4}$
    National/8 percent account $E_4(L) = 0.1(\alpha)^{4.5}$

III. Empirical model: (fitting to points above 0.95)
    Local/20 percent account $E_5(L) = 0.1(\alpha)^{4.8}$
    National/8 percent account $E_6(L) = 0.1(\alpha)^{3.2}$

Note: The extraordinary constancy of the estimates of u was caused by the relative constancy of the estimates of expected losses for all stances and models in the interval about $\alpha = 1.00$. These were invariably in the range $0.10 to $0.13.

In our exploration of the sensitivity of the planning model to parameter changes we use four different values of z: 3.2, 4.3, 5.4, and 12.0. These effectively cover the range of results presented in Table 35, and it seems likely that they span the "true" values.

Now that we have our functions relating chosen inadequacy levels to expected drought losses, we need only one more bit of information to be able to construct the planning model: an estimate of the cost of improving the level of system adequacy.

CHAPTER 13

THE COST OF ADDITIONS
TO SAFE YIELD

We now turn to the estimation of the costs of increasing safe yield. We present the results of two alternative approaches, the first based on a general published study of the costs of water supply; the second based on analysis of a number of reservoir projects proposed to several Massachusetts towns over the last 60 years by consulting engineering firms.

A THEORETICAL APPROACH

The problem of determining the cost of additions to safe yield may logically be separated into two subsidiary problems. First, one must determine for a particular stream, subject to a particular climate, the amount of storage required to produce a given (say daily) draft with a given level of assurance. Second, it is necessary to estimate the costs associated with the provision of the required amount of storage.[1]

The first consideration, that of the draft-storage relationship, is clearly bound up with the matter of climatic uncertainty discussed above. The cost of reservoir construction, on the other hand, is conceptually a deterministic function of reservoir size, along with other variables such as terrain and type of construction used. We consider this latter relationship first.

---

[1] These costs may, in the simplest case, consist of the capital costs of construction of the required dam and the annual Operation-Maintenance-Repair costs required for the new storage facility. More realistically, any decision to provide additional safe yield for a water system will probably also imply costs for conveyance from the new facility to the area of use, and also for construction and operation of treatment facilities. In this study, we concentrate on the capital cost of reservoir construction.

To the extent that other costs are a function basically only of the size of the safe-yield increment, their inclusion then will encourage postponement of construction. If certain costs are time-dependent (in particular, if certain costs can be expected to increase with time) their inclusion will work in the opposite direction by rewarding early construction.

Capital Cost of Increased Storage Volume

The cost functions we present here are based largely on the data provided by Louis Koenig.[2] Koenig presents the results of analysis of the costs of over 1,000 U.S. reservoirs. The cost figures were adjusted to 1962 prices on a regional basis, using the *Engineering News Record* 20-Cities Construction Cost Index.[3] They are presented as median costs ($ per acre foot) for different size classes of reservoirs. For the New England region, data were provided for only four size classes: 10,000; 100,000; 1,000,000; and 10,000,000 ac.ft.

The applicable cost function was obtained by fitting to these points, by eye, on log paper, a straight line. If the total cost function is of the form $C(V) = a \cdot V^\beta$ where V is storage in acre feet and β is the scale parameter, then the average cost function is of the form $C(V)/V = aV^{\beta-1}$ or in log-log form, $\log C(V)/V = \log a + (\beta - 1) \log V$ and a and β may be estimated directly from average cost data. The estimates obtained for 1962, New England storage capacity cost parameters were: $a = 19,900$ ($\log a = 4.299$) and $\beta = 0.52$.

The results for the scale parameter accord generally with the expectations expressed by Thomas: "The scaling factor, β, usually lies in the range 0.5 to 0.8. It may be as low as 0.3 for some types of storage dams and irrigation canals, and as high as 0.9 for large modern sewage treatment plants with many replicate units."[4]

Sample total costs for various sizes of reservoir are included below in Table 36 to provide the reader with a "feel" for the orders of magnitude involved.

TABLE 36. ILLUSTRATIVE COSTS FOR RESERVOIRS OF DIFFERENT SIZES, NEW ENGLAND, 1962

Storage provided (*ac. ft.*)	Approximate total capital cost ($)	Approximate average cost ($ per ac. ft.)
1,000	724,000	724
10,000	2,400,000	240
100,000	7,940,000	80
1,000,000	26,300,000	26
10,000,000	87,100,000	9

[2] Louis Koenig, "Cost of Conventional Water Supply," in *Principles of Desalinization*, K. S. Spiegeler, ed. (New York: Academic Press, 1966), Ch. 11.

[3] See our later comments on this point.

[4] H. A. Thomas, "Capacity Expansion of Public Works," Harvard University, Department of Engineering and Applied Physics, unpublished.

The Draft-Storage Relation

The amount of storage required in a particular situation to assure a given sustained level of draft from a stream at a given probability of failure is given by a draft-storage relation. In general, as the desired draft approaches the mean flow of the stream, the amount of storage increases without limit, but the actual form of the relation will vary across the regions of the country with the variability of streamflow.

We have estimated a draft-storage relation for Massachusetts based on the work of Hazen and Koenig[5] and under the following assumptions:

The required level of assurance is 95 percent (i.e., 5 percent chance of failure);

The average water supply system has available to it a range of stream sources ranging in size from about 10 to about 500 mgd.

The resulting relation, expressed in the form $V = b(D)^x$, where V is again volume and D is draft, is:[6]

$$V = 34.7 \, (D)^{1.49} \tag{13-1}$$

The Cost of Changing Safe Yield

Now, we combine the results for the cost-of-storage and the storage-draft relations straightforwardly as follows:

$$C(V) = a(V)^\beta \text{ (where } V \text{ is storage in acre feet)} \tag{13-2}$$

$$V = b(D)^x \text{ (where } D \text{ is dependable draft at about the}$$
$$\text{95 percent assurance level, in mgd),} \tag{13-3}$$

and therefore,

$$C(D) = ab^\beta D^{\beta x} \text{ which we rewrite as } C(D) = K(D)^Y. \tag{13-4}$$

Our estimates give us, then,

$$C(D) = 1.28 \times 10^5 (D)^{0.78}; \tag{13-5}$$

---

[5] See Koenig, "Cost of Conventional Water Supply," and Allen Hazen, "Storage to be Provided in Impounding Reservoirs for Municipal Water Supply," *Transactions of the American Society of Civil Engineers*, LXXVII (1914), 1539–1640. See also Allen Hazen, *American Civil Engineering Practice*, R. W. Abbett, ed., as revised by Richard Hazen (New York: Wiley, 1930).

[6] Actually, this relation was estimated from a scatter of points representing individual draft storage relations for 46 Massachusetts streams of various sizes as indicated above. The R^2 for this regression was 0.69; the standard deviation for x was 0.20; and, with log b estimated as 1.54, its standard deviation was 0.38.

or since $D = \Delta SY$[7]

$$C(\Delta SY) = 1.28 \times 10^5 (\Delta SY)^{0.78}, \tag{13-6}$$

(1962 construction dollars for Massachusetts in streams with mean daily flows between 30 and 450 mgd). Table 37 gives some sample costs for various safe-yield increments.

TABLE 37. ILLUSTRATIVE SAFE-YIELD COSTS, NEW ENGLAND, 1962

Desired firm draft increment (ΔSY) (in *mgd*)	Estimated total capital cost ($)	Estimated cost (*$ per mgd*)
1	128,000	128,000
10	776,000	77,600
100	4,700,000	47,000
1,000	28,000,000	28,000
10,000	169,000,000	16,900

In the actual planning model we consider the result of considering scaling factors of 0.68 and 0.88 as well as 0.78. This amounts roughly to checking one standard deviation on either side of 0.78, when we treat 0.52 as exact.

AN EMPIRICAL APPROACH

Based on our study of reports prepared by consulting engineers for several Massachusetts cities over the past 60 years, we were able to undertake a direct, empirical estimation of the costs of increases in water system safe yield. In essence this approach involved simply the search of engineering reports for projects for which the reservoir costs per million gallons per day of safe yield were identifiable; the "inflation" of earlier year costs to make them comparable in 1962 dollars; and, then, a regression of the log of unit cost on the log of the safe-yield increment. The sample of projects constructed numbered 20, ranging in size from 0.25 to 12.6 mgd in safe yield. The inflation of the reservoir costs of these projects was carried out using the Bureau of Public Roads Construction Cost Index.[8]

---

[7] This function is implicitly based on costs of initial development of a stream. The costs of incremental development of existing storage sites may, of course, be the relevant factor for many towns. Our empirical work includes data for projects involving both new development and expansion of existing sites.

[8] From the *Historical Statistics of the United States* and the *Statistical Abstract of the United States, 1966*, Series N-101. This index was used in preference to the familiar *Engineering News Record* index because the latter is weighted with base weights. It thus reflects the construction technology of 1913, the base year, and exaggerates the increase in costs over the past 55 years. The construction industry today is highly capital-intensive relative to 1913, as capital has been substituted for the relatively more expensive factor labor.

Estimating from these data, the function $C(\Delta SY)/\Delta SY = K(\Delta SY)^{y-1}$ in log-log form we obtain the results shown in Table 38.

TABLE 38. REGRESSION RESULTS

$$\log \frac{C(\Delta SY)}{SY} = 5.4844 - 0.2428 \log(\Delta SY)$$
$$(0.0496) \quad (0.0766)$$
$$\text{or } C(\Delta SY) = 305,000 \, (\Delta SY)^{0.76}$$

$r^2 = 0.358$; F-ratio test significant at 1 percent

t = tests for coefficients both significant at 1 percent

95 percent confidence intervals

$\log K = 5.4844 \pm 0.1195 \; (232,000 \leq K \leq 402,000)$

$\log y - 1 = -0.2428 \pm 0.1846 \; (0.57 \leq y \leq 0.94)$

The most striking result is the excellent agreement between the scale parameter estimate here (0.76) and that found above (0.78).[9]

In our planning model, then, we use as our basic safe-yield cost function the following:

$$C(\Delta SY) = 1.28 \times 10^5 (\Delta SY)^{0.78}; \tag{13-7}$$

and we vary y, the scale factor, using 0.68 and 0.88 as well. K is not varied.

[9] Our empirical estimate of the constant, K (the cost of a 1 mgd project) is a little less than 2½ times greater than the one we found above. One possible explanation of this difference is easy to see. Since our empirical data are drawn from suggested alternatives, only a few of which were ever actually undertaken, whereas Koenig's data represented projects actually chosen, we may expect that our cost data are biased upward relative to his. This will be true so long as a city's choices of actual projects are at least partially based on considerations of unit-cost minimization. To reflect this bias, we have used the K-estimate based on Koenig's work, ignoring the higher value found by the empirical method.

CHAPTER 14

A CAPACITY EXPANSION PLANNING MODEL FOR MUNICIPAL WATER SUPPLY SYSTEMS

The model presented in this chapter is designed to provide a framework for balancing expected drought losses as a function of chosen adequacy level against the costs of improving that adequacy level. As mentioned above, it is in the tradition of inventory-adjustment/capacity-expansion models applied by others, although most such applications have taken deterministic forms. Because of the probabilistic nature of our capacity variable, there is no distinction in our model between under- and over-capacity, no line at which costs *begin* to be incurred. This feature, the fact that inadequacy is entirely a relative concept, results from the lack of any upper limit to drought severity. In principle, no matter how large a system's safe yield relative to its demand, a drought can occur that will be severe enough to cause shortage for that system.[1]

The choice variables controlled by the planners, subject to certain constraints, are the timing and sizes of increments to the system's safe yield. By choosing a time path of the level of system safe yield with given information about the rate of growth of demand, the planners determine a total present value of capital costs and a discounted sum of expected annual drought losses. The optimal plan for given growth rates and other parameters is the one which minimizes the total of these discounted costs and losses. We choose to work with a planning horizon of 60 years.

[1] In practical computations, of course, one has to draw the line on significant decimal places somewhere. If that line is drawn for probabilities at the fourth decimal place (numbers smaller than 1×10^{-4} are counted as zero), then any system with a D/Y ratio less than 0.3 is effectively drought-proof.

148

BASIC STRUCTURE OF THE MODEL

In Figure 21, we represent schematically the choice variables and resulting time paths of key variables for a particular plan choice. Note that we limit the decision variables to six: four increments, two of which must be constructed in years 0 and 60, and two at intermediate times. Each of these variables is continuous and, naturally, all are constrained to be non-negative. The times are further constrained to be less than 60.

In order both to make provision for the post-horizon future, and to standardize the set of possible paths, we introduce the constraint that at the end of year 60, the total safe yield constructed as part of the plan must equal the total growth in demand over the horizon. Thus, if we start with

(A) SCHEMATIC OF POSSIBLE TIME PATH OF WATER SYSTEM

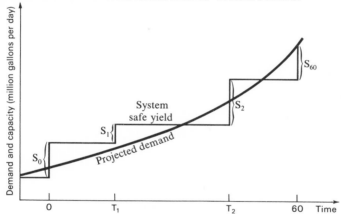

(B) THE TIME PATH OF SYSTEM INADEQUACY

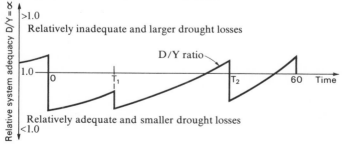

Figure 21. Schematic of choice variables and resulting time paths of key variables for a particular plan choice.

projected demand equal to safe yield in year zero, the same must be true at the end of year 60. This particular method of handling the bequest problem is recommended by its simplicity, but it also seems in some sense fair: we bequeath the same situation we have inherited in terms of our measure of relative adequacy.

FUNCTIONAL FORMS: A REVIEW AND CONSOLIDATION

We assume, first, that population and per capita demand grow exponentially according to the formulae:

$$\text{Population in year "}t\text{"} = N_t = N_o e^{\beta t} \tag{14-1}$$

$$\text{Projected Per Capita Demand}^2 \text{ in year "}t\text{"} = P_t = P_o e^{\gamma t} \tag{14-2}$$

We may thus express the total demand in year t as

$$D_t = N_t \cdot P_t = N_o P_o e^{(\beta+\gamma)t} = D_o e^{\alpha t} \tag{14-3}$$

where $N_o \cdot P_o = D_o$ and $\alpha = \beta + \gamma$.
The capital costs of safe-yield expansion are given by:

$$C(\Delta SY) = K(\Delta SY)^y$$

or, if $\Delta SY \equiv s_t = s_0, s_1, s_2$ or s_{60} (14-4)

$C(s_t) = K(s_t)^y$; (y generally < 1).

And so the present value of the cost of the increment s_t is:

$$PV[C \cdot (s_t)] = K(s_t)^y e^{-\rho t} \tag{14-5}$$

where ρ is the discount rate.

Now, the treatment of the expected losses from water shortage is, of necessity, more complex. From Chapter 12, we recall that expected annual per capita losses from drought for time t accrue at the rate

$$EAL_t = U[D_t/Y_t]^z \tag{14-6}$$

for given projected demand and chosen level of safe yield. In order to express this function in the terms we are presently employing, we define, $\bar{s}$ = level of safe yield inherited from the past. Then Equation 14-6 becomes:

$$EAL_t = U\left[\frac{D_o e^{(\beta+\gamma)t}}{\bar{s} + s_0 + \ldots}\right]^z \tag{14-7}$$

where $Y_t = \bar{s} + s_0 + \ldots$, and the exact composition of the denominator will depend on how many increments have been added prior to time t.

---

² We shall express both demand and safe yield in average daily terms. Our cost functions are standardized for arguments in millions of gallons per day (mgd). Hence, P_t is per capita daily demand in millions of gallons per day.

This implies that the *total* expected losses during a small period Δt, occurring at time t will be:

$$TEL_t = U\left[\frac{D_o e^{(\beta+\gamma)t}}{\bar{s} + s_0 + \dots}\right]^z N_o e^{\beta t}\Delta t = UN_o\left[\frac{D_o}{\bar{s} + s_0 + \dots}\right]^z e^{(\alpha z+\beta)t}\Delta t$$

(14-8)

where, we recall, $\alpha = \beta + \gamma$.

The present value of the total expected losses for the periods Δt at time t will then be:

$$PV(TEL_t) = UN_o\left[\frac{D_o}{\bar{s} + s_0 + \dots}\right]^z e^{(\alpha z+\beta-\rho)t}\Delta t$$

(14-9)

The next step is the computation of the total contribution to the present value of losses of a period between additions of safe yield. Let us, for example, consider the total present value of the losses suffered between time T_1 and T_2. Integrating, we have:

$$\text{Total } EL_{(T_2,T_1)} = \int_{T_1}^{T_2} UN_o\left(\frac{D_o}{\bar{s} + s_0 + s_1}\right)^z e^{(\alpha z+\beta-\rho)t}dt$$

(14-10)

which is particularly simple because t only appears in the exponent of e. Equation 14-10 gives us

$$\text{Total } EL_{(T_2,T_1)} = \left(\frac{UN_o}{\alpha z + \beta - \rho}\right)\left(\frac{D_o}{\bar{s} + s_0 + s_1}\right)^z \cdot [e^{(\alpha z+\beta-\rho)T_2} - e^{(\alpha z+\beta-\rho)T_1}].$$

(14-11)

The objective function for the planning model may then be written in its entirety:

Total present value of costs and losses $= \theta(S_0, S_1, S_2, S_{60}, T_1, T_2)$

$$= \sum_{t=0,T_1,T_2,60} K(s_t)e^{-\rho t} +$$

$$+ \frac{N_o U(D_o)^z}{\alpha z + \beta - \rho}[(\bar{s} + s_0)^{-z}(e^{(\alpha z+\beta-\rho)T_1} - 1)$$

$$+ (\bar{s} + s_0 + s_1)^{-z}(e^{(\alpha z+\beta-\rho)T_2} - e^{(\alpha z+\beta-\rho)T_1})$$

$$+ (\bar{s} + s_0 + s_1 + s_2)^{-z}(e^{(\alpha z+\beta-\rho)60} - e^{(\alpha z+\beta-\rho)T_2})].$$

(14-12)

The constraint set includes:[3]

$$\sum_{t=0,T_1,T_2,60} S_t = D_o(e^{60\alpha} - 1)$$

(14-13)

[3] If we wish to allow for an inequality we may write:
$$s_0 + s_1 + s_2 + s_{60} - s_s = PD_o(e^{60\alpha} - 1)$$
where s_s is a slack variable and $s_s \geq 0$. This formulation might be useful where demand is growing slowly or not at all and some capacity above the minimum required to cover that growth might reduce drought losses by enough to be worth while.

$$S_t \geq 0 \text{ all } t$$

and,[4]

$$0 \leq T_1 \leq 60,$$
$$0 \leq T_2 \leq 60,$$

The following constants retained the values indicated for all runs:[5]

$$N_o = 10^5$$
$$D_o = 10(\text{mgd})$$
$$P_o = 10^{-4}(\text{mgd})$$

and,

$$K = 1.28 \times 10^5;$$
$$U = 0.1.$$

GENERAL COMMENTS

The capital-cost portion of the objective function is concave (since $y < 1$). Thus, without consideration of drought losses, the minimum-cost plan would be the construction of the entire required increment in the final year.[6] When, however, we include drought losses the situation becomes at once more complicated and more promising for meaningful minimization solutions.

METHODS OF SOLUTION

Two methods were used in finding the solutions to this programming problem. First, as a method of developing some familiarity with the behavior of the solutions, a rather simple search technique was employed. Then, a nonlinear programming algorithm based on the method of

---

[4] The objective function as formulated above depends on T_1 being less than T_2. It might seem that it would be necessary to add a constraint to this effect; for example, writing $T_1 + T_s = T_2$, with $T_s \geq 0$, a slack variable. In practice, however, this problem did not arise in any of our many solution runs, and we have not included such a constraint. One conjectures that since one increment must necessarily be added later than the other (unless $T_1 = T_2$) the problem is only one of labeling.

[5] As noted later, a few runs were made with $N_o = 50,000$ in connection with comparison of our optimality "rules of thumb" and the actual expansion histories of three Massachusetts systems.

[6] Since there is effectively one constraint, the extreme point vector will have only one non-zero element. This implies the economically sensible result that either s_0 or s_{60} must be non-zero, since the other four variables are, in a sense, paired. At a positive discount rate, everything will be built in year 60; with a zero discount rate, the planner would be indifferent between the first and last years.

Zoutendijk was applied.[7] These methods are both discussed in somewhat more detail in Appendix H, while the actual results are discussed below.

RESULTS OF SOLUTION OF THE MODEL FOR VARIOUS PARAMETER VALUES

We are interested here in changes in total costs and in the elements of the solution vector in response to changes in the scaling factor, the discount rate (ρ), and the key drought loss-function parameter (z). The combinations of parameters for which the model was solved are listed in Table 39.

TABLE 39. COMBINATIONS OF INITIAL VECTORS AND PARAMETER VALUES USED IN COMPUTER RUNS

Initial vectors	Loss function parameter z	Safe yield scale factor y	Discount rate ρ	Population rate of growth β	Per capita daily consumption rate of growth γ
$\begin{bmatrix} 1 \\ 2 \\ 3 \end{bmatrix}$	$\begin{bmatrix} 3.2 \\ 4.3 \\ 5.4 \\ 12.0 \end{bmatrix}$	$\begin{bmatrix} 0.88 \\ 0.78 \\ 0.68 \end{bmatrix}$	$\begin{bmatrix} 0.07 \\ 0.05 \\ 0.03 \end{bmatrix}$	$\begin{bmatrix} 0.015 \end{bmatrix}$	$\begin{bmatrix} 0.020 \end{bmatrix}$

(108 runs total)

$\begin{bmatrix} 2 \\ 3 \end{bmatrix}$	$\begin{bmatrix} 4.3 \\ 12.0 \end{bmatrix}$	$\begin{bmatrix} 0.78 \end{bmatrix}$	$\begin{bmatrix} 0.05 \end{bmatrix}$	$\begin{bmatrix} 0.000 \\ 0.015 \\ 0.030 \end{bmatrix}$	$\begin{bmatrix} 0.000 \\ 0.020 \\ 0.040 \end{bmatrix}$

(36 runs total)

The "best" solution vectors and costs are shown in Table 40 for the 36 combinations of y, ρ, and z. We report here the total costs, capital costs, and drought losses to the nearest thousand dollars. Times (T_1 and T_2) are reported to the nearest tenth of a year and capacity increments to the nearest hundredth mgd.[8] ($\beta = 0.015$; $\gamma = 0.020$.)

[7] See G. Zoutendijk, *Methods of Feasible Directions* (Amsterdam: Elsevier, 1960).
[8] For a comparison of the results found using the search technique with the programming solutions, see Appendix H.

TABLE 40. SENSITIVITY OF RESULTS TO PARAMETER CHANGES

(costs given in $1,000)

Z	Y	ρ	Total cost	Capital cost	Drought loss	T_1	T_2	S_0	S_1	S_2	S_{60}
12.0	0.88	0.07	1,339	1,182	157	15.2	34.5	4.52	12.66	34.78	19.71
12.0	0.88	0.05	1,898	1,723	175	17.4	37.4	5.99	15.04	34.95	15.67
12.0	0.88	0.03	2,922	2,743	178	20.1	40.0	8.12	18.06	35.68	9.80
12.0	0.78	0.07	1,088	971	117	15.2	34.6	4.81	13.18	36.40	17.27
12.0	0.78	0.05	1,497	1,372	125	17.5	37.7	6.37	15.87	36.79	12.63
12.0	0.78	0.03	2,214	2,130	84	20.8	42.8	9.59	21.28	40.80	0
12.0	0.68	0.07	883	799	84	15.7	35.3	5.37	14.13	37.76	14.41
12.0	0.68	0.05	1,179	1,092	87	18.7	39.5	7.32	18.04	37.88	8.42
12.0	0.68	0.03	1,712	1,623	89	26.0	53.0	13.54	32.98	25.63	0
5.4	0.88	0.07	1,145	838	307	14.8	34.8	2.14	10.11	25.90	33.51
5.4	0.88	0.05	1,727	1,382	345	17.1	37.5	3.69	12.31	27.36	28.30
5.4	0.88	0.03	2,836	2,461	374	19.4	40.1	5.85	15.20	30.02	20.60
5.4	0.78	0.07	980	734	246	14.5	34.9	2.40	11.11	28.27	29.88
5.4	0.78	0.05	1,419	1,156	263	17.3	38.2	4.22	13.75	30.26	23.44
5.4	0.78	0.03	2,214	2,031	183	22.5	46.4	9.30	22.42	39.94	0
5.4	0.68	0.07	835	651	184	15.6	36.4	3.28	12.85	30.76	24.78
5.4	0.68	0.05	1,159	970	189	18.8	40.3	5.48	16.41	33.44	16.33
5.4	0.68	0.03	1,697	1,508	189	23.3	46.4	8.80	25.06	37.80	0
4.3	0.88	0.07	1,059	602	457	13.2	34.3	0	9.52	23.38	38.76
4.3	0.88	0.05	1,655	1,239	417	16.5	37.2	2.56	11.26	24.65	33.19
4.3	0.88	0.03	2,794	2,339	455	19.0	39.9	4.90	14.17	27.68	24.91
4.3	0.78	0.07	906	504	402	12.8	34.1	0	10.92	22.77	37.97
4.3	0.78	0.05	1,382	1,052	329	16.1	37.7	2.82	12.77	27.94	28.13
4.3	0.78	0.03	2,203	1,960	243	23.8	48.5	8.88	23.49	39.29	0
4.3	0.68	0.07	798	392	406	14.2	37.5	0	13.59	29.99	28.08
4.3	0.68	0.05	1,141	923	218	20.9	45.8	5.36	20.15	46.15	0
4.3	0.68	0.03	1,712	1,528	185	24.5	47.0	9.93	26.05	35.68	0
3.2	0.88	0.07	948	426	522	19.9	44.1	0	12.20	23.63	35.83
3.2	0.88	0.05	1,523	920	603	15.5	38.6	0	10.76	22.05	38.85
3.2	0.88	0.03	2,711	2,005	706	11.5	34.0	0	10.26	26.14	35.26
3.2	0.78	0.07	836	377	459	19.4	43.5	0	14.22	32.28	25.16
3.2	0.78	0.05	1,294	813	480	15.8	41.6	0	15.39	34.09	22.18
3.2	0.78	0.03	2,147	1,732	415	7.8	36.4	0	14.86	32.08	24.72
3.2	0.68	0.07	708	312	396	16.3	37.7	0	11.39	21.98	38.29
3.2	0.68	0.05	1,088	546	492	16.5	42.2	0	17.51	25.64	28.51
3.2	0.68	0.03	1,708	1,392	317	22.4	47.7	6.10	24.00	41.57	0

By far the most striking of our findings is the insensitivity of total losses to changes in z. We note, for example, that when $y = 0.68$ and $\rho = 0.03$, the difference in total costs between the $z = 12$ and the $z = 3.2$ situations is only \$4,000 or about 0.18 percent. It is not true, of course, that we can dismiss the problem of determining the proper z, for the similarity in total costs noted above was only achieved by following quite different optimal paths. In particular, if z is large, we wish to build considerably more capacity in the initial year (13.54 mgd vs. 6.10 mgd in our example).[9] The remaining elements of the two plans are not very different, though $\hat{S}_1$ is also larger when $z = 12$.

Indeed, another interesting feature of the solution data is the relative insensitivity of these remaining elements of the optimal plan to changes in z. For example, for $y = 0.78$, $\rho = 0.05$, as z changes from 12 to 3.2, the timing portion of the solution vector changes only from $T_1 = 17.5$, $T_2 = 37.7$ to $T_1 = 15.8$, $T_2 = 41.6$. We may contrast this with the change in timing for $z = 5.4$, $y = 0.78$ as ρ goes from 0.07 ($T_1 = 14.5$, $T_2 = 34.9$) to 0.03 ($T_1 = 22.6$, $T_2 = 46.4$). Similar, if less pronounced, differential sensitivity may be observed in the capacity elements of the solution vectors.

The observed differences in total plan cost between $z = 12$ and $z = 3.2$ situations are considerably greater under other combinations of y and ρ. In general these differences seem to be greater, the greater y and ρ. When $y = 0.88$ and $\rho = 0.07$, the cost difference is about \$400,000, or 30 percent. But even this difference is small compared to those observed as ρ varies from 0.07 to 0.03 for given z and y. For example, when $z = 5.4$, and $y = 0.88$, the difference between total costs at 3 percent and at 7 percent discounting is about \$1,700,000, or 60 percent of the larger figure (150 percent of the smaller). *It seems clear that both total costs and the values of $\hat{T}_1$, $\hat{T}_2$, etc. are most sensitive to the discount rate.*

The heavy impact of this parameter is not surprising. When z is large, the model seeks a path which includes a bit more capacity early in the period to keep the D/Y ratio down in the area around 1.00 for which drought losses per capita are small even for large z.[10] But when ρ is smaller, whatever the optimal path involves it is bound to cost more, since ρ acts symmetrically on capital costs and drought losses. The only trade-offs

---

[9] The cost of misspecification of z may be found for two situations: if we build the plan optimal for $z = 3.2$ and z is "really" 12, then we lose over \$740,000 in increased drought losses. If we build for $z = 12$ when it is really 3.2, we lose about \$75,000. This represents the net of \$230,000 in increased capital costs and \$155,000 in reduced drought losses. See below for further evidence on the importance of z.

[10] This strategy results in lower total drought losses, for given y and ρ when $z = 12$ than when $z = 3.2$, 4.3, or 5.4. The somewhat higher total costs for larger z reflect the higher present value of capital costs implied by building early.

possible here involve time, for postponement either of capital costs or of losses is less well rewarded under a smaller discount rate.

We note that the model's sensitivity to changes in ρ extends more deeply than a mere increase in the present value of total expected costs and losses. When ρ changes, so do the two elements of the plan vector particularly important to planners; i.e., the size of the increment to be built in year zero and the time to the next increment. For the parameter combination $z = 5.4$, $y = 0.88$, when ρ falls from 0.07 to 0.03, $\hat{S}_o$ increases from 2.14 to 5.85, or by well over 100 percent.

It is interesting that *while total costs show some sensitivity to changes in y, the composition of the optimal path shows virtually none at all.* Thus, for example, when $z = 4.3$, and $ρ = 0.07$, as y changes from 0.68 to 0.88, total costs increase from \$798,000 to \$1,059,000 or by about 25 percent of the lower figure. But, over this same interval, the optimal vector changes very little in terms of the generally sensitive variables $\hat{S}_o$ and $\hat{T}_1$.[11]

By way of tentative summary we may suggest that an accurate estimate of the appropriate interest rate is at least as important for effective planning as exact knowledge of either the loss function or the scaling factor (given that the latter are in the range we use). This is true even though we realize that in determining the optimal plan, the planners need make no irrevocable decisions except what size to make S_o.

[11] As discussed below, we had hoped that in each run the solution vectors found using the three different initial vectors would be the same. Had this invariably happened, we would have been reasonably confident that we were finding the global minimum. Unfortunately, however, we did not achieve such ideal results. Indeed, of the 36 parameter sets solved with separate initial vectors, only 12 (about 33 percent) gave results which could be classified as triple agreement on a single optimum. Three different kinds of problems could be distinguished in the 24 cases of nonagreement, all resulting from the nonconvexity of the surface. First, for certain parameter combinations, the partial derivatives show perverse sign behavior in the neighborhood of one or more of the starting vectors. In these instances the program reports as the solution a minor modification of the particular starting vector. (These "solutions" are recognizable even without knowledge of the global optimum and there is very little danger of their acceptance in an actual series of computations.) Second, when one of the increment sizes naturally tends to be small because of the particular parameter combinations, corner solutions again turn up. This is particularly troublesome in the fairly large number of cases for which s_o tends to zero. Here no solution is obviously incorrect, but all are highly suspect and only the performance of a large number of runs gives any assurance that the solution accepted is close to the best attainable. Third, what appear to be classical local optima within the constraint region are occasionally turned up.

Generally, the method worked best when z was 5.4. For large z, the program tended to find starting-vector corner solutions when ρ and/or y were small; when ρ and y were large the program moved more securely to a single optimum. When z was small (3.2), the problem created by the tendency of s_o to zero cropped up frequently. We may place the most faith in the results found for $z = 5.4$ and 4.3, the least on the results for $z = 3.2$.

We move on now to examine the sensitivity of the solutions to changes in the growth rate of demand and to investigate the implications for the planning process of uncertainty about these rates of growth. We shall note that good estimates of these rates are more critical to effective planning than is knowledge of any of the other key parameters.

EFFECT OF UNCERTAINTY IN PROJECTIONS OF THE GROWTH OF DEMAND

Our first step is to look at the solutions to the planning model under 9 combinations of population and demand rates of growth. We then calculate the costs of adopting programs optimal under one set of growth rates, when the actual rates of growth are different. The calculations are performed under two sets of assumptions, one of which represents an extreme view of the possible losses to be incurred, and the other of which is an attempt to capture a more realistic set of losses. The difference between the two cases is the time at which we assume the growth-rate discrepancy is discovered and a return to the optimal path effected.

OPTIMAL PATHS AND RESULTING COSTS UNDER VARIOUS SETS OF GROWTH RATES

In Table 41 we summarize the values of costs and of the choice variables under 9 different combinations of assumed growth rates of population and per capita demand. We report the results for two different sets of basic parameters: (i) $z = 12$, $y = 0.78$, $\rho = 0.05$; and (ii) $z = 4.3$, $y = 0.78$, $\rho = 0.05$.

These results do not hold any particular surprises, although they do illustrate that the total costs are relatively sensitive to changes in growth rates. Thus, let us compare the results for an overall growth rate of demand of 0.015 with those for a rate of 0.070. This represents an increase in the growth rate of about 4.7 times. When $z = 4.3$, this produces a difference in costs of 7.3 times, and when $z = 12$, of 9.8 times. Drought losses do not vary nearly so much over this range—only by factors of about 2 in each case. The large differences in total costs thus reflect proportionally even greater changes in capital costs (on the order of 10 or 11 times). These increases are, in turn, based on the fact that total demand growth to be covered by construction increases far more than in proportion to the increase in the rate of growth. (As the growth rate goes from 0.015 to 0.070, the total growth of demand over 60 years increases by a factor of 45.) The capital cost increases are, however, dampened by two factors. First, of course, economies of scale hold down the costs of build-

TABLE 41. SENSITIVITY OF RESULTS TO GROWTH RATE CHANGES

ζ	β	γ	Total cost	Capital cost	Drought loss	T_1	T_2	S_0	S_1	S_2	S_{60}
12.0	0.000	0.000	180	80	100	—	—	5.47	—	—	—
12.0	0.015	0.000	633	540	93	27.1	46.3	3.88	5.54	5.18	—
12.0	0.030	0.000	1,275	1,161	114	17.6	38.0	5.55	13.18	28.50	3.27
12.0	0.000	0.020	764	676	88	16.7	42.2	3.02	7.21	12.97	—
12.0	0.015	0.020	1,497	1,372	125	17.5	37.8	6.37	15.87	37.03	12.40
12.0	0.030	0.020	2,736	2,549	188	20.1	41.9	13.31	46.40	93.45	37.77
12.0	0.000	0.040	1,753	1,610	143	18.4	39.6	7.56	21.64	45.90	25.13
12.0	0.015	0.040	3,167	2,953	214	20.4	41.6	15.30	53.50	120.71	71.62
12.0	0.030	0.040	6,181	5,965	216	27.4	53.6	42.13	299.59	283.48	31.66
4.3	0.000	0.000	190	—	190	—	—	—	—	—	—
4.3	0.015	0.000	659	343	315	8.6	51.4	—	4.84	7.30	2.46
4.3	0.030	0.000	1,274	957	317	16.3	38.4	2.67	12.33	26.53	8.95
4.3	0.000	0.020	712	378	334	10.8	49.2	—	5.39	11.16	6.21
4.3	0.015	0.020	1,382	1,052	329	16.1	37.7	2.82	12.77	27.94	28.13
4.3	0.030	0.020	2,470	2,055	415	18.3	39.5	6.97	29.51	88.23	66.15
4.3	0.000	0.040	1,500	1,161	339	16.2	37.5	3.09	13.50	29.79	53.86
4.3	0.015	0.040	2,685	2,253	432	18.3	39.3	7.28	31.06	93.98	128.81
4.3	0.030	0.040	4,817	4,235	582	22.7	45.1	17.41	106.00	231.04	302.42

ing more capacity. And, second, under the higher growth rate relatively less of the total required construction is undertaken in the first year of the period. (Under the 0.015 growth rate, 26.6 percent of the total construction is carried out in year zero. When the overall growth rate is 0.070, only 6.4 percent is done in the first year.)

Losses From Incorrect Demand Projections: The Case of the Obtuse Planners

If we assume that planners are faced with a range of possible growth rates for population and per capita demand, we may ask what kinds of losses (excess costs) are involved in acting on the basis of one such combination when another combination, in fact, describes the state of nature over the planning period. In order to obtain an estimate of the largest possible losses for a given strategy, given parameter values, and given range of growth rates (and given that the bequest constraint is met), we first assume that the planners involved are extremely obtuse: so much so that they proceed with the chosen plan right through the period, ignoring any evidence of a discrepancy between the assumed and actual rates of growth. Only in year 60 do they realize their mistake. At that time they build, if it is necessary, an increment large enough to meet the bequest constraint.

For simplicity, we consider the set of possible growth-rate combinations to include only the following 9 elements:

Population Growth, (β)	0.000	0.015	0.030	0.000	0.015	0.030	0.000	0.015	0.030
Per Capita Demand Growth, (γ)	0.000	0.000	0.000	0.020	0.020	0.020	0.040	0.040	0.040
Total Demand Growth	0.000	0.015	0.030	0.020	0.035	0.050	0.040	0.055	0.070

[We assume $y = 0.78$ and $\rho = 0.05$, in what follows. Results are reported for $z = 4.3$ and $Z = 12$. We futher assume that a single rate of growth holds over the entire period, whether this rate is the one assumed by the planners or not.]

We assume that the planners accept the pair $\beta = 0.015$ $\gamma = 0.020$, as the best estimate of the future growth rates, and that they act to follow the plan optimal for this pair. In Table 42 we show the losses resulting from such a policy when each of the other growth rates in fact turns up. These losses represent the difference between the actual costs implied by the assumed strategy and those which would have been incurred under

TABLE 42. RESULTS OF NON-OPTIMAL POLICIES, WITHOUT REVIEW

(all costs expressed in $1,000)

$Z = 4.3$

Actual growth rates		Total cost		Capital cost		Drought losses	
			Difference from		Difference from		Difference from
β	γ	Actual	optimal	Actual	optimal	Actual	optimal
0.000	0.000	1,010	820	970	970	40	(150)
0.015	0.000	1,050	392	970	627	80	(235)
0.030	0.000	1,280	6	1,000	43	280	(37)
0.000	0.020	1,050	348	970	592	90	(244)
0.015	0.020	1,380	—	1,050	—	330	—
0.030	0.020	7,540	5,070	1,280	(775)	6,260	5,845
0.000	0.040	1,510	10	1,120	(41)	390	51
0.015	0.040	9,960	7,275	1,390	(863)	8,570	8,138
0.030	0.040	577,000	572,200	1,920	(2,300)	575,000	574,500

$Z = 12.0$

β	γ	Actual	optimal	Actual	optimal	Actual	optimal
0.000	0.000	1,330	1,150	1,330	1,250	0	(100)
0.015	0.000	1,332	699	1,330	790	2	(91)
0.030	0.000	1,370	95	1,330	169	40	(74)
0.000	0.020	1,334	570	1,330	654	4	(84)
0.015	0.020	1,500	—	1,370	—	130	—
0.030	0.020	1.9×10^6	1.9×10^6	1,610	(900)	1.9×10^6	1.9×10^6
0.000	0.040	2,070	317	1,440	(170)	630	487
0.015	0.040	2.6×10^7	2.6×10^7	1,730	(1,200)	2.6×10^7	2.6×10^7
0.030	0.040	2.4×10^{12}	2.4×10^{12}	2,260	(3,700)	2.4×10^{12}	2.4×10^{12}

Note: Figures in parentheses indicate savings.

certainty by using the plan appropriate to the actual growth rate. As such, they may be thought of as costs of uncertainty.

We note from Table 42 that the results of such doggedly incorrect decision-making could be literally disastrous. We note, however, that the magnitude of the problem varies enormously with the size of z, the drought loss function. It is in this area of uncertain demand projections that we find the first signs that the planning process is seriously sensitive to z. Clearly it is important to know what z is in order to choose among alternative strategies for dealing with this problem.

Losses From Incorrect Demand Projections: A More Realistic Case

Let us consider the same combination of parameter values and the same assumptions about the range of possible growth rates. In this example, however, we assume that the planners act so as to retain some flexibility in the face of uncertainty about these rates. Specifically, before building the increment $\hat{s}_1$, optimal for $\hat{T}_1$ under the assumed growth rates $\beta = 0.015$ and $\gamma = 0.020$, the planners check these assumed rates against evidence from the world. Let us assume that the evidence indicates that the actual rates of growth are $\beta = b$ and $\gamma = g$. (We assume that these rates have, in fact, held since the year 0 and will hold to the horizon.) With these rates of growth and given the information about z, y and ρ, there is associated an optimal plan vector, T_{1bg}, T_{2bg}, s_{0bg}, s_{1bg}, s_{2bg}, s_{60bg}. The planners, acting on their discovery, build increment s_{1bg} in time $\hat{T}_1$, instead of continuing with their original plan. Subsequently they build s_{2bg} in time T_{2bg}, and an amount in year 60 determined by the bequest constraint.

TABLE 43. RESULTS OF NON-OPTIMAL POLICIES, WITH REVIEW

$Z = 4.3$ *(all costs expressed in $1,000)*

Actual growth rates		Total cost		Capital cost		Drought losses	
β	γ	Actual	Difference from optimal	Actual	Difference from optimal	Actual	Difference from optimal
0.000	0.000	353	163	287	287	65	(125)
0.015	0.000	695	36	529	186	166	(149)
0.030	0.000	1,270	0	970	15	300	(15)
0.000	0.020	759	47	590	212	169	(165)
0.015	0.020	1,380	0	1,050	0	329	0
0.030	0.020	2,560	90	1,850	(205)	710	295
0.000	0.040	1,500	0	1,140	(30)	360	30
0.015	0.040	2,800	115	2,030	(220)	760	335
0.030	0.040	5,520	705	3,970	(270)	1,560	975

$Z = 12.0$

β	γ	Actual	Difference from optimal	Actual	Difference from optimal	Actual	Difference from optimal
0.000	0.000	543	363	542	462	1	(99)
0.015	0.000	800	167	791	251	9	(84)
0.030	0.000	1,290	15	1,220	59	70	(44)
0.000	0.020	916	152	906	230	10	(78)
0.015	0.020	1,497	0	1,372	0	125	0
0.030	0.020	3,740	1,000	2,270	(275)	1,460	1,275
0.000	0.040	1,770	17	1,560	(50)	210	67
0.015	0.040	5,400	2,333	2,600	(353)	2,800	2,233
0.030	0.040	62,400	56,209	5,990	25	56,400	56,184

Note: Figures in parentheses indicate savings.

The results for this example are contained in Table 43. We note that, with one exception, the total costs associated with early adjustment to incorrect demand projections are of the same order of magnitude as those resulting from proper projections. Only in the situation for which $z = 12$, and the overall growth rate of demand is, in fact, 0.070 (i.e., when $\beta = 0.030$, $\gamma = 0.040$) does a really larger loss show up. This observation puts into better perspective the question of over-building as a hedge against uncertainty. *The indication is that only in relatively unusual circumstances would even a serious underestimate of demand growth imply very large losses, if the planners take the reasonable precaution of checking their assumptions.*

With the above evidence in mind on the existence of persuasive reasons for a bias toward "overbuilding" of water supply systems, it will be particularly interesting to turn to a consideration of the practical planning process. In the next chapter, we discuss rules of thumb, based on our computational results, for use in the making of municipal water supply decisions.

PART V

PRACTICAL SYSTEM PLANNING

CHAPTER 15

RULES OF THUMB FOR OPTIMAL PLANNING

It now seems appropriate to ask whether the formal model set up in Part IV might find application in the practical planning of municipal investments in water supply system capacity. It does seem clear that if it is left to each town, or even each engineering firm, to formulate a version of the model and to estimate the applicable parameters on a case-by-case basis, little will be done. On the other hand, it is conceivable that some agency could put together a suitable general model, run it many times while varying the parameters over relevant ranges, and publish in a handbook or similar form a summary of the results.

In order to illustrate this possibility on the basis of the relatively simple model presented here, we have calculated two summary measures which would answer the key questions of the optimal timing and size of capacity increments for given sets of parameter values.[1] Both these measures are based on the already familiar concepts of projected demand (and its rate of growth) and safe yield, for we felt that these are key terms in the existing planning process, and that it would be wise to minimize breaks with present practice.

OPTIMAL TIMING OF CAPACITY INCREMENTS

We first examined the timing question by looking at the ratio of demand to safe yield (the inadequacy level) existing at times $\hat{T}_1$ and $\hat{T}_2$ (the times at which increments were added) for each program run. Those ratios were generally not exactly equal for a particular parameter combination, but

---

[1] Note that in calculating these measures we must generally use solution values generated for times T_1 and T_2 (increments s_1 and s_2) only, since in time zero and time 60 the model was free to choose only increment size and not timing.

165

TABLE 44. OPTIMAL INCREMENT TIMING

For $z = 12$

and if $\rho =$	0.03	0.05	0.07
If $y = 0.88$	1.11	1.15	1.16
0.78	1.08	1.12	1.15
0.68	1.06	1.12	1.12

For $z = 5.4$

and if $\rho =$	0.03	0.05	0.07
If $y = 0.88$	1.24	1.33	1.39
0.78	1.14	1.29	1.34
0.78	*	1.25	1.30

For $z = 4.3$

and if $\rho =$	0.03	0.05	0.07
If $y = 0.88$	1.30	1.42	1.58
0.78	1.21	1.36	1.57
0.68	1.18	1.35	*

Notes:
The table entries indicate the safe-yield ratio at which expansion should be undertaken.
No table has been provided for $z = 3.2$ because of the generally lower quality of the computational results achieved in those runs.
* Solutions not reliable.

the differences were almost always small. To illustrate the kind of planning aid we have in mind, we present as Table 44 a sample handbook timing table. Entering the table for the appropriate value of z (depending on stance, climate, etc.) for one's situation, one runs down the left-hand side to the applicable scaling factor (y, depending primarily on terrain and climate), and across this row to the discount rate column describing the cost of capital to the town. The entry gives the adequacy level at which it is optimal to plan to add an increment of safe yield.[2]

The results presented in the table follow a very plausible pattern. For given z, with higher interest rates (greater savings from postponement) and less important economies of scale, it is optimal to let system adequacy fall farther (let D/Y grow larger) before building an addition to capacity. For given interest rate and scaling factor, a lower value of z (indicating less

[2] In fact, except under very special conditions on the relative sizes of the parameters, α, β, and y, the ratio of demand to safe yield at which an increment is added will change over time. This change will nearly always be fairly small (on the order of 5 percent total over 20 years) and so we feel justified in ignoring it.

spectacular growth in expected losses with deteriorating adequacy) also encourages longer postponement of additions to adequacy.

OPTIMAL SIZE OF CAPACITY INCREMENTS

We express our results for increment sizes in terms of years of demand provided for. Specifically, we calculate the ratio of the system safe yield *with* the new increment to that existing before, and determine what period in years is implied by that ratio, where we treat safe yield as though it were growing at the rate α, the rate of growth of total demand. Symbolically, we define the optimal increment size τ at building time T as:

$$\tau = \frac{1}{\alpha} \ln \left[\frac{\bar{s} + s_o + \ldots + s_T}{\bar{s} + s_o + \ldots + s_{T-1}} \right] \qquad (15\text{-}1)$$

Note that this measure of increment size is in units which we would expect to be independent of the rate of growth of demand, in the sense that whether this rate of growth is high or low, for given z, ρ, and y the optimal increment should cover the same number of years. The physical size of a τ-year increment will depend, of course, on the rate of growth.[3]

We present in Table 45 sample handbook pages for the planning of increment sizes. The method of entering the tables is the same as for Table 44; here the entry tells the manager how big his increment should be in terms of years. To translate into physical size, he uses the formula

$$\Delta S = S \text{ (existing) } (e^{\alpha \tau} - 1), \qquad (15\text{-}2)$$

where τ is the table entry and α is the estimated rate of growth of demand for his system.

The general patterns of the table are, again, in keeping with economic common sense. The lower the interest rate, for given scale factor, the larger the optimal increment size. For given ρ, decreasing the scale factor increases the optimal increment size.[4] Perhaps the most surprising feature is, however, the marked lack of sensitivity of the increment size of z.

---

[3] That the model actually does give us the same information on optimal increment size was checked by calculations over the several growth rate combinations used in the calculations for Chapter 14. Since these runs were made with constant z, y, and ρ, we hypothesized that for each growth rate the model would build for the same number of years of demand growth. This was, in fact, the case within the limits of error implied by our computational problems.

[4] As with the timing rule, there is a problem introduced because the optimal increment size will, in general, change from time $\bar{T}_1$ to time $\bar{T}_2$. Because of the complexity of the partial derivatives with respect to increment sizes, it is difficult to make any conclusive formal argument showing how the increment sizes should vary from $\hat{s}_1$ to $\hat{s}_2$ for particular parameter values. Examination of the computational results indicates, however, that the problem will be greatest when y and ρ are both relatively large, and that if ρ is small, the problem may be insignificant.

TABLE 45. OPTIMAL INCREMENT SIZE

For $z = 12$			
and if $\rho =$	0.03	0.05	0.07
If $y = 0.88$	19.7	18.9	17.9
0.78	22.6	19.4	18.2
0.68	25.0	20.4	18.6

For $z = 5.4$			
and if $\rho =$	0.03	0.05	0.07
If $y = 0.88$	19.2	18.3	17.3
0.78	22.0	19.4	18.3
0.68	*	20.6	19.4

For $z = 4.3$			
and if $\rho =$	0.03	0.05	0.07
If $y = 0.88$	19.1	18.3	19.1
0.78	23.0	19.8	21.1
0.68	23.9	23.9	*

Notes:
The table entries indicate the number of years the increment constructed should be designed to cover.

We note that, calculated on the basis described in the text, the optimal sizes change very little with the large change in z. We earlier calculated increment sizes on a somewhat different basis, in which the level of demand existing when an increment was built was explicitly included. On this basis there was a sharp increase in optimal sizes with the increase in z. The basis we adopt here seems "purer" since we cannot be picking up influences which should be reflected already in the choice of optimal D/Y ratio (the timing problem).

* Solutions not reliable.

If we agree to accept these rules of thumb as rough standards for optimal system expansion over time, what can we say about investment records of actual systems? Within the limits of the information available to them, do system managers generally seem to build too much or too little capacity? Do they plan to build too early or too late? Or are they, by some rough, intuitive process homing in on nearly optimal recommendations? We attempt to answer these questions by examining the world of practical water-system planning, the actual expansion histories of five Massachusetts systems, and the costs implied by these histories in the context of our planning model. These results may then be compared with the results achievable through the use of our rules of thumb.

CHAPTER 16

THE FRAMEWORK FOR
WATER SUPPLY DECISIONS

We have seen from the foregoing that through the application of formal economic analysis the problem of planning municipal water system expansion is amenable to solutions which minimize the total costs to the community. We hardly need point out; however, that the average municipal water system is not planned using a model including drought losses and taking account of the trade-off between these losses and capital costs of safe-yield expansion. The world of municipal water supply management is a world of pragmatists (political and otherwise) who tend to be seeking two goals: they wish to provide the community with safe, low-cost water; and they usually wish to retain or advance their personal positions. Because of the contrast between the "economic man" of sophisticated analytical abilities and the *homo realitus* of community government, we feel it will be useful to describe how planning is actually carried out, who the planners are, what sources of information they have, and how they make use of the information they receive from these sources. Hopefully we will be able to provide in conclusion some comments on the prospects for the inclusion of some tool such as our rules of thumb in the practical planning process.

MAJOR PARTICIPANTS IN THE WATER-MANAGEMENT SYSTEM

Although there are several forms of local government in Massachusetts, they differ only in detail. In these governmental situations, the water-management system itself is usually made up of three component parts, although there may be variations in organization. These parts are the elected community officials, the bureaucratic or departmental personnel, and the external advisors.

Elected Officials

The elected community officials, namely the mayor and the city councilors, are responsible for all functions that the government performs.[1] Final decision-making power on water supply matters rests in the hands of these elected officials. In Massachusetts the city government can authorize the issuance of bonds by the vote of the city council. Town governments, on the other hand, may issue bonds only with the consent of the voting public at town meeting.

Some communities have a board of water commissioners made up of three elected officials who are responsible, in an advisory capacity, for matters relating only to water supply. They have the power to act as agents for the city or town but do not have the power to raise funds.

The ultimate power regarding any large expenditure of funds by the water department rests with the elected officials. The information on the operation and expansion of the water supply system which the elected officials use in exercising this power generally comes from the city water department or from external specialists hired as consultants. Information on the performance of the water supply system (as distinct from its operation) comes to the elected officials from many other sources as well, including members of the general public.

In matters dealing with additions to water supply capacity the elected officials lean heavily on the advice of departmental personnel and consulting engineers. The goal of providing safe, efficient water supply which is built into the elected positions, and which becomes a part of the water manager role, is pursued subject to the constraint that the achievement of the personal goals of the individual officials, such as reelection, prestige, recognition, power, and so forth, is at least not jeopardized.

The mayor of a city (or the manager in the case of a city manager form of government) holds a critical position in terms of water supply, as he

[1] The entire area of the Commonwealth of Massachusetts is divided into municipal governmental units. Municipalities are either cities or towns. There are seven different types of city charter which may be adopted in the state. Space does not permit a discussion of their differences here; but see Commonwealth of Massachusetts, *General Laws*, Ch. 4, Sec. 7. There is only a single form of town government consisting of a board of selectmen carrying out executive functions, with legislative power in the hands of the general citizenry at town meeting. The finance committee of the town meeting is the body which actually allocates money to the selectmen so that town services may be provided. Under most of the *city* charters in Massachusetts this allocative function is performed by the city council. Although there are some towns in our sample, our discussion is simplified considerably by confining our descriptive passages to organization at the city level. In the further interest of simplicity the "typical" city government will be assumed to consist of a mayor or manager performing executive functions and a city council allocating funds.

does in other types of decision-making. It is the mayor who must request the city council to issue bonds or otherwise make funds available. The mayor must also balance the community's demand for water with its demands for all other city services. It is this elected official who most directly reaps the political gains and losses associated with choosing one service over another in the allocation of money.

The city council acts in a more passive way in water supply matters, although there are isolated examples of council members having an active interest in the development of the water system. Such examples generally arise because a councilor perceives some political advantage in using an active voice in water supply matters.[2]

The water supply system retains a unique position in that it is a source of revenue for the city and, at least theoretically, is capable of providing funds for its own development. Financial arrangements dictated by state law are permissive in this regard, and allow the water department to retain a portion of its revenues for future construction if the city government so desires. The fact that only half of the water departments in the 46 municipally operated systems we surveyed retained any control at all over their revenues testifies that the water departments generally must compete for development funds with other city departments.

In addition to the municipal officials, the state legislature also has a supervisory hand in local water management under two provisions of state law. First, it has established the ground rules under which the whole system operates, giving to the Department of Public Health its powers and occasionally creating new entities such as the Metropolitan District Commission. Secondly, it approves all increments of supply that involve crossing of municipal boundaries. In most cases its approval comes quickly as a matter of course. Occasionally, however, the state legislature may actually exercise very strong and direct control over the shape of the urban water supply system.[3] Thus while not a major decision-maker, the state legislature may operate as a constraint and a court of last resort in the provision of water supply.

[2] Two examples show how the councilor may be influential in specific decisions. In one community a councilor was reported to have a reputation for denigrating the recommendations of the water superintendent to the point that personal animosity existed between the two. In another case, a councilor's challenge to the recommendation of a consulting engineering firm resulted in the eventual rejection of expert advice.

[3] See, for example, the discussion of the legislature's role in the Brockton, Mass., water crisis in Roger Kasperson, "Environmental Stress and Municipal Political System: The Brockton Water Crisis of 1961–66," a paper presented at the 1968 Meetings of the Association of American Geographers.

Departmental Personnel

There is wide variance among communities in the structure of water departments themselves. In most places the water department is separate and headed by the water superintendent. In other places the water superintendent may be a member of the public works department.

The typical manager of an urban system in Massachusetts is not an engineer and often lacks any formal technical training. He is usually a municipal employee who began in the system in plant operation, water distribution, or even in meter reading. He rose through the civil service or its equivalent, and his present skills reflect primarily experience and on-the-job training. (See Table 46.) He knows best the distribution problems of the system, for these are his day-to-day concern. For most problems connected with the provision of supply capacity he relies heavily on his external advisers. Problems of projecting demand, choosing further increments of supply, or seeking out alternative sources, are almost universally referred to the consulting engineer in the first instance, and then, for approval, to the Massachusetts Department of Public Health.

TABLE 46. BACKGROUND OF INTERVIEWED WATER SUPERINTENDENTS

Background and training	Number	Percentage of total
City Water Department employee—no special training	23	48
City Water Department employee—with special training	8	17
Long-time employee with engineering degree	7	15
Managerial experience and training in another profession	5	10
Other than above	3	6
Not ascertained	2	4
Total	48	100

Nevertheless the water supply manager is the individual in the community whose role is most directly related to the system. As such he is frequently called upon to present his views as to system needs and expansion to the elected officials and the community at large, and he may prove to be quite influential. Managers do not have impressive knowledge of factors relevant to investment decisions about water supply, such as hydrology, economics of alternative supply, and projection of demand. But since they are deeply committed to the safety of the supply and they desire to satisfy all potential demand at the existing price, they are usually ardent advocates of system expansion and modernization.

External Advisers

On almost all questions that he cannot answer the manager turns to his consulting engineer for assistance. This assistance is provided in two ways: formal preparation of a report; or frequent, informal, personal consultation. In theory, consulting engineering firms prepare specific reports and analyses on the request of a water system. When a new increment of supply is authorized they then design the works and supervise their construction. But most firms also provide informal consultation for which they do not usually bill their clients, much as the family doctor is (or used to be) prepared to give minor advice or even prescriptions by telephone without fee.

The State Department of Public Health is required by law to approve all proposals and plans for public water supply before their implementation. It is responsible for approving the purity of the present supplies and the adequacy and safety of future supplies. Like the consultant engineer, the DPH serves informally, through its district engineers, as a source of advice and counsel in the day-to-day functioning of systems. The files of the department give ample testimony that managers turn to it for advice as well as consent on a variety of problems of supply, treatment, and distribution.

INTERACTION BETWEEN THE SYSTEM PARTS: THE FRAMEWORK FOR DECISIONS

A typical water supply management system is shown schematically in Figure 22. Here, the three key participants identified above interact with each other and with the system's customers. The initial impetus for discussion and decision of a system change may come from the elected officials, department personnel, or the water-users. Department personnel are interested in maintaining a relatively adequate system in terms of safety, aesthetic quality, and abundance. Their interest in price will depend on the pressures on them to be self-supporting and the extent to which they control the allocation of water revenues. They will probably be the source of proposals for expansion in times when the system is apparently performing well, for they have a real interest in insuring continued success and no particular responsibilities for other areas of the municipal budget. Such proposals must be "sold" to the elected officials and their public, and this may be a difficult task in the absence of clear "need." The department may seek out, on its own, the expert opinion of its consultants and use this to bolster its case.

The elected officials can hardly be against safe, clean, cheap, and abundant water, but they do have responsibilities in other areas. Faced with

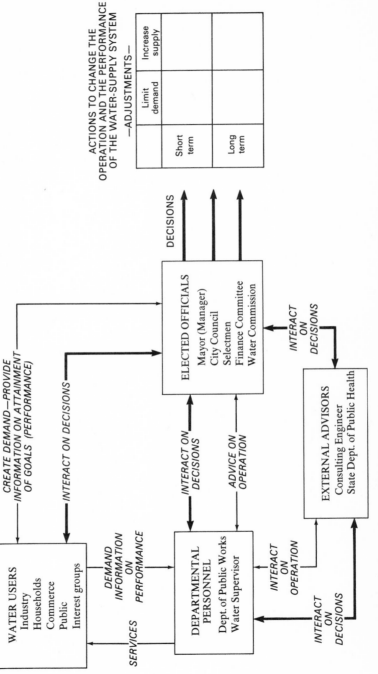

Figure 22. The municipal water-management system.

chronically insufficient local tax revenues, these officials must balance competing interests. They may agree publicly with a system expansion proposal, while maneuvering in private to delay or kill the measure. They may, on the other hand, attack the informational basis of the proposal; for example, by questioning demand projections.

The public, anxious for service, but equally anxious not to see increased debt or taxes may be reluctant to approve system expansion in normal times. If, however, a drought occurs or if distributional inadequacies are exposed, public concern may align itself with proposals for investment in new sources or transmission facilities. Indeed, a serious enough dry spell may find the public or its elected officials taking the lead in demanding system improvement. It seems often to be the case that drought serves in this respect as a determinant of increment timing, creating public acceptance of previously prepared plans. Moreover, as we showed in Chapter 8, it may spark the formulation of additional plans.

In the planning process, the scope of the debate is generally set by the consulting engineers. They define the alternatives, make the demand projections, and provide the cost information. They are, of course, constrained by existing attitudes of both officials and public; for example, it is generally true that all concerned are committed to obtaining "clean, upland sources" and the consultants tend to accept this, giving relatively short shrift to alternatives involving treatment of nearby but polluted sources. Within these constraints, they generally provide the town with a small set of alternatives, and these are generally discrete projects of set size.[4] Certain projects are generally recommended for stated reasons; these usually include some discussion of the implied safe yield of the total system and the projected level of demand. This discussion may give the impression that safe yield is really safe, and no discussion of the economic implications of choosing greater or lesser system adequacy is provided. This is entirely in keeping with the general antipathy among all concerned towards discussion of system failure (shortage) prior to its occurrence.

Now, it is certainly true that in the real world, our actors, even those in the water department, have concerns competing with long-run planning for their attention. We have stressed the planning role because of our interest in the application of better methods in this area. We have indicated, however, in Figure 22 that there are three other important decision categories involving our management system. We have discussed the matter of long-run efforts to limit demand, whether through metering, price changes, or permanent restrictions. We have specifically assumed away these im-

---

[4] We use "size" here to refer to estimated safe yield. This bit of information is peculiarly the province of the engineers, based as it is on technical methods.

portant areas in constructing our model, after having noted that they are not, in general, popular with managers.

The short-run decisions are typically those necessitated by supply shortage or distributional inadequacies. We have observed and commented on the kinds of short-run decisions made during the recent drought; we also noted that advance planning of such short-run measures as restrictions could have a great impact on long-run needs. But, again, our model takes account of the short run only as such decisions give rise to costs (as of emergency supplies), and we do not attempt to discuss optimal short-run actions.

SUMMARY: THE EXISTING SITUATION AND ECONOMIC OPTIMALITY

It is clear from the above discussion that there are serious obstacles in the way of attaining economic optimality in water system planning. This is true even if we agree to confine ourselves to seeking optimal capacity expansion paths.[5] There are any number of ways to categorize these obstacles, but we choose to divide them into those which are and those which are not in principle amenable to improved methodology.

There are two broad problem areas in the water supply planning process which are essentially immune to improvements in planning techniques. One of these areas is a problem for every management system in the local government structure such as the schools and police; indeed, to mention it is to risk stating a truism. That is, since the decision-making process is tied up with a democratic political process, the influences of personalities and pressure groups will contend with and often dominate considerations of efficiency.[6]

The other such problem area is perhaps unique to water supply, for it is here that public attitudes towards the service provided become quasi-mystical. Water is somehow special; that is the public feeling, and we are hardly the first to note it. This problem, however, is basically one of education, though changing this attitude may take a long and intensive campaign, since the traditions involved are old and the symbolism powerful.[7]

[5] We confine ourselves to efficiency considerations and do not become involved in a discussion of the importance of and method of dealing with other goals, such as the redistribution of income.

[6] This is not necessarily bad. Indeed, it is the essence of the process of making decisions about the provision of public goods. See Robert Dorfman, "General Equilibrium with Public Goods," Working Paper No. 95, Institute of Business and Economic Research, University of California, Berkeley, June 1966.

[7] See R. W. Kates, "Stimulus and Symbol: The View from the Bridge," *Journal of Social Issues*, XXII (1966), 21–28.

Several of the existing obstacles to planning are in principle subject to improvements in methodology. In practice, however, they promise to be with us for a considerable time. Among such long-term practical obstacles is the fact that water supply planning is hampered by the chronic lack of public funds at the local level. As things now stand, the preparation of elaborate optimal plans would seem, as often as not, to be a fruitless exercise for economists and engineers, for actual investment decisions would still be made after balancing competing demands at the political level. This pessimistic view ignores, however, the possibility of truly inclusive local planning. Were the costs and benefits in other areas of municipal concern quantified, one result could be the discovery of the shadow price for investment and/or operating funds within a limited city budget. The iterative process by which optimality might be attained has been described elsewhere.[8] We may confine ourselves to noting that the impact of overall planning on our sub-optimizing model could come through the assumed value of ρ, the discount rate. Instead of naively using the financial cost of capital funds, our planners could use the opportunity cost of funds withdrawn from the next most "productive" use.

Another obstacle which could, in principle, be dealt with is the preference of public and planners alike for clean upland supplies. Difficult as it might be, there is no reason why it should not be possible to measure the strength of people's desires in this regard. Perhaps all that would need be done would be to present alternatives on this issue explicitly—to say, "How much are you willing to pay for clean upland sources?"

A third set of problems which may be attacked via better methods are those surrounding the matter of uncertainty. We have not faced these problems squarely, having fallen back on expected values of losses and having treated only briefly the problems raised by uncertainty in demand projections. There has been and continues to be, however, a great amount of work in this area by professionals of several disciplines. It is conceivable that a practical way could be found to apply some of the more fruitful techniques to local planning problems. It seems most likely that such approaches would first be used in attacking the hydrologic sources of uncertainty, as a growing literature testifies is even now being done.[9] The problem of the uncertainty of demand projections is somewhat more

[8] See, for example, J. Kornai and T. Liptak, "Two-level Planning," *Econometrica*, 33 (1965), 141–69.

[9] For an approach to the evaluation of the relative importance of various sources of uncertainty in investment decisions, see Ivan James, Blair Bower, and Nicholas Matalas, "Relative Importance of Variables in Water Resources Planning," to be published in *Water Resources Research*.

difficult for two reasons: apparently it has a very great impact on the size of the cost incurred; and the probability distributions are particularly ill-defined.

The final problem area we discuss, and the one to which our suggested improvement is addressed, is that of the poor quality of information and the lack of *any* explicit economic considerations (except project cost) in the present planning process. Consulting firms provide population and per capita demand projections for the future. These are seldom of high quality, but, in any case, there is now no information given on the relative costs attached to building the recommended increment now or later or not at all. The lower system adequacy brought about by postponement is treated as a bad thing. Though there may be some discussion of the recurrence frequency of the event required to produce shortage under two different levels of capacity in relation to demand, there is no discussion of what this might mean in terms of losses.

CHAPTER 17

HISTORICAL PROFILES OF FIVE MASSACHUSETTS WATER SUPPLY SYSTEMS: COMPARISON OF ACTUAL AND ATTAINABLE RESULTS

We have suggested that the planning process through which decisions are made concerning the growth of water supply systems in Massachusetts could be improved by explicit inclusion of information about the trade-off between greater system capacity and smaller expected drought losses. The rules of thumb set out earlier appear to offer a way of influencing the decisions of practical men in this direction. At this point it is natural to wonder how the decisions produced historically compare with those which would have been made under our rules of thumb. In this chapter, then, we describe the histories of five Massachusetts water supply systems and compare these histories with the implications of our rules of thumb for system growth.

We present the histories of four systems serving individual communities—Fall River, Fitchburg, Pittsfield, and Worcester[1]—and also that of the Metropolitan District Commission, the regional system serving Boston, its suburbs, and certain other towns.[2] The four communities are all of medium size (serving populations of between about 40 and 190 thousand

[1] The town of Braintree in which interviews were conducted with various community leaders in our research was not used as a case study for two reasons: (a) it has a town form of government with a Board of Water Commissioners, reducing its comparability with the other communities which are cities, and (b) the series of engineering reports available to trace the history of the water supply system is neither as extensive nor as comprehensive as the series of reports available for the 4 cities studied.

[2] The historical development of the MDC was studied by Donald J. Volk as part of the overall research effort of this project.

people), and they all face mixed domestic, industrial, and commercial demand. The MDC also has mixed demand but is distinguished from the community systems both by its very large size and by its regional authority character.[3] The MDC serves about one third of the population of the entire state—about 1,650,000 people in Boston, its suburbs, and other communities.

SYSTEMS HISTORIES

The history of development for each of the five supply systems is shown diagrammatically in Figures 23 through 27. On these diagrams the esti-

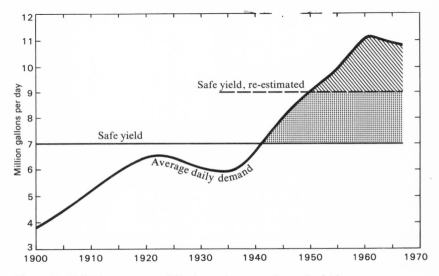

Figure 23. Fall River: average daily demand compared to safe yield.

mated safe yield of the system is shown, along with average daily use (both in million gallons per day) on the ordinate. The years from 1900 through 1966 appear on the abscissa. The line representing demand growth is smoothed considerably and may be thought of as a trend line about which daily, annual, and seasonal variations in average daily demand might be

[3] All 4 of the cities used as case studies export some water to sections of neighboring communities. Worcester sells water to a section of the town of Auburn; Pittsfield supplies a section of Dalton; the town of Westminster uses one of the Fitchburg reservoirs as its source of water; and Fall River exports water to the town of Tiverton, R.I. In no case, however, is the amount of exported water greater than 3 percent of the larger city's demand.

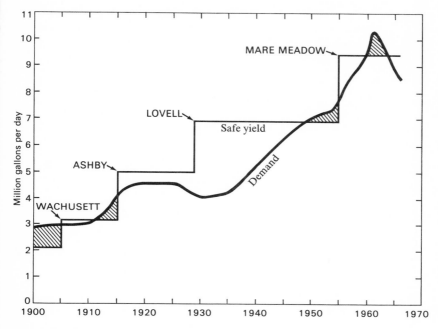

Figure 24. Fitchburg: annual daily demand compared to safe yield.

distributed.[4] Development prior to 1900 is not shown because of the difficulty of acquiring accurate information on safe yield and demand. (The *hatched areas* in Figures 23–27 indicate periods when demand exceeded safe yield.)

The cities of Fitchburg (Figure 24) and Fall River (Figure 23) show highly contrasting patterns of development. In Fitchburg the development profile strongly suggests a tendency to establish excess capacity and thus to lower the long-term risk of water shortage. Fitchburg's development has been unique among the four towns in one respect. The addition of Lovell Reservoir, in 1929, is the only municipal example of a project being constructed when the inadequacy ratio was less than one ($D/Y < 1$). This apparently resulted primarily from the influence of a single elected official.[5]

[4] It is closely related, but not identical to the regression trend lines estimated in Chapter 4.

[5] In an interview in June 1966, J. Andre Provencial, Fitchburg's water superintendent, stated that the mayor in office in 1929 believed in leaving visible evidence of his tenure in the city's strong-mayor form of government and that he was particularly fond of water supply development as opposed to other types of municipal construction.

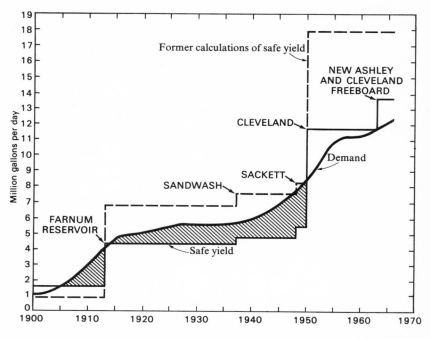

Figure 25. Pittsfield: average daily demand compared to safe yield (*broken lines* indicate prior evaluation of safe yield).

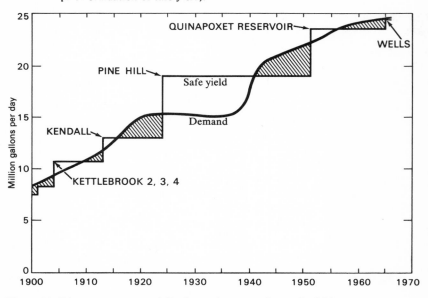

Figure 26. Worcester: average daily demand compared to safe yield.

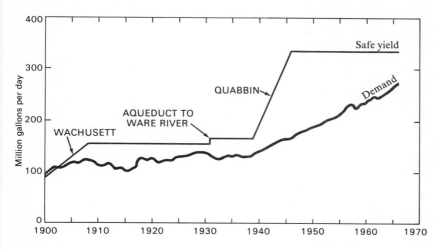

Figure 27. Metropolitan District Commission: average daily demand compared to safe yield.

Fall River provides an example of the early establishment of a natural source of water which fortuitously insured the city against the effects of water shortage for many years. We say fortuitously because when Fall River's source of supply was studied by engineers in 1910 the expected safe yield (as then measured) of the source was 6.5 mgd, not greatly above the demand for that year. In later years the same supply proved to have a safe yield substantially above 6.5 mgd.[6]

Worcester and Pittsfield have displayed mixed patterns of growth. Pittsfield (Figure 25), has had a number of re-evaluations of safe yield which increased the apparent risk of shortage but have not resulted in immediate compensating additions to capacity. Worcester (Figure 26) has added relatively often to its system, but the average size of these additions (as a percentage of the existing system size) has been relatively small. (See Table 47 for comparisons of increment sizes and timing for the four municipal systems.)

One interesting feature of the operating policies of the various towns, which helps to explain the observed differences in growth paths, is the extent to which emergency supplies have been relied on to augment the normal system during dry periods. As we see in Table 48, Worcester has done this very frequently, Fitchburg hardly at all. Pittsfield is second in terms of the number of years in which emergency supplies have been tapped. Even though the Massachusetts Department of Public Health, which has authority to approve sources for such supplies, does not look

[6] See the comments on predicted and observed shortages in Chapter 7.

TABLE 47. ADDITIONS TO THE CAPACITY OF THE FIVE SAMPLE WATER
SUPPLY SYSTEMS IN MASSACHUSETTS, 1900–1966

City	1966 safe yield (in *mgd*)	Capacity added since 1900 (in *mgd*)	Number of additions since 1900	Average size of addition (in *mgd*)	Average size of addition as percentage of existing capacity	Average time between additions (*years*)
Worcester	24.5	19.5	6	3.3	14	11
Pittsfield	14.7	12.1	5	2.4	16	13
Fitchburg	9.4	7.5	4	1.8	19	14
Fall River	9.0	0.0	0	0.0	0	>65
MDC	350.0	260.0	2	130.0	100	35

Source: Unpublished Engineering Reports, available at the Massachusetts Department of Public Health.

TABLE 48. USE OF EMERGENCY WATER SUPPLIES IN
4 MASSACHUSETTS CITIES, 1900–1966

City	Number of years used since 1900	Percentage of years since 1900
Fall River	8	12
Pittsfield	10	15
Fitchburg	4	6
Worcester	18	27

Sources: Unpublished Engineering Reports, available at the Massachusetts Department of Public Health.

with favor on the development of "permanent" emergency supplies, Worcester and Pittsfield have effectively done just that.[7] This development has given these two systems a degree of flexibility not available to the other two.

The MDC, of course, because of its tremendous size cannot plan on having any emergency supplies available during a dry spell; no sufficiently large alternative source exists except for the major rivers, the Connecticut and the Merrimac, which are presently unacceptable. While smaller systems may count on the local recreation pond (or the MDC), the MDC must be its own supplier of last resort. This observation immediately suggests the reason for the differences between the growth path of the

[7] Worcester has made use of emergency water supply available from the Boston MDC's Wachusett Reservoir, part of which actually lies within the city limits of Worcester. Pittsfield has used emergency supply from a recreational lake, located in the city. Both of these cities have constructed permanent pumping facilities at the sources of their emergency supply.

MDC and those of the other systems. Only two capacity additions have been made to the MDC system since 1900, but both of these increments have been very large. Even more significant, at no time has the ratio of average demand to safe yield been allowed to go above one. That is, the relative system adequacy has consistently been maintained at a high level compared to those levels tolerated by the other systems at different periods in their histories.[8]

This discussion suggests that one important caution should be borne in mind in our examination of the differences between actual and optimal paths of growth: availability of emergency supply sources will probably have a significant effect on the growth path of the system. Our model will not take this into account. When emergency sources become institutionalized by frequent use, or even more definitely by the construction of permanent pumping stations and lines (as in Pittsfield), it hardly seems that they retain their emergency quality. The difference from our point of view is that even these quasi-permanent sources are generally not artificial impoundments but natural lakes and ponds, and the city lucky enough to have such a source at hand may effectively enlarge its system's capacity while avoiding most of the costs we include in the planning model. The fact that such increments cannot be matters of official policy where the Department of Public Works is concerned means also that no planning tools which are to receive official sanction can move into this grey area.

With this problem in mind, we move on to a consideration of the observable differences between the actual growth paths followed by our sample systems, and the path which our rules of thumb suggest would be optimal.

COMPARISON OF ACTUAL AND OPTIMAL PLANNING RESULTS

We need first to translate our historical data on increment size from millions of gallons per day of safe yield to years of demand growth and data on increment timing from calendar time to adequacy ratios. This translation, in turn, involves us in explicit assumptions about the kinds of information the system decision-makers could be expected to use.

Once we translate our data, we do the comparison in two steps. First, we check the average size and timing of increments for agreement with our rules of thumb, for reasonable assumptions about key parameters. (At the

[8] There are, of course, other important factors which differentiate the MDC. It maintains its own engineering staff and need not rely on infrequent consultations with one or another Boston firm for recommendations and projections. It also has greater powers to take land and greater flexibility in the raising of funds when development has been decided upon.

same time, we compare the towns themselves to see if there are explainable differences in average timing and size choices.) But we should like to be able to say more than just that the towns tend to build bigger or smaller increments earlier or later than would be optimal. For to say that the average increment is 10 percent too big, or that it is added 5 percent too early is not to say much. Whether this is a relatively good, bad, or indifferent performance depends on the implications of the alternatives for total costs over some horizon—and, of course, *as of* some chosen date.

Thus our second approach to the actual/optimal comparison is to take the necessary steps to fit both into the framework of our planning model, noting the differences in total present value of costs under different assumptions about the parameters. This approach requires a second, essentially inverse, set of translations; the size and timing "rules" implied by our model and those discovered in the historical experience of our sample towns must be used to construct vectors $\{T_1, T_2, s_o, s_1, s_2, s_{60}\}$ which can be run through the model to give a total cost result.

TRANSLATING HISTORICAL SIZE AND TIMING DATA

We have historical data on the size of chosen increments in terms of their safe yields, and on the timing of those increments in terms of calendar years. Our discussion of optimal planning has been couched in terms of increments of size τ years added when the adequacy (D/Y ratio) of the system is k. The practical gap between these two is not so great as it might seem, for most system managers are accustomed to discussions of how long an increment will "last" in terms of growing demand. And most also think of adequacy in terms of some relation between their community's water use and their system's safe yield. We think, then, that it is fair to assume that managers acted as if they calculated τ and k, and the central question becomes what information we may reasonably expect them to have had and used at the time of the decision. More particularly, we must decide:

1. What date to accept as "the" date of the decision to build, since no public notice is generally given of the decision *per se*.

2. What information on the level of system adequacy would have been available at that date.

3. On what basis could increment size in safe-yield terms have been translated into a τ figure, i.e., what information on the rate of growth of demand was available.

Our choice of a date for the decision to build had to be chosen from the three times that we were able to tie down for each project from our study of engineering reports and available town and state records. We know the date of the engineering report in which the project was introduced, the date of the loan authorization related to construction, and the date of completion of the project. In these circumstances, it seems clear that the date which best represents the decision to build is that of the loan authorization. In answer to our second question, then, we propose that the ratio of water use to safe yield in the year of the loan authorization be taken to be the adequacy ratio "chosen" for the timing of the addition. The principal problem with this decision is that it is probably reasonable to assume that system managers take account of the various lags between the decision and the time the increment is actually operating. We note below the results of assuming that the managers are able to predict construction lag and demand growth rate perfectly; that is, we calculate the system adequacy ratios for the years of completion of the various projects.

Finally, we adopt as the appropriate measure of demand-growth expected by decision-makers the rate of growth projected by the consulting engineers in the report introducing the project in question.

RESULTS OF TRANSLATING HISTORICAL DATA

The actual calculation of the size and timing values implied by the towns' decisions is straightforward once we have made the assumptions discussed just above. The water-use/safe-yield ratio (WU/SY) for any year needs no explanation, while the size in years, τ, of an increment is calculated from the formula

$$\tau = \frac{1}{\alpha} \ln \left(\frac{s + \Delta s}{s} \right) \tag{17-1}$$

where ln denotes the natural log, and s is the existing safe yield before an increment, Δs (s and Δs are measured in flow units, such as millions of gallons per day).

In Table 49 we show the results of these calculations averaged for individual towns and across the entire sample. For timing, we confine ourselves to simple averages of the WU/SY ratios at the time of loan authorization and of construction completion. For size, however, we include both weighted and simple averages, with and without two very large (in terms of τ) projects.[9] Because of the size of our sample, these large observations affect the averages very strongly, and it is best to keep in mind that the very large average increments sizes found with these two projects may not, in fact, be representative. It would, of course, be possible

---

[9] The weighted averages are calculated using the safe yields of the several projects as weights.

TABLE 49. ACTUAL AND OPTIMAL TIMING AND SIZE DECISIONS

Timing (PD/SY)	Fitchburg	Pittsfield	Worcester	All
Projects[a]	4	4	4	12
Average WU/SY ratio at time of loan authorization	1.00	1.41	1.12	1.17
Average WU/SY ratio at time of completion of construction	1.12	1.51	1.14	1.25

Optimal PD/SY ratios from model[b]
and, for $\begin{cases} y = 0.78 \\ \rho = 0.05 \end{cases}$

for $z = 12$;　$PD/SY = 1.12$
for $z = 5.4$;　$PD/SY = 1.29$
for $z = 4.3$;　$PD/SY = 1.36$

Size: (τ years)	Fitchburg	Pittsfield	Worcester	All
Projects[a]	3	3	2	8
Simple average of all projects	51.2	70.7	27.0	52.5
Weighted average of all projects	56.5	145.0	28.0	70.7
Simple average without two largest	25.6	22.7	27.0	25.1
Weighted average without two largest	25.6	22.8	28.0	26.3

Optimal τ from model
and, for $\begin{cases} y = 0.78 \\ \rho = 0.05 \end{cases}$

for $z = 12$;　$\tau = 19.4$
for $z = 5.4$;　$\tau = 19.4$
for $z = 4.3$;　$\tau = 19.8$

Notes:

[a] The number of projects represented in the timing and size calculations reflects the availability of the necessary data on intended safe yield, demand growth projections, etc., within a universe of projects referred to in the system histories.

[b] These rules of thumb were calculated from computer runs for which the initial population was set at 100,000. Subsequently, they were checked from the results of runs for which $N_o = 50,000$. In general, optimal sizes (τ) were the same in both circumstances; there was an apparent tendency for the optimal adequacy ratio to be larger (the construction time later) for the smaller town.

to argue that these large projects are simply evidence of overbuilding in public water supply. This seems particularly dangerous here, however, since the rates of growth of demand connected with these two projects, as shown in the engineering reports, were so very low that the town officials might not have taken them completely seriously.[10] We also include in the table the optimal rules of thumb given by our model for three values

[10] One project, at the projected growth rate of 0.4 percent per year, covered 167 years of demand growth. The other, at 0.3 percent, covered 102.5 years. In neither case did simple extrapolation of existing trends, at the times of the reports and of the loans, suggest that such low rates were realistic.

of the loss-function parameter (z), when the scale factor (y) is 0.78 and the interest rate (ρ) is 0.05. The values of y and ρ have been chosen to reflect the most likely situation; our best empirical estimate of y was about 0.76, and our study of municipal water bonds suggests that an interest rate of 5 percent is a good approximation to the cost of capital in the minds of the planners.

Certainly in terms of the timing of capacity expansion, the evidence in Table 49 is that towns have not been doing badly. If we accept the rules for $z = 5.4$ as our standard, building seems, on the average, to be occurring somewhat early (at adequacy ratio 1.17 instead of 1.29). If, however, we look at the WU/SY ratios at the times of project completion, we find this tendency has essentially disappeared. Thus, under the most generous allowance for managers' ability to plan around construction lags, we find them on target in their timing decisions.

The size decisions made by our study towns involve, by any measure, increments larger than the optimal. Here the rule of thumb appears to be independent of the value of z and to call for increments of about 19½ years. Even if we remove the influence of the two very large projects mentioned above, the average of actual decisions is between 25 and 27 years, depending on averaging technique. And, if we include these very large projects, average actual increment size grows to somewhere between 50 and 70 years. Thus, the weighted average project size for all towns and projects is more than three times the optimal size!

None of the towns exhibits a tendency to build smaller than optimal increments, but Pittsfield takes the honors for the largest. The weighted average of Pittsfield projects is 145 years; almost 7½ times optimum size. Worcester projects generally are the smallest, averaging only 27 to 28 years. It is interesting to note that Pittsfield waits longest and builds largest. It is probable that by waiting, overbuilding is encouraged, since the lower adequacy ratios tend to increase average annual shortages and thus to increase public concern about the water system. And public concern seems, in turn, frequently to be translated into highly visible system improvements.

The above comments are, of necessity, essentially qualitative, for in the absence of information on the cost implications of various policies, we have no basis for saying how much better it is to build an optimal increment on time than to build a relatively large increment a bit too early. To make some quantitative judgments about the degree of success of actual system planning, we translate policies into costs, and in order that this be done on a standardized basis, we go back to our planning model with a fixed 60-year horizon and a constraint on the minimum total increment over the horizon.

COSTS OF VARIOUS POLICIES

We now compare the cost implications of observed system expansion policies with those both of our rules of thumb and of the programming model solution itself (without the approximations subsumed in the rules of thumb). We use the actual expansion policies obtained from the town experiences averaged both with and without the two largest projects. Our calculations are done for a city of initial size of 50,000, an initial per capita water use of 100 gpd, and an initial safe yield of 5 mgd.[11]

In Table 50 we show, for each parameter combination, the total present value of costs from the planning model using the vectors implied by the appropriate rule of thumb and the two policies estimated from historical data. In addition, for all but two combinations, we have available a cost benchmark in the form of a programming solution to the planning model. We indicate in the table the percentage differences between the several suboptimal results and this benchmark.

In general our expectations are confirmed by the pattern of results. For given z and α, the costs implied by the town policies including all projects (the largest τ) are significantly larger than those achievable by the programming solution. The largest observed difference between the costs of this policy and those found for the optimal policy is 38 percent; the average difference is about 21.5 percent. The costs implied by the smaller-increment town policy are generally closer to the best attainable mark (average difference = 10.4 percent). And the rules of thumb perform, as we would hope, relatively very well by this test (average difference = 5.4 percent).

If we are willing to accept the evidence of our limited sample that towns are building increments averaging over 50 years of demand growth in size, then we may conclude that the total of costs they are incurring over any particular planning period are significantly above both the best attainable and those attainable using the rules of thumb. These increased total costs will reflect very much larger capital outlays, not balanced by corresponding reduction in expected drought losses. This indicates that the familiar charge of water-supply "overbuilding" may be valid and relatively serious. The present value of the extra cost burden imposed by this overbuilding may be $250,000 to $300,000 for a town with initial population of 50,000 and growth rate of demand of 0.035 over 60 years. We should remember, however, that the managers' best information may include an estimate of a relatively low rate of growth of demand. If such a growth rate in fact prevails, the maximum extra costs, those implied by following the "large

---

[11] The actual translation of policy rules into size and timing vectors for the capacity expansion model is basically only a reversal of the technique described above for deriving the rules of thumb in the first place.

TABLE 50. TOTAL PRESENT VALUE OF COSTS IMPLIED BY VARIOUS CAPACITY-EXPANSION POLICIES

α		z = 4.3			z = 5.4			z = 12.0		
		Total present value of costs ($)	Percentage difference from programming solution	Percentage difference from rules of thumb	Total present value of costs ($)	Percentage difference from programming solution	Percentage difference from rules of thumb	Total present value of costs ($)	Percentage difference from programming solution	Percentage difference from rules of thumb
0.003	Programming solution	a			a			150,600		
	Rule of thumb	128,900	a		137,500	a		190,800	21.1	
	Small increment policy[b]	130,000	a	0.8	137,800	a	0.2	205,800	30.0	2.6
	Large increment policy[c]	130,000	a	0.8	137,600	a	0.1	203,400	28.4	1.4
0.015	Programming solution	312,000			324,000			340,400		
	Rule of thumb	315,900	1.2		d	d		353,300	3.8	
	Small increment policy	321,100	2.9	1.6	325,000	0.3	d	361,900	6.3	2.4
	Large increment policy	347,400	11.4	10.0	350,200	8.1	d	373,000	9.6	5.6
0.035	Programming solution	763,900			803,000			860,900		
	Rule of thumb	797,500	4.4		807,100	0.5		871,400	1.2	
	Small increment policy	877,100	14.82	10.0	930,600	15.9	15.3	881,500	2.4	1.2
	Large increment policy	1,053,900	38.0	32.2	1,059,000	31.9	31.2	1,058,900	22.9	21.5

[a] For two parameter combinations, the programming algorithm proved to be completely unreliable. Apparently the previously discussed zero-increment (s_o) problem was exaggerated by the generally small size of all the increments when α is very small.

[b] "Small-increment policy"—based on $\tau = 26.3$, the weighted average project size determined without considering the two largest projects. (From historical data.)

[c] "Large-increment policy"—based on $\tau = 41.6$, somewhat less than the simple average product size with all projects included. (Historical data.)

[d] For $z = 5.4$, the rule of thumb derived from the solution for $\alpha = 0.035$ did not prove satisfactory for $\alpha = 0.015$. Since for $\alpha = 0.035$, $s_o \neq 0$ while for $\alpha = 0.015$, $\hat{s}_o = 0$ is probably true, we surmise that this is another manifestation of the zero-increment problem.

increment" policy, are significantly lower. For example, the average difference between best and worst costs when $\alpha = 0.015$ is only a little over 8 percent. Thus, if managers expect low growth rates, it may not seem worth their while to exert themselves in the search for better planning rules. This consideration is, of course, quite independent of questions about political constraints, alternative objectives, etc., which we have raised previously.

CHAPTER 18

DROUGHT AND WATER SUPPLY: CONCLUDING COMMENTS

This study has moved from observation of a natural event to the construction and application of a model for investment planning. Accordingly, it seems natural to arrange our concluding comments in two categories: first, the significance of our findings about the experience of Massachusetts water-supply systems during the 1962–66 drought; and second, the significance of our effort to go beyond the drought into the area of policy prescription. Broadly speaking, the results of our study of the drought itself indicate that this was a very severe and correspondingly rare event on the physical scale, but one with a surprisingly small economic impact on municipal water supply systems and their customers. On the significance of our generalization from these observations, we feel that our planning model and rules of thumb point the way to potentially significant savings but that there are notable obstacles to their use (beyond the obvious problems of data-gathering and computation).

SUMMARY OF FINDINGS

More specifically, we may summarize our findings on the recent drought as follows:

Recurrence Frequency. As measured by our pooled rainfall record (a rough average experience for the state) the drought, as a 4-year event, had a recurrence frequency of about 1/150, i.e., it was roughly the 150-year drought. It was considerably more severe than the drought used to define "safe yield," that of 1900–1911, which had a recurrence frequency of about 0.03, or was roughly the 30-year event.

Physical Impact on Water Systems. In the sample of cities (26) for which we were able both to predict and observe the physical stress created by the drought, we observed no annual water shortages of greater than 30 percent.[1] On the other hand, a reasonable model of the physical impact of the drought projected shortages of over 50 percent for several towns. In general, those cities for which very large shortages were projected were observed to have smaller-than-projected shortages. A number of systems for which no shortages were projected actually suffered significant shortages.

In explanation, it was suggested that shortages could be created for a relatively adequate system by a system manager who wished to hedge against worse conditions ahead through conservation today. At the other end of the scale, it seemed likely that potentially hard-hit systems might find, in extremis, that their actual water availability was greater than that indicated by their safe yield. This would be a natural result of the pressures on consulting engineers for "safety" of supply.

Reactions in the Short Run.   Our data indicated that in the short run, when faced with a potential shortage, municipalities find it most desirable to cut back water use through restrictions, especially on lawn-sprinkling and car-washing. Restrictions were placed on industrial and commercial uses by fewer municipalities; those that did introduce such restrictions were generally facing larger shortages than those that restricted only domestic uses. The most frequently used restriction on commercial and industrial use was one requiring that air-conditioning cooling water be recirculated. No efforts were made to ration water through higher prices on such price-elastic uses as lawn-sprinkling.

Those systems which were in a position to do so obtained additional supplies by sinking new wells, improving old ones, by tapping recreational lakes, or by purchasing water from a more adequate system.

Economic Impact.   We observed that after correction for future investment returns and for certain other considerations, the economic impact of drought was small in absolute terms. The fully corrected annual "loss" figures, at a 20 percent discount rate and local accounting stance, for our sample cities in the last year of the drought (self-suppliers as well as municipal system customers) ranged from $5.46 per capita in Braintree (with a 10 percent shortage), to $5.33 in Pittsfield (14 percent shortage), to $13.05 in Fitchburg (22 percent shortage). After removing the influence of self-supplied users, these figures became, respectively: $5.42 in Braintree, $4.53 in Pittsfield, and $11.07 in Fitchburg. Changing the interest rate to 8 percent and the accounting stance to a national one changes the loss picture substantially. Indeed, before separation of self-supplied users,

---

[1] The reader will recall that observed shortages are measured after correction for emergency supplies provided, so that actual consumption might equal projected demand when we "observe a shortage."

Fitchburg had an aggregate *net gain* under these assumptions of $26.05. This reflected almost entirely the profitability of certain recirculation investments undertaken by Fitchburg industrial firms.

INVESTMENT PLANNING LESSONS OF THE OBSERVED EXPERIENCE

Based on our study of the drought, we constructed expected drought-loss functions which we then used in an investment-planning model. The computational results from this model were in turn used to construct sample handbook tables for the use of practical planners, tables which answered the questions of how much safe yield to add and when to add it. This method is capable of refinement and complication to a degree limited only by the time and money devoted to additional research. In particular, alternatives to system expansion could be included in considering the optimal path for system adequacy over the planning horizon. By refining the present treatment of climatic variation, it would be possible to take account of the seasonal nature of shortages and resulting losses. The ultimate refinement would be to introduce demand and price considerations, to do away with the assumption of given constant prices and hence of equivalent gross benefit streams for all plans.

But is it, after all, realistic to expect the acceptance of a planning criterion which explicitly incorporates a positive failure rate or average annual loss from water shortage? We found that the municipal water system planning process is significantly constrained, not only by the familiar local governmental constraints of lack of money and susceptibility to special interests but by the public's attitude toward water and water supply. This attitude stresses the "specialness" of water and discourages rational pricing and informed discussion of shortages.

Our fundamental conclusion is that significant savings could be effected in system design if account were taken of the real nature of the loss functions from water shortage. The present implicit assumption is that loss functions rise essentially vertically from zero shortage. Such is not the case. Indeed, if more flexibility in the application of short-run measures such as restrictions were politically feasible, it might be possible to take advantage of slack in the adoption of water-saving technology by industry significantly to reduce the real impact of drought. Even in the absence of this opportunity, however, system shortages do not mean disaster, and perhaps if more effort were made to spell out beforehand the consequences of various "failure" levels, public acceptance could be won for more rational planning. In short, "drought" need not constitute, as it now does, a convenient natural cloak for hiding past planning failures or garbing for public acclaim plans for building expensive monuments to the "right" to cheap water.

A PRELIMINARY TEST OF
THE DEMAND PROJECTIONS

This appendix presents a comparison of our projected levels of per capita daily demand with the consumption actually observed in communities which neither restricted use nor augmented normal supply sources during the drought. For these communities (9 of the 28 for which projections were made) there is no reason to believe that response to the drought should have interfered with the accurate prediction of actual levels of demand. In Table 51 we summarize the results of this comparison. For each system and year we show the predicted level of per capita daily demand, the 95 percent confidence interval for that prediction, the observed per capita daily consumption and the percentage difference between the projected and observed quantities. This last figure is computed as:

$$\% \text{ Difference} = \frac{P_{it} - [C_{it}/(N_{it} \cdot 365)]}{P_{it}} \times 100; \qquad \text{(A-1)}$$

where C_{it} is the observed annual consumption. Thus, positive percentage errors in Table 51 imply that our regression parameters produced overestimates of demand.

The most important thing to note about Table 51 is the extent to which we were or were not able to predict realized demand (actual consumption) as measured by the percentage error of each projection. In these terms it appears to be possible to divide the systems into three groups: three (11, 24, 27) show excellent accuracy in prediction with no errors over 6 percent in any year; four others (16, 19, 29, 42) show generally good results with most errors on the order of 10 percent and the largest error

197

TABLE 51. TEST OF DEMAND PROJECTIONS

System	1963				1964			
	$\hat{P}$	95% confidence interval	$\dfrac{C}{N.365}$	% Error	$\hat{P}$	95% confidence interval	$\dfrac{C}{N.365}$	% Error
11	116.5	121.1 / 111.9	113.7	+ 2.4	120.3	126.7 / 113.9	116.9	+2.8
16	136.2	147.7 / 134.7	127.0	+6.8	143.7	157.7 / 129.7	136.4	+5.1
19	138.4	147.8 / 129.0	130.7	+5.6	143.0	155.7 / 130.3	133.9	+6.4
20	148.0	161.7 / 134.3	141.2	+4.6	153.3	169.8 / 136.8	134.7	+12.1
21	127.5	144.1 / 110.9	141.4	−10.9	111.5	144.7 / 78.3	142.1	−27.4
24	116.7	124.4 / 109.0	121.3	−3.9	120.0	128.9 / 111.1	122.5	−2.1
27	106.5	112.4 / 100.6	106.2	+0.3	106.2	112.0 / 100.4	102.7	+3.3
29	69.7	75.3 / 64.1	79.7	−14.3	70.3	78.3 / 62.3	80.1	−13.9
42	136.3	148.2 / 124.4	124.8	+8.4	140.4	156.0 / 124.8	124.6	+11.2
Average error				−0.1%				−0.3%

TABLE 51—continued

$\hat{P}$	1965 95% confidence interval	$\dfrac{C}{N.365}$	% Error	$\hat{P}$	1966 95% confidence interval	$\dfrac{C}{N.365}$	% Error	Average town error over 4 years
								(*percent*)
124.6	132.6 116.6	118.2	+5.1	126.7	135.5 117.9	119.4	+5.8	+4.0
152.5	171.8 133.2	128.7	+15.6	156.8	180.9 132.7	140.1	+10.6	+9.5
147.8	164.3 131.3	127.9	+13.5	151.1	170.2 132.0	135.2	+10.5	+9.0
159.9	181.3 138.5	121.5	+24.0	163.5	185.5 141.5	117.7	+28.0	+17.2
108.9	182.3 35.5	150.6	−38.2	100.9	178.9 22.9	147.8	−46.5	−30.8
123.3	133.6 113.0	126.7	−2.8	126.1	137.1 115.1	127.7	−1.3	−2.5
110.7	118.9 102.5	113.8	−2.8	114.5	123.7 105.3	120.8	−5.5	−1.2
80.8	100.3 61.3	95.4	−18.1	81.4	99.0 63.8	89.8	−10.3	−14.2
145.7	165.8 125.6	125.1	+14.1	149.0	170.7 127.3	132.4	+11.1	+11.2
			+1.2%				+0.3%	Overall average +0.3%

18.1 percent;[1] two (20 and 21) show great inaccuracy, with maximum error almost 50 percent. In one of these last two classes (system 20) our projections were much too high; this may be partially explained by calls for voluntary restriction of use made by the city's officials at various times during the last three years of the drought. To attribute the entire error to these calls would, however, be at variance with other evidence from the study that voluntary restrictions are notably ineffective.

Although the projections for certain of the individual systems are inaccurate, the average percentage error (across the systems) for each year is very small; in no year is this average error greater than about 1 percent. This suggests that our simple regression/projection equation fails to capture some influences on per capita daily demand which are essentially random and symmetric with respect to an aggregate of communities, one or more of which may influence significantly an individual town's demand over a period. Examples of such influences might be the existence of distributional inadequacies; sudden shifts in the composition of the local industrial sector; or shifts in domestic habits (as in the substitution of disposals for garbage collection).

[1] For this group there is an interesting tendency for projection errors to peak in 1965. This is true for each of the 4 systems. The explanation of this behavior may be that for 3 of these systems, the peak of the drought, as measured by the Palmer Index, occurred in 1965.

NOTES ON DATA USED
IN THE VARIOUS TESTS

The following notes on data used will be useful to the reader.

Number of Observations. Of the 33 towns for which significant regression relations were found in Chapter 4, 5 were eliminated (as discussed in Chapter 5) because of missing observed-consumption data in the drought years. Of the remaining 28 towns, 4 were eliminated because they either had essentially unlimited safe yield or no safe-yield estimates at all. Four additional towns depended entirely on groundwater supplies; here the concept of safe yield did not apply, and there was no reason to expect the model itself, based on precipitation as a surrogate for streamflows, to apply. This same principle was applied to systems with combinations of ground- and surface-water sources, except where the latter provided a very high percentage of the total system supply. This resulted in the elimination of three additional systems. Finally, two systems were not used in this shortage/adequacy analysis because in the previously reported analysis of "adequate" systems (see Appendix A above—"adequate" systems were those reported as adequate by their managers and not requiring restrictions or emergency supplies at any time during the drought) our projections of demand had appeared to perform very badly. For these two "adequate" systems our projections indicated shortages in *every* drought year of between 5 and 30 percent. The final sample of towns used in the regression analysis was thus reduced to 15.

Calculation of Shortages. Shortages were calculated from the formula given in Chapter 5, Equation 5-4. Figures on emergency supply were obtained from water system managers in the 5 towns which resorted to emergency supplies. In all these instances, the equipment required was loaned to the towns by the Massachusetts Civil Defense organization, and

TABLE 52. CUMULATIVE RAINFALL DEVIATIONS AND α'_t

	1911	1963	α'_t 1964	1965	1966
Cumulation period	(1908–11)	(1960–63)	(1961–64)	(1962–65)	(1963–66)
Cumulated deficiency (average for state) (*inches*)	−23.0	−8.3	−28.3	−30.1	−32.7
Calculated α'_t from Equation (6–10)	1	2.77	0.81	0.76	0.70

Note: For each town in each year, the appropriate value of α'_t was subtracted from the estimated actual P/Y ratio to find the proper independent variable for the regression Equation (7-5).

in return the agency required reports of water pumped and general comments on the need for the water and the uses to which it was put. Investigation of these records and discussion with responsible officials at the agency indicated that 3 of these towns in certain drought years used some fraction of their emergency pumpage, not to meet current demands but to refill reservoirs drawn down during the earlier dry years. Use of the total emergency pumping figures for these towns and years would then overstate the size of the current shortage. Unfortunately, the records did not allow an allocation of the pumping figures between these two uses. Our strategy was to reduce the recorded emergency pumpage by amounts which, though basically arbitrary, were based on the comments of the Civil Defense staff and on those recorded in the reports submitted by the towns.

The projected demand figures were calculated as described above. Observed consumption figures were obtained from the records of the towns themselves and those of the Massachusetts Department of Public Health.

Safe Yields. These were obtained, where available, from the system managers in the interviews held with them. In some cases, changes in system safe yields came "on stream" during the drought. Our data on the times of such changes were, again, taken from the interviews.

Calculation of α'_t from Precipitation Data. For each year of the drought (1963–66), the 4-year cumulative rainfall deviations from one station in each of the three Massachusetts climatic divisions (western, central, and coastal) were averaged. The resulting state average deviation was divided into a similar average for the 1908–1911 period.[1] The results of these computations are summarized in Table 52.

[1] It is unfortunate, given what we have observed of the differences in drought timing, that it was not possible to deal with each section of the state separately. This would, however, have resulted in very small samples for each of the regional regressions.

DROUGHT ADJUSTMENTS BY THE METROPOLITAN DISTRICT COMMISSION

The Metropolitan District Commission (MDC) is an independent authority created by the Commonwealth of Massachusetts. We present the MDC experience because it affords an opportunity to see the effectiveness of partial restrictions on water use. During most of the 4-year drought, there were no restrictions on water use for MDC customers. However, during a 5-week period late in the summer of 1965, certain restrictions were in force. After a call for voluntary reductions in water consumption failed to produce any decrease in use, mandatory restrictions on "non-essential use of water" were proclaimed by the Massachusetts Department of Public Health upon recommendation of the MDC commissioner.[1] The restrictions were not enforced by MDC, but by the communities which it serves under threat of water cutoff for noncompliance. The ban prohibited the use of water for watering lawns and gardens; for washing cars, driveways, sidewalks, and streets; and for use in non-recirculating air-conditioning equipment, swimming pools, wading pools, and fountains.[2]

The emergency restrictions were proclaimed, not because of a shortage of water *per se* but because of inadequacies in the water distribution system combined with unusually high demand resulting from the dry weather. Wachusett Aqueduct, which carries water from Wachusett Reservoir to MDC customers, has a maximum capacity of 290 million gallons per day (mgd). On several days during the month prior to initiation of the ban, water use in the district exceeded 330 million gallons, with a peak day's consumption of 380 million gallons.[3] The excess of demand over aqueduct

---

[1] Office of Public Information, press release, August 11, 1965.

[2] *Ibid.*

[3] *Ibid.*

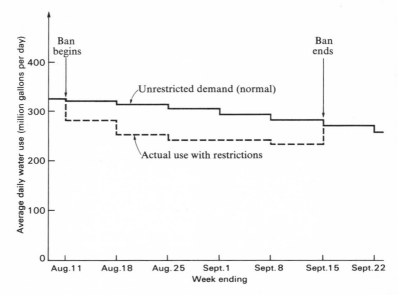

Figure 28. Impact of restrictions on water use by Metropolitan District Commission ↓ customers, August 4–September 22, 1965.

capacity had to be drawn from Sudbury Reservoir, which has only a limited storage capacity. The ban was proclaimed, therefore, to bring daily demand down to a level which could be supplied by Wachusett Aqueduct.[4]

How well did the ban work? The immediate purpose of the ban was achieved within the first week, when water use dropped to 280 mgd. (It dropped further in subsequent weeks and did not again rise above 280 mgd during 1965.)[5] The reduction in average consumption amounted to 40–65 mgd, with an average of 55 mgd. For the 5 weeks during which the ban was in force, a reduction in use of about 2 billion gallons total was achieved. This amounts to 2 percent of total use during 1965, or about 0.5 percent of total use during the 4-year drought period.

On the basis of results achieved by the 1965 water ban it appears that a reduction of perhaps 20 percent in water use during the months of peak demand might be expected under such restrictions. This would probably mean a reduction of no more than 10 percent in average yearly consumption.

[4] The Wachusett Aqueduct bottleneck has since been circumvented by construction of the Wachusett-Marlborough Tunnel completed a year later, which should prevent the recurrence of a similar situation.

[5] Unpublished MDC records.

Additional water was made available by MDC to communities it does not normally supply. Such emergency aid was given to the second and third largest cities in Massachusetts—Springfield and Worcester—neither of which is normally supplied by MDC. Other communities, only partially supplied by MDC, managed to avoid problems by taking larger than normal amounts from MDC during the drought. In both cases, the MDC system was subjected to greater stress because accelerated demand increases came at the time that supplies were most critical. The use of MDC water is, for these communities, a relatively painless way of coping with drought emergencies.

APPENDIX D

MEASUREMENT OF BUSINESS LOSSES FROM SHUTDOWN

Consider the case of a firm forced to shut down for a short period by a lack of water. We apply the same principle as in the test—that losses equal gross benefits less costs avoided—but we find a somewhat more complex and subtle problem because of the nature of the firm and conflict between the firm's view and that of society as a whole.

Our first task is the measurement of gross benefits. In this we are assisted by a theorem which states that a firm's willingness to pay, under the usual competitive assumptions, for w_o units of water as an input, can be measured either as:

1. The area up to w_o under the firm's derived demand curve for water as an input, or

2. The difference between the gross value of output using w_o (and the associated optimal input combination) and the (true opportunity) cost of all other inputs involved.[1]

As stated, this theorem seems to give our measure of gross benefits. We must, however, note that the theorem is applicable to the longest-run, to system design, when everything is assumed adjustable. That is, we implicitly assumed in stating the theorem that all inputs other than water may be hired at any required level and that these inputs are mobile between employments. In brief, the assumption was that all non-water input costs were avoidable by the firm and society. This is clearly not the case when we are dealing with temporary shutdown due to shortage. A great many costs are fixed for the firm in the short run, and we will maintain that even more

---

[1] See Arthur Maass et al., *The Design of Water Resource Systems* (Cambridge: Harvard University Press, 1962), p. 27. The proposition can easily be shown to be true for simple examples such as a two-factor, decreasing-returns, Cobb-Douglas production function.

are fixed for society. These considerations increase the losses from shutdown relative to the statement of the theorem by reducing the amount of cost deducted from the gross value of production lost.

In the short run, the firm will be able to avoid a large part of its variable costs when it shuts down. Wages of most workers, raw materials, housekeeping, and most process-energy requirements are among the most important of such avoidable costs.[2] Thus, from the firm's point of view, the (say daily) losses from the drought are roughly:

$$pY - V_C - P_w w_o$$

where pY is the value of output per day using w_o units of water and the appropriate combination of other inputs; V_C is the avoided variable-cost total except for water costs; and $P_w w_o$ is the daily water bill not paid.

From society's standpoint, the firm's estimate of its losses is too small, for society recognizes a broader sweep of factor immobility than the firm. We note, first, that fixed costs are clearly not avoidable on the part of the firm. Neither are they for society, for the resources, especially capital and entrepreneurship, represented by the fixed payments, are not free in the short run to migrate to alternative employment.[3] Society is paying an opportunity cost for their employment by the firm; this opportunity cost does not vanish merely because of shutdown. This consequence of immobility is recognized by accepting the firm's view of fixed costs as unavoidable. The problem of immobility, however, applies also to certain inputs under variable costs—most importantly to labor. In the short run, the labor force of a firm is very largely immobile, and society must take into account the opportunity cost of this arrangement in estimating costs avoided. Since the impact of odd jobs, expanded moonlighting, etc., is undoubtedly quite small, it seems reasonable to amend the firm's estimate of its losses, in moving to the social view, by subtracting from costs avoided (adding to losses) the value of wages per day. Thus the firm's daily losses corrected for the social cost of labor immobility would be:

$$pY - (V_C - WL) - P_w w_o$$

where WL is the wage bill per day.

If the firm is a self-supplier this expression must be corrected directly for the daily avoided costs of water supply. If it buys from the city we may begin by counting the city's daily lost revenue and correcting that for costs avoided.

[2] We here accept some vaguely "normal" definition of variable costs. To be strictly correct, we should probably maintain the tautological nature of the terminology and call only avoidable costs "variable," all others being "fixed" in the run under discussion.

[3] This ignores any rents or other transfers, just as we ignored them under variable costs.

Thus, $P_w w_o - H_A$ = cost to city of interrupted production, where H_A represents the avoided costs of water supply. It is clear that in any case the aggregate social cost per day is:

$$pY - (V_C - WL) - H_A.$$

It is interesting and important to note that $V_C - WL$ is composed of raw material and energy costs and that hence $pY - (V_C - WL)$ is essentially value added by the firm. (In our example, it is value added per day.) Hence, we arrive at the intuitively plausible and appealing result that value-added per day is a good first measure of business losses from shutdown. This, of course, is before any consideration of transferral or deferral of production and, indeed, before taking account of avoided water losses. Notice, however, that for both domestic and industrial losses, the basic measures discussed directly above and in the text of Chapter 9 are valid for all accounting stances above the individual firm or household.

LOSSES FROM RESTRICTIONS ON LAWN–SPRINKLING

This appendix describes in some detail the method used to estimate the losses accruing to the domestic sector because of restrictions on household use of water for sprinkling purposes. We remind the reader that the losses accruing to the municipal sector because of these restrictions were estimated separately in Chapter 9 as "Lost Revenue."

It was not feasible to gather data on these losses by the same methods used for the industrial and commercial sectors because, again, of manpower and money constraints on our efforts. Fortunately, Howe and Linaweaver's work[1] on demand functions for domestic water was completed and available in time to be used for an aggregate level attack on the problem. Our approach was to use their demand function for summer sprinkling water applicable to the eastern United States in areas with metered water and public sewers.

$$q_{s,s} = 0.164 \, b^{-0.793}(w_s - 0.6r_s)^{2.93} \, P_s^{-1.57} v^{1.45} \qquad \text{(E-1)}$$

Here,

$q_{s,s}$ = average summer sprinkling demand in gallons per day per dwelling unit;

b = irrigable area per dwelling unit;

w_s = summer potential evapotranspiration in inches;

r_s = summer precipitation in inches;

P_s = marginal commodity charge applicable to average summer total rates of use (cents per 1,000 gal);

---

[1] Charles W. Howe and F. P. Linaweaver, Jr., "The Impact of Price on Residential Water Demand and Its Relation to System Design and Price Structure," *Water Resources Research*, I (1965), 13–32.

v = market value of dwelling unit in \$1,000.[2]

We chose values for the parameters b and w_s from the table provided by Howe and Linaweaver (Table 2, p. 8). In particular, we used the average values for these parameters reported for the 11 eastern areas used in estimating the demand equation.

$$b = 0.147 \text{ acres per dwelling unit}$$
$$w_s = 16.84 \text{ inches per acre}$$

The average value of r_s given by this same table is 10.96 inches per acre. We use 5.00 in/ac in our calculations to reflect the significantly lower rainfalls of drought summers, without aspiring to greater accuracy for this parameter than for the others. Hence $(w_s - 0.6r_s)$ equals 13.84 in/ac. Under average rainfall conditions, $(w_s - 0.6r_s) = 10.26$ in/ac.

Values of v appropriate to each town were calculated from data in the 1960 *Census of Housing*, vol. I, part 4, especially Table 21. v was taken to be a weighted average house value for the town, where the numbers averaged were the midpoints of the various value intervals reported in the table, and the weights were the number of dwellings in the town in each interval. P_s was taken to be the first block rate; that is, the one applicable to lowest total use, since this is invariably the one applicable to domestic decisions about sprinkling. (See Table 53.)

In one significant respect, we depart from the general procedures outlined in the text. That is, for the sprinkling losses of Braintree and Fitchburg, we include in Table 22 the average of the 1965 and 1966 losses. This stretching of our self-imposed rule to use only 1966 losses for these 2 towns was undertaken with the aim of adequately capturing domestic sector sacrifices. (Many of the early critical comments received in connection with this study suggested that we were somehow "missing" some of the drought's domestic sector impact.) To the extent that one of our central findings is the surprisingly small amount of loss (after correction), this policy is distinctly conservative.

As is argued in the text of Chapter 9, the calculation of sprinkling losses in situations in which all sprinkling is forbidden is straightforward. The integral under the given demand curve up to the quantity implied by the price existing before the prohibition will be the measure of total willingness to pay.[3] The net loss to the domestic user will be this area corrected for

[2] A different form for this demand function was reported by Howe in "Water Pricing in Residential Areas," *Journal of the American Water Works Association*, LX (1968), 497–501.

[3] As we note in the text, we assume that water is a small enough factor in the budget that we may use the simple consumer surplus argument.

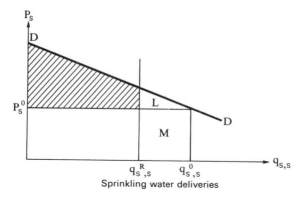

Figure 29. Losses from a partial ban on lawn-sprinkling.

water bills avoided (or consumer surplus). In our present framework, the measure which emerges is in terms of per-dwelling-unit per-day and must be multiplied by the number of dwelling units in the town and the number of days "per summer" to arrive at a total annual loss for the town. This simple situation applied in Fitchburg in 1965, when no sprinkling at all was allowed.

An additional complication is, however, introduced when, as in Braintree in 1965 and 1966, sprinkling is not completely forbidden but only restricted in time. For example, in 1965, Braintree allowed only 1 hour of sprinkling each day; in 1966, this was increased to 2 hours per day. Now, the situation before and after such a restriction may be represented as in Figure 29, where the time restriction appears as a limit on the quantity which can be purchased even though the original price schedule remains in effect. The new net benefit to the consumer is the *shaded area* under the demand curve above the existing price and out to the allowed quantity. The loss *to the consumer* of the restriction is the area L; the gross loss is $L + M$, of which M is borne by the town. The central problem under this situation is, then, to estimate the quantity $q_{s,s}^{R}$, the amount of which will be used in the restricted time at the existing price.

Our method here was to estimate on the basis of casual empiricism that the average garden use of water would be at the rate of 1 gpm or 60 gph.[4]

[4] This estimate of sprinkling rate is low by comparison with those estimated in the "Final and Summary Report on Phase One of the Residential Water Use Research Project," John C. Geyer, Jerome B. Wolff, F. P. Linaweaver, Jr. (Johns Hopkins, Dept. of Sanitary Engineering and Water Resources, October 1963), p. 10. The rates estimated in that study ranged from 2.90 to 6.19 gpm. Our use of the lower rate is conservative in that it tends to increase the size of losses by decreasing the amount available under restrictions.

Then the use one *could* get per day in Braintree in 1965 was 60 gallons (assuming one hose per house); in 1966, 120 gal. The loss is established by first comparing the possible use, with the desired demand as given by the demand equation. Clearly, if the possible use is greater than the desired, there will be no loss from the restriction (ignoring any psychic losses from not being able to water whenever one wished, etc.).

The Pittsfield situation was, on its face, similar to that of Braintree. Here the restrictions put in effect in 1964 and 1965 allowed 12 hours of sprinkling every other day. But Pittsfield sells domestic water on an annual flat-rate basis, and so the measurement of losses from these restrictions did not seem at all simple; especially since Howe and Linaweaver stress that their results show that the demand for water under a flat-rate is not the same as that implied by a zero price at the margin in the regular demand function. In searching for a measure of willingness to pay for Pittsfield, we came across the information that a very similar city in western Massachusetts, also flat-rate, sells a sprinkling *privilege* exactly equivalent to the Pittsfield restrictions (12 hours every other day). This privilege costs $34.00 per season and is subscribed to by roughly 10 percent of the system's customers who have a need for outside use.[5] It seemed reasonable to conclude that a restriction equivalent in severity to a rather expensive privilege could hardly have resulted in economic losses. Accordingly, we estimated that there were no domestic-sector losses from sprinkling restrictions in Pittsfield. As already noted, no revenue would have been lost in any case, since domestic use is flat-rate.

The actual calculations for Braintree and Fitchburg involved, first, finding the desired quantity of sprinkling water (per dwelling unit per day) in each town at the existing price ($q_{s,s}^\circ$). Then the demand equation was solved for its inverse (p as a function of q), and this was integrated up to $q_{s,s}^\circ$. The form of the inverse is such that the lower limit could not be taken as zero; we chose for simplicity to use 1 as the lower limit of integration. The subsequent corrections to this total willingness to pay estimate to cover the Braintree and Fitchburg examples are straightforward. To obtain annual totals for the towns, 120 days was used for the length of the sprinkling season. The previously calculated number of owner-occupied dwelling units from the *Census of Housing* was used for each town as an estimate of the number of dwelling units affected by the restrictions.

It is interesting to note that the estimates for both towns of total annual household willingness to pay for sprinkling water under average rainfall

[5] The normal sprinkling privilege is 2 hours every other day and costs $8.75 per year. Compare with the 1966 Braintree restriction.

The reason for this rationing of sprinkler time is the distributional inadequacy of this particular system, rather than any shortage of water to deliver.

conditions are quite close to the $8.75 normal-privilege price charged by the town referred to above. These "normal" estimates of willingness to pay are included in Table 53 along with the loss estimates for Braintree and Fitchburg in 1965 and 1966 under the assumed summer rainfall of 5 inches.

TABLE 53. DOMESTIC LOSSES FROM SPRINKLING RESTRICTIONS

	Braintree	Fitchburg
1. Number of owner-occupied dwellings	6,806	4,173
2. V = average value per dwelling ($1,000)	15.4	12.3
3. P_s = price of domestic water ($\cent$/1,000 gal.)	47	33
4. $q_s, {}^o_s$ = desired quantity (gpd/dwelling unit)		
a. under average rainfall	85.9	108.4
b. under 5 inches of summer rain	206.5	260.6
5. Willingness to pay for the desired quantity ($/year/dwelling unit)		
a. under average rainfall	$10.70	$9.70
b. under 5 inches of summer rainfall	$27.43	$24.64
6. Total annual willingness to pay—assuming 5 inches of summer rainfall	$186,700	$101,800
7. Allowed use of water (gpd/dwelling unit)		
1965	60	0
1966	120	no restrictions
8. 1965 loss calculation:		
a. TWTP (Item 6 above)	$186,700	$101,800
b. TWTP for 60 gpd	$107,800	not applicable
c. Market value of difference between desired and allowed purchases (M in Figure 29)	$56,200	not applicable
d. Market value of desired purchases	not applicable	$43,000
Losses = a-b-c-d (as applicable)	$22,700	$58,800
9. 1966 loss calculation:		no loss
a. TWTP (Item 6 above)	$186,700	
b. TWTP for 120 gpd	$147,700	
c. Market value of difference between desired and allowed purchases (M in Figure 29)	$33,200	
Losses = a-b-c (L in Figure 29)	$5,800	
10. Losses included in Table 22 et seq.	$14,200	$29,400 (see text)

APPENDIX F

CORRECTIONS FOR
INVESTMENT RETURNS

First, we must distinguish between three aspects of a firm's "use" of water as an input. Usually, a certain quantity of water per unit of time is required to *flow through* the plant. For example, given information about plant efficiency, load factor, condenser design, etc., for a thermal electric plant we can predict the total quantity of water required to pass through the condensers per year. It is not, however, necessary that the plant *withdraw* from its source(s) an amount equal to the total flow-through use. Water use technology offers the manager a range of water use patterns from once-through use to a very high degree of recirculation and consequently low withdrawal requirement relative to flow-through use. (In the thermal-electric case, the manager may decide to erect cooling towers through which the condenser cooling water is recirculated to reduce its temperature by evaporation. The water may then be reused in the condenser.) In most uses of water, some of the water withdrawn is *lost*. (Evaporative losses in the cooling towers or in the stream warmed by the condenser water effluent are the relevant losses in our thermal electric example.)[1]

Within this framework we can discuss the effect of investment projects on annual water costs in very simple terms. In the case of wells, what is at stake is usually the substitution of one source for another. That is, firms and individuals drilling wells are most often interested in substituting their own for city water with its attendant restrictions. No change in total use, withdrawals, or losses is involved.[2] The changes are only in the sources of

[1] Blair T. Bower, "The Economics of Industrial Water Utilization" in *Water Research*, Allen V. Kneese and Stephen C. Smith, eds. (Baltimore: Johns Hopkins Press for Resources for the Future, 1966).

[2] Note that wells might also be dug to replace surface water self-supply or to augment existing wells or surface supplies.

withdrawals and consequently in their price. For example, let us define the following variables:

$$T(1{,}000 \text{ gal}) = \text{total annual withdrawals before adjustment}$$

$$L(\$ \text{ per } 1{,}000 \text{ gal}) = \text{marginal block rate for city water}$$

$$v = \text{fraction of required withdrawals supplied by the new well}$$

$$V_w(\$ \text{ per } 1{,}000 \text{ gal}) = \text{variable costs of well water}$$

$$F_w(\$ \text{ per } 1{,}000 \text{ gal}) = \text{fixed costs of well water (annual capital charge; we ignore other possible fixed charges)}$$

We also define

$$Q = \frac{(1 + r)^N - 1}{r(1 + r)^N} = \text{present worth factor for a constant stream of future earnings. Here } r \text{ is the rate of discount and } N \text{ is the length of the stream (project life).}$$

Then,

$$\frac{1}{Q} = \frac{r(1 + r)^N}{(1 + r)^N - 1} = \text{capital recovery factor,}$$

the annual charge which, if the discount rate is r and the life of the project N years, will produce a constant-cost stream of present value K, the original capital investment. Then in our notation

$$F_w = (K_w/Q) \cdot (1/vT) \tag{F-1}$$

where K_w is the capital cost of the well.
Further define:

$$S_w = V_w + F_w = \text{total annual cost per } 1{,}000 \text{ gal of well water.} \tag{F-2}$$

Now, before the adjustment, the total annual cost of water to the firm was: TL (approximately only, because of the usual block rate structure). After the adjustment, the total annual cost is:

$$vTS_w + (1 - v) TL \tag{F-3}$$

For there to exist a net savings in water costs during each year of the well's life it must be true that:

$$TL - [vTS_w + (1 - v) TL] > 0 \tag{F-4}$$

or that L be greater than S_w. This same condition will insure that the project's present value will be positive, for that requirement is that,

$$Q[TL - (\nu TS_w + [1 - \nu] \, TL)] > 0 \qquad (F\text{-}5)$$

and $Q > 0$ necessarily if $1 > r > 0$. Expressed in terms of variable costs, the requirement is that

$$Q[TL - (\nu TV_w + [1 - \nu] \, TL)] > K_w.^3 \qquad (F\text{-}6)$$

The formulae required for the discussion of recirculation projects are somewhat more complex but the basic ideas are equally straightforward. Recalling the variables defined before, but replacing the subscript w with R, let us consider a particularly simple example. We assume that before adjustment the firm's T thousand gallons of withdrawals from city water represent also its flow-through use. (The plant's use of water is once through.) As above, costs before adjustment are approximately TL. Now, we assume that the firm installs a cooling tower with capital cost K_R capable of recirculating Y thousand gallons per year. The relationship between Y and K_R depends on the cooling requirements, climatic conditions, and hours of operation.[4] Of the total recirculation volume some fraction, m, will have to be made up from city water due to evaporation and blow-down losses. Defining S_R to be average total cost per 1,000-gallons exclusive of make up costs, we may write total water costs after the adjustment as either:

$$(S_R + mL) \, Y + (T - Y) \, L, \qquad (F\text{-}7)$$

or

$$S_R Y + (T - Y + mY) \, L. \qquad (F\text{-}8)$$

For the adjustment to produce a stream of benefits (net water cost savings) over its life, it must be true that:

$$TL - [S_R Y + (T - Y + mY) \, L] > 0, \qquad (F\text{-}9)$$

or that,

$$L(1 - m) > S_R. \qquad (F\text{-}10)$$

For example, Equation F-10 says that for a water-cost saving to exist with 10 percent make-up feed, the average total cost of the recirculated water

[3] The equivalence of Expressions F-5 and F-6 is easily proved by substituting from F-1 and F-2 into F-5.

[4] See, for example, Paul Cootner and George O. G. Löf, *Water Demand for Steam Electric Generation* (Baltimore: Johns Hopkins Press, 1965), Ch. 6.

(exclusive of make-up costs) must be less than 90 percent of the local block rate. (By the same reasoning used above, this is sufficient for the project to have a positive present value.) Alternatively, in terms of variable costs we have the requirements,

$$QY[L - mL - V_R] > K_R. \tag{F-11}$$

Again, the equivalence of the statements in terms of S_R and V_R follows directly from the definition of S_R.

PRODUCTION LOSSES AND NET EARNINGS REMITTALS UNDER VARIOUS ACCOUNTING STANCES

If we assume that production is "lost" at one time or place but made up at some other time or place, our estimate of the extent of factor employment at the latter will be directly relevant to our assessment of the cost this transfer represents to society. If full employment holds for the time or place to which the shift occurs, then the cost of increasing production is measured by the marginal cost of leisure foregone (wages), of increased depreciation (if capital is also fully employed), and of the cost of spreading managerial ability thinner. Interest and rent charges would not increase. Discussion of profits in this context is made very difficult by the lack of agreement among economists as to just what profits are. If profits are a return to managerial ability, our comments above apply. If, however, profits are a return for the bearing of uncertainty, the making of decisions, or the introduction of innovations, it is more difficult to see just what the impact of transfer or deferral would be. One might adopt an assumption tying the supply of the relevant function to the level of employment of other factors. Thus, if full employment were the rule, there will also be some social cost of drawing out a bigger supply of the risk-bearing or decision-making function.

Given this framework of principle, we must decide what corrections to make in practice. We first note that the important variable here is the extent of labor unemployment. We may think of capital as nearly always underemployed in a social sense so long as one shift is the general rule. Alternatively we can take the view that whether or not it is said to be fully

218

employed is irrelevant, since we can intensify its use with a negligible increase in social cost. Similarly, we may ignore the other factors in worrying about the impact of unemployment. We further agree to consider only two cases called "unemployment" and "full employment" and to assume that at full employment a given amount of "lost" value added can be replaced at a different time or place at a social cost approximately equal to the money costs of hiring the required labor (or persuading the required labor to give up leisure at the margin). We may then say that that part of the lost value-added attributable to wages represents the social cost of its replacement at a different time or place under full employment. To this basic cost must be added the increased transport charge in the case of spatial transfer or the cost of waiting where a temporal shift is involved. Thus, we summarize in Table 54 the costs if under a given accounting stance we determine that transfer or deferral of production losses must have occurred.

TABLE 54. COSTS OF "LOST" PRODUCTION UNDER TRANSFERRAL OR DEFERRAL

Transfer		Defer	
Full employment	Unemployment	Full employment	Unemployment
Wages and transport costs	Transport costs	Wages and waiting costs	Waiting costs

In translating this scheme into use with our data, we follow work done by Kates in the field of flood losses.[1] In this work Kates reached, by a rather different line of reasoning, conclusions essentially the same as we have set out above. In particular, we make use of his approximation of transport and waiting (he uses a different term here) costs of 2 percent of the gross value of production "lost." Not only does this figure appear intuitively reasonable, but our use of it is a step in the direction of comparability of losses from various natural "disasters." Potentially, then, even with our limited consideration of unemployment possibilities, we have an infinity of situations to consider, depending on the degree of transferral or deferral assumed under each of the accounting stances. In order, again, to limit our task to reasonable proportions, we originally considered the following situations:

[1] See Robert W. Kates, *Industrial Flood Losses: Damage Estimation in the Lehigh Valley*, Department of Geography Research Paper No. 98. (Chicago: University of Chicago Press, 1965), pp. 47-57.

At Each Discount Rate—8 percent and 20 percent

Local Stance   a. no transfer/defer
                   b. 50 percent transfer/defer—full employment
Regional Stance   c. 25 percent transfer/defer—unemployment
                   d. 50 percent transfer/defer—unemployment
National Stance   e. 75 percent transfer/defer—full employment
                   f. 100 percent transfer/defer—unemployment

The same principles apply and the same methods are used in correcting retail-sector business losses as for the production losses in the industrial sector. The same set of situations is considered in order to preserve consistency even though it seems clear that deferral is almost certainly the rule for these losses given sufficient time.

The second basic question we must deal with here is that of the method of allowing for the remitting of net returns to central headquarters by the divisions of national firms represented in our survey. The impact of this correction will be to decrease the positive present value (perhaps even driving it negative) associated with the aggregate of industrial investments in the local and regional accounts. This correction is made under the following assumptions:

1. That 95 percent of net earnings of national firms are drained out of the local area.

2. That 80 percent of net earnings of such firms are drained out of the region (the state).

3. That we may ignore international transactions and treat 100 percent of such earnings as accruing to the nation's account.

In actually reporting the results of our calculations, we have confined ourselves to 4 of the 12 sets originally considered—the local 0 percent deferred, and national, 100 percent deferred accounts at each discount rate. This selection has the effect of keeping down the volume of information competing for the reader's attention; it is, however, justified as discussed in the text, on the basis of the relevance of two of the chosen accounts for key decision-making levels. The other two are presented primarily to show the effect of changing interest rates.

METHODS OF SOLUTION

Initially, solutions to the model under various combinations of parameter values were sought using a simple search technique on the time-sharing computer. This technique was chosen after we had first gone over the response surface fairly carefully under one set of parameters and found apparently only one optimum vector. In the general search procedure, an initial vector $\{T_1^1, T_2^1, S_0^1, S_1^1, S_2^1\}$ was chosen. A program was written which looked at the 125 vectors formed by considering $x_i^1 - \Delta x_i^1$, $x_i^1 + \Delta x_i^1$ for each element, x_i^1, of the initial vector. The program chose that vector giving the minimum value to total cost. The initial T_i's were always chosen as follows:

$$T_1^1 = 20; \quad \Delta T_1^1 = 10$$

$$T_2^1 = 40; \quad \Delta T_2^1 = 10.$$

The s_i^1's were chosen differently depending on the total increment which had to be provided from Equation 14-13, which equals $D_o(e^{60} - 1)$. In general, it had to be true that for $\{S_0^1 + \Delta S_0^1, S_1^1 + \Delta S_1^1, S_2^1 + \Delta S_2^1\}$, s_{60} was non-negative.

The vector giving minimum cost in the initial search was chosen as the base vector for a second round in which the intervals used were reduced to $\frac{1}{2}$ those used in the first run ($\Delta x_i^2 = \frac{1}{2}\Delta x_i^1$). This procedure was repeated until the resulting reduction in the total costs was less than some $\epsilon > 0$.

The results obtained from this technique were encouraging in that the changes in optimal solution values of the vector $\{x_i\}$ with changes in the important parameters (particularly ρ, y, and z) were generally intuitively acceptable. It seemed, however, that a more efficient method of taking into account the possibility of multiple local optima was needed. Accordingly, it was decided to attempt to use a non-linear programming package based on the Zoutendijk method of feasible directions.

The basic outline of the Zoutendijk method is well known. It is applicable to the problem of minimizing a function, $f(x)$, subject to a set of linear constraints, $Ax = b$, defining a closed, convex region; and to non-negativity constraints, $x > 0$. If $f(x)$ is strictly convex, the method will find the global optimum.

There are two essential subproblems involved at each step in the iterative procedure: the direction-finding problem and the step-size problem. The process is initiated at some feasible vector (one satisfying the set of constraints). In the direction-finding problem the method attempts to find a direction in which to move away from the initial (or subsequent) vector. This direction should be as close as possible (in some sense) to the negative of the gradient of $f(x)$ at that initial (or subsequent) vector, subject to the restriction that some movement may be made in that direction without leaving the feasible region. The actual choice of the direction of movement involves specification of a normalization rule which protects us from choosing directions with infinite components.

The step-size problem involves the choice of the best distance to move along the feasible direction. This problem may be solved by a search technique or through a sub-program optimizing the step-length for the given gradient information.[1]

Because our objective function is non-convex, we must concern ourselves with the possibility that the solutions obtained are merely local optima. We attempted to deal with this problem by using three different starting vectors for each of our solution runs, hoping that the same solution vector would be found from each starting point. In a six-dimensional space, of course, it may be argued that using only three vectors does not even begin to answer the question; that there are just too many nooks and crannies which will be ignored unless we use a large number of different initial vectors, perhaps choosing them at random.[2] Our problem is, however, simple enough that we may hope to be able to make use of economic intuition in choosing a small set of vectors spanning a large relevant portion of the space. In particular, the vectors we chose to use are shown in Table 55.[3]

[1] For a fuller explanation of the methods involved, see Douglas Shier, "The Zoutendijk Method: A Computational Analysis," unpublished undergraduate honors thesis for the Department of Applied Mathematics at Harvard College, May 1968.

[2] For example, we could use the method developed by Peter Rogers. See his "Random Methods for Non-convex Programming," Doctoral dissertation presented in 1966 to the Division of Engineering and Applied Physics at Harvard University.

[3] Because of the form of the partial derivatives of the objective function, the initial vector could not be chosen with any zero capacity increments (except, of course, for the

TABLE 55. STARTING VECTORS

Elements	1	2	3
T_1	5	5	29
T_2	10	55	30
s_0	$D_0(e^{60\alpha} - 1) - 3$	$\dfrac{D_0(e^{60\alpha} - 1)}{4}$	1.0000
s_1	1.0000	$\dfrac{D_0(e^{60\alpha} - 1)}{4}$	$\dfrac{D_0(e^{60\alpha} - 1)}{2} - 1$
s_2	1.0000	$\dfrac{D_0(e^{60\alpha} - 1)}{4}$	$\dfrac{D_0(e^{60\alpha} - 1)}{2} - 1$
s_{60}	1.0000	$\dfrac{D_0(e^{60\alpha} - 1)}{4}$	1.0000

Thus, the differences between the vectors are large in terms of the timing of the major part of the required capacity expansion. In Vector 1, nearly all the total addition to safe yield is constructed early in the planning period. In Vector 3, a large block of capacity is added at the middle of the period; while under Vector 2, about half is built early, half rather late.

The rules for the termination of the program, that is, for identification of an optimum, were the following:

1. The program terminated if no feasible direction of movement could be found; that is, if either the solution to the direction-finding problem was a zero vector, or if the only feasible step length in the best direction was zero.

2. The program also terminated when along a feasible direction the optimal step length resulted in a reduction in the value of the objective function of less than 10^{-7}.

3. Finally, the program terminated if accumulated round-off errors in the interim solution vector resulted in that vector becoming infeasible (violating the constraint) by more than 10^{-6}.

COMPARISON OF PROGRAMMING AND SEARCH RESULTS

We present in Table 56 the results of comparing the total costs of the "optimal" solutions found by the programming algorithm with those

---

slack element). In principle, such an element would make the problem impossible because terms in one or more of the partials would not be defined. In practice, the computer adopts some approximation, and whether or not a meaningful solution is reached depends on the parameter values being run; for some values, the program is derailed almost immediately, while for others, it may perform as well as when started from a legitimate vector.

discovered using the search technique. These results are presented for 27 combinations of z, y and ρ; no search results were available using $z = 12.0$. Most striking, perhaps, is the closeness of agreement between the two sets of costs. The difference between the two figures is only once larger than 5 percent and is often less than 1 percent. (Small percentage differences in the total costs generally imply considerably larger differences in the elements of the choice vector, but where the cost agreement is particularly close, the optimal paths are also nearly identical.)

TABLE 56. COMPARISON OF SEARCH RESULTS WITH PROGRAMMING
SOLUTIONS: TOTAL COSTS

			Minimum Total Cost			
z	y	ρ	Search routine	Programming solution	Lower cost	Percentage difference
5.4	0.88	0.07	$\$1.151 \times 10^6$	$\$1.145 \times 10^6$	Program	0.52
5.4	0.88	0.05	1.729×10^6	1.727×10^6	Program	0.11
5.4	0.88	0.03	2.837×10^6	2.836×10^6	Program	0.03
5.4	0.78	0.07	0.964×10^6	0.980×10^6	Search	1.65
5.4	0.78	0.05	1.419×10^6	1.419×10^6	Program	0
5.4	0.78	0.03	2.235×10^6	2.214×10^6	Program	0.95
5.4	0.68	0.07	0.800×10^6	0.835×10^6	Search	4.37
5.4	0.68	0.05	1.162×10^6	1.159×10^6	Program	0.25
5.4	0.68	0.03	1.729×10^6	1.697×10^6	Program	1.88
4.3	0.88	0.07	1.052×10^6	1.059×10^6	Search	0.66
4.3	0.88	0.05	1.662×10^6	1.655×10^6	Program	0.42
4.3	0.88	0.03	2.794×10^6	2.794×10^6	Program	0
4.3	0.78	0.07	0.895×10^6	0.906×10^6	Search	1.23
4.3	0.78	0.05	1.356×10^6	1.381×10^6	Search	1.84
4.3	0.78	0.03	2.225×10^6	2.203×10^6	Program	1.00
4.3	0.68	0.07	0.756×10^6	0.798×10^6	Search	5.55
4.3	0.68	0.05	1.102×10^6	1.141×10^6	Search	3.54
4.3	0.68	0.03	1.736×10^6	1.712×10^6	Program	1.40
3.2	0.88	0.07	0.914×10^6	0.948×10^6	Search	3.71
3.2	0.88	0.05	1.514×10^6	1.522×10^6	Search	0.52
3.2	0.88	0.03	2.702×10^6	2.711×10^6	Search	0.33
3.2	0.78	0.07	0.798×10^6	0.835×10^6	Search	4.63
3.2	0.78	0.05	1.264×10^6	1.294×10^6	Search	2.73
3.2	0.78	0.03	2.141×10^6	2.147×10^6	Search	0.28
3.2	0.68	0.07	0.692×10^6	0.708×10^6	Search	2.31
3.2	0.68	0.05	1.049×10^6	1.088×10^6	Search	3.72
3.2	0.68	0.03	1.691×10^6	1.708×10^6	Search	1.00

The search method we used is rather simple. For it to arrive successfully at the optimum requires a simple shape for the objective function; otherwise, each time we halve the search distance, we risk missing the area in which the optimum is located. Thus, the fact that this method leads us to solutions either very close to or better than those achieved by the programming algorithm may be seen as evidence that our objective function is, in fact, quite well behaved.

It is also significant that the search method tends to produce the better results for those parameter combinations with which the program had the most trouble. In particular, when z equals 3.2, the search method invariably turns up the lower total cost figure, while when $z = 5.4$, the search solution is lower cost in only two instances. We noted above that the problems the program experienced for low values of z were due to the tendency for zero-capacity increments to appear in the solution vector under those conditions. It is not surprising to find that a technique making relatively large steps in each direction in searching for the optimum is less sensitive to the corner-solution problem, a symptom of the myopia of the methods of the calculus. What is, perhaps, surprising is that the programming solutions do as well as they do. The available evidence suggests that while there are some difficulties in assuring the discovery of the global optimum (particularly when z is small), we may be confident that the actual solutions found do not give rise to total costs more than 5 percent above the best attainable.

INDEX

Page numbers for sources in tables and figures are in italics

THE WHO REVEALED

Publisher and Creative Director: Nick Wells
Project Editor and Picture Research: Sonya Newland
Art Director: Mike Spender
Layout Design: Vanessa Green
Digital Design and Production: Chris Herbert

Special thanks to: Helen Crust, Amanda Leigh, Geoffrey Meadon, Polly Prior, Sara Robson and Digby Smith

First Published 2010 by
FLAME TREE PUBLISHING
Crabtree Hall, Crabtree Lane
Fulham, London SW6 6TY
United Kingdom

www.flametreepublishing.com
Music information site: www.flametreemusic.com

Flame Tree is part of the Foundry Creative Media Company L
© 2010 The Foundry

10 12 14 13 11
1 3 5 7 9 8 6 4 2

The CIP record for this book is available from the British Library.

ISBN: 978-1-84786-883-1

MATT KENT (Author) saw his first Who show in 1971 and has remained a fan ever since. In 1995 he organized the London Who Convention and founded *Naked Eye*, the successful fanzine in its wake. He worked for Pete Townshend between 1998 and 2006, running his websites, and now spends most of his time in photography pits at music shows. He has co-authored a previous book on The Who and has contributed to many Who related magazine, TV and DVD projects. To contact Matt visit his website at www.mattkent.co.uk. Matt Kent wishes to thank Michelle, Pat, Steve, Andy, Ross, Nick and Roxana for their help, advice, time and above all friendship. He also thanks and acknowledges the numerous scribes that have detailed The Who's history over the years. Many thanks go to Pete Townshend for taking the time to answer questions and finally to Pete and Roger for keeping the flag flying. *This book is dedicated to the inspirational Nick Goderson and to the memory of the 11 Who fans who tragically lost their lives in Cincinnati.*

PAUL DU NOYER (Introduction) began his career on the *New Musical Express*, went on to edit *Q* and to found *Mojo*. He also helped to launch *Heat* and several music websites. As well as editing several rock reference books, he is the author of *We All Shine On*, about the solo music of John Lennon, and *Wondrous Place*, a history of the Liverpool music scene. He is nowadays a contributing editor of *The Word*.

Picture Credits

Alamy Images: David Hickes: 70; M&N: 44 (l), 72; Trinity Mirror/Mirrorpix: 78, 114, 128, 133, 160–61; Pictorial Press Ltd: 19, 22–23, 30–31, 43, 45, 46–47, 52–53, 55, 76–77, 105, 110, 124, 132, 135, 141. **Corbis:** Bettmann: 71, 139; Henry Diltz: 63; Jacques Haillot/Apis/Sygma: 28; Hulton-Deutsch Collection: 21; Richard Melloul/Sygma: 140; Neal Preston: 106 (t), 118–19, 168–69; Leonard de Raemy/Sygma: 81. **Foundry Arts:** 17 (cr), 23 (r), 26 (cr), 35 (r), 44 (r), 46 (l), 53 (r), 60 (c), 79 (cl), 82 (l), 90 (r), 92 (l), 106 (b), 109 (r), 126 (l), 142 (r), 147 (c), 151 (b), 165 (l), 188 (b). **Getty Images:** 65, 104, 152–53, 170, 174, 175, 177, 179, 187, 189, 194, 196; AFP: 171, 190; FilmMagic: 164; Hulton Archive: 12–13, 14, 15, 41, 49, 50, 51, 64, 89, 92 (r), 107, 111, 122–23, 129, 144–45; Estate of Keith Morris: 62; NY Daily News: 60 (t), 117; Michael Ochs Archives: 27, 38, 40, 42, 48, 95, 121, 126–27, 158; Terry O'Neill: 125, 150; Popperfoto: 16, 18; Redferns: 17 (t), 20, 32, 33, 36–37, 39, 54, 58, 59, 61, 66–67, 68, 69, 73, 74–75, 79 (t), 82 (r), 83, 84–85, 86, 87, 88, 90 (l), 91, 94, 96–97, 98, 100–01, 102, 103, 115, 136, 138, 142 (l), 143, 146, 147 (t), 148–49, 151 (t), 156–57, 159, 165 (r), 166, 186, 195; Time & Life Pictures: 137, 162; WireImage: 99, 163, 172–73, 178, 184–85, 191, 192–93. **Matt Kent Photography:** 176, 180–81, 182, 183, 188 (t), 197. **London Features International:** 26 (t), 29, 34–35, 80, 108–09, 112–13, 134; AH: 116; Neil Jones: 93. **Mirrorpix:** 120. **TopFoto:** Curzon Fritz/Arena PAL: 167.

Printed in China

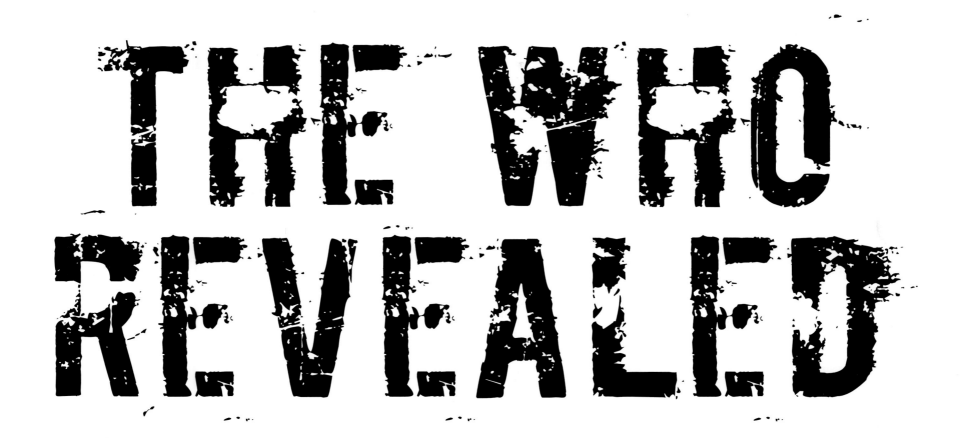

THE WHO REVEALED

BY MATT KENT

INTRODUCTION BY PAUL DU NOYER

FLAME TREE
PUBLISHING

CONTENTS

INTRODUCTION

The greatness of The Who is that they were two contradictory things at the same time. On the one hand was the sheer physical *noise* they made, an eruption of volcanic force that left bystanders stupefied. But on the other was a purely intellectual force. In their chief songwriter Pete Townshend, The Who had a true rock theorist, probably the first there ever was. And we cared about his theories because he had a magnificent band – a 'People's Band' – who could express it all with brutal finesse.

Thinkers are not unknown in rock music, and nor are barnstorming stadium acts. But The Who at their peak took each of those qualities and jammed them into a single, unstoppable body of work.

The two sides of The Who were evident from their very beginnings on the London scene of the early 1960s. Like so many of his contemporaries, including John Lennon, Keith Richards and Ray Davies, Pete Townshend was an art student. As such he was encouraged to look at popular culture with a more thoughtful eye than the typical teen consumer. Rock'n'roll had just outgrown the

unselfconscious passion of its earliest years and the second wave of players had a more analytical take. The British acts, especially, could filter this basically American art through a different sensibility, giving it unexpected twists of irony, social observation and even sexual ambiguity.

Townshend was still a rocker, nonetheless. And so were the young men who joined him: singer Roger Daltrey, bassist John Entwistle and drummer Keith Moon. Between them was a love for jazz, blues and soul, but their common ground was the guitar-driven rock of Eddie Cochran and Johnny Kidd & The Pirates. Although a quartet, instrumentally The Who were a power trio, with all the ramped-up energy that demands. No lead guitar or keyboard frills were available to them, unlike rival acts on the circuit of 1963. Townshend's rhythm guitar had to do all the heavy lifting. In other bands, too, the bass and drums were only a chugging, reliable engine room, but in the agile hands of Entwistle and Moon they were flamboyant elements with their own starring roles.

The belligerent roar of vocalist Roger Daltrey was the final defining feature. The group were perfecting a violent sound they liked to call 'Maximum R&B' and it left no room for a singer who couldn't match the fire power. Daltrey could, with ammunition to spare.

Though The Who were a rock band, their first audience was the mods, that fanatical sect of sharply-dressed soul boys, and the group's style was consciously tailored in that direction. (For a time they changed their name to The High Numbers, a nod to mod slang.) The tribal elitism of the mod underground was fascinating to Townshend and the group's early manager Pete Meaden; the band offered those fans a stand-in for the faraway black American stars that British club-goers had little chance of seeing. The Who dressed as mods for a time, but without the puritanical dedication. The group's visual leanings were in fact towards pop art, and the dark suits and short hair gradually gave way to more adventurous looks.

As was usual in British bands of the early 1960s, The Who soon emulated The Beatles by developing their own material rather than relying on US imports. And at this point Townshend really came into his own, writing an astonishing series of songs that would define the new London scene as dramatically as anything by The Rolling Stones (an act that The Who had watched and studied, right down to Keith Richards' 'windmilling' arm swing on guitar). Townshend's apprenticeship in mod circles, combined with his flair for the conceptual overview, led to classic anthems of youth culture including 'My Generation' and 'The Kids Are Alright'.

The stutter of 'My Generation', like another hit 'I Can't Explain', signalled the desperate urge to communicate, conveyed through a persona too uneducated (or perhaps pilled-up) to articulate smoothly. Other numbers such as 'I'm A Boy' and 'Happy Jack' addressed questions of identity versus conformity. In just a couple of years, The Who's emblematic character had moved from the triumphant insider of 'I'm The Face' to the agonized outsider of 'Substitute'. In the long decades that stretched ahead, Pete Townshend's writing would rarely indicate any lasting equilibrium or inner peace.

Maybe it was accidental but, as in The Beatles, the four bizarrely varied members of The Who looked uncannily destined for one another, forming that proverbial whole that exceeds the sum of its parts. In The Who's case, the combination was not so much harmonious as dynamic, and often looked combustible. In a band less intensely aggressive, the contrasting personalities might have made for a Monkees-style cartoon image. But this was no contrivance. Everything about The Who was – in the parlance of the day – 'heavy'.

Conflict was in their DNA. Roger and Pete were a case in point. Unlike almost all the other great rock acts, whether it's The Stones, Kinks and David Bowie, or Led Zeppelin, U2 and Bruce Springsteen, the singer of The Who was not its lyricist (nor even, by and large, a songwriter). The bluntly straightforward Daltrey was seldom on the same page, mentally, as the eternally searching Townshend, which made their partnership a fractious one. It's obvious that each man needed the other, but the result was necessarily a sort of rock ventriloquism. Both would try to forge careers outside The Who, but were always driven back into the belly of the beast.

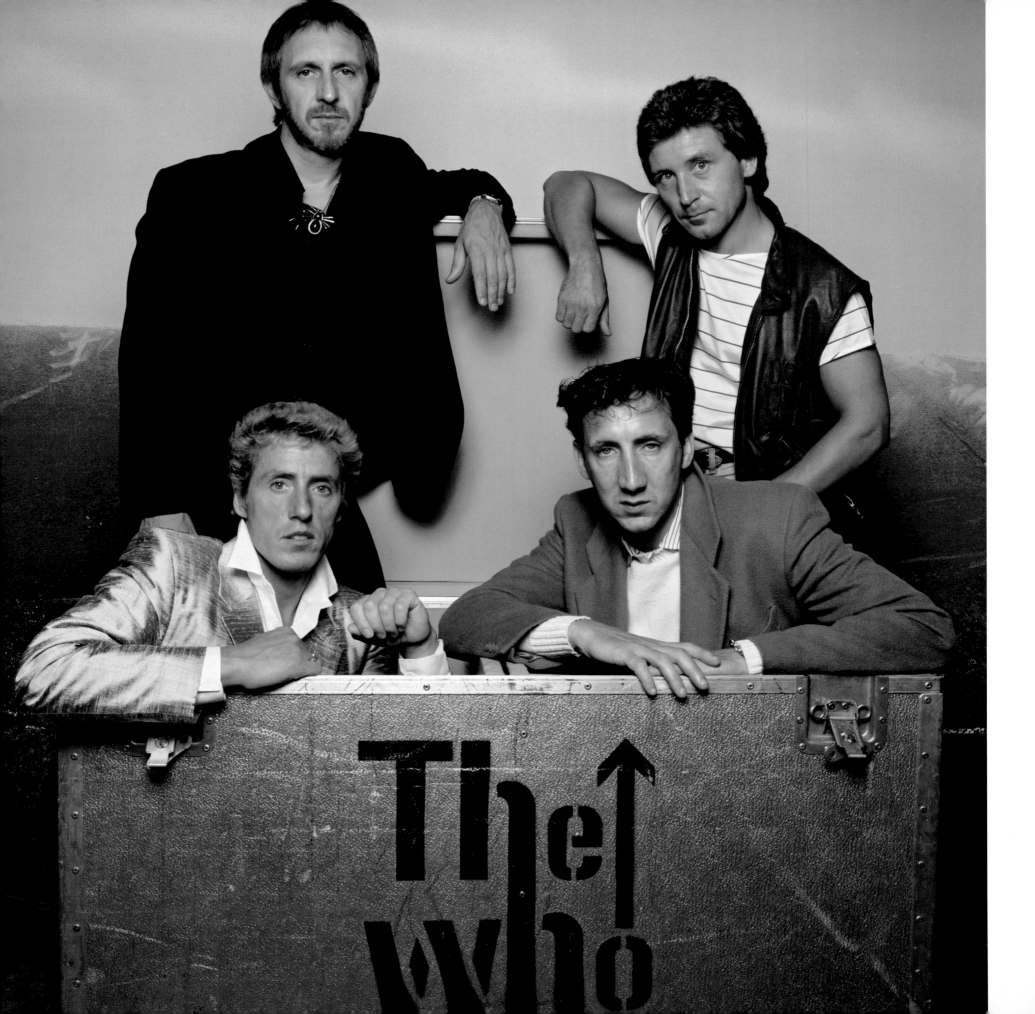

Keith Moon's wildly unpredictable nature had all the manic energy of his drumming but with a darkly self-destructive edge. Next to him, John Entwistle ('The Ox') cut the most amazingly stolid figure, as ominously still as Moon was fiery. The sight of such extremes within a single rhythm section would have been comical in any other band – but not, somehow, amid the thunderous tumult of The Who.

The Who defied all expectations. Their live sound grew ever louder and more savage, yet their material was now verging on the spiritual. They might play around with cameos of working-class London ('Dogs', 'A Quick One While He's Away') but also absorbed serious classical influences. Pete Townshend's 1969 rock opera Tommy was as daring as anything attempted in that decade of reckless experiment. Pushing against rock's boundaries, he was arguably the first to discover its limitations. Individual standouts like 'Pinball Wizard' and 'See Me, Feel Me' are all but lost in the confusion. But the scale of their ambition was inspiring.

There was no slackening of the musical attack, as is proven by that great document of 1970, *Live At Leeds*. The Beatles had stopped performing on stage since 1966, but now technology and logistical expertise were improving dramatically. In the next decade it was The Who, The Stones and Led Zeppelin who took live rock to new heights of ribcage-rattling power.

Townshend, as ever, cherished his aggression and refused to conform to conventions of hippie bliss. Instead of flowers and beads he wore bovver boots and boiler suits; through all the changes, his was still a People's Band. In *Tommy* The Who had satirized rock's new psychedelic pretensions, and even a starring part at Woodstock left them unimpressed by the counterculture. Still resisting, always reacting, Pete's defiant manifesto was 'Won't Get Fooled Again'. In that other epic undertaking, *Quadrophenia*, he drew upon the band's old mod connection to consider individuals who must, inevitably, confront their own lives when youth movements let them down.

In the eyes of posterity The Who will be defined by 'My Generation', but it's a song that Pete Townshend has, in a sense, been un-writing ever since 1965. 'Hope I die before I get old' was always a line that offered a hostage to fortune and it's haunted him – not to mention the youth-fixated

generation he celebrated – right up to the present day. It was The Who's destiny to travel onwards with their audience, to age with them (as well as attracting new recruits along the way) and to affirm rock music as a lifelong focus for community.

The passing of Keith Moon and John Entwistle lent sombre weight to the legend of The Who. Excellent as their replacements may be, the potent four-way chemistry of the band could never be reconstituted. But nobody wants to close this story down. Townshend and Daltrey have intermittently reunited. Their nostalgic live shows are more applauded than the recent records, but the pair look at peace together in ways they never did before. Perhaps Pete and Roger have come to realize what it truly means to be a People's Band. The Who does not belong to them, or to the ghosts of Keith and John. The Who belongs to its audience.

UP AND RUNNING: 1962-65

1962-65

The inauspicious backdrop of Acton County Grammar School provided the foundation for one of the world's most exciting, articulate, explosive and entertaining rock'n'roll bands – The Who. Roger Daltrey (b. 1944), John Entwistle (1944–2002) and Pete Townshend (b. 1945) showed a proclivity towards music at an early age and came together when Entwistle and Townshend joined Daltrey's band, The Detours, in 1962.

They were a competent and popular live act, but were never going to set the world on fire. The discovery of a group going by a similar name prompted a change to The Who, and in 1964 a new member, Keith Moon (1946–78), took his place on the drum stool. Rechristened The High Numbers by publicist Pete Meaden in an attempt to appeal to the mod movement that was sweeping Britain, the band released one single. It flopped, and The High Numbers quickly found themselves bought out of their contract by budding filmmakers Kit Lambert and Chris Stamp.

The band reverted to the name The Who, and the new management wasted little time turning their young charges into stars. The Townshend-penned composition 'I Can't Explain' broke them into the Top 10. On stage, The Who gained an explosive reputation. Off stage, however, the group constantly seemed in danger of implosion, as arguments threatened The Who's fledgling existence.

1962–63
ORIGINS OF THE BAND

Acton County Grammar School in West London would not, on the face of it, seem a likely melting pot of teenage angst. But it was here that Roger Daltrey, Pete Townshend and John Entwistle – having served their apprenticeships with various bands – came together as The Detours in 1962. Although they enjoyed some success on the West London club circuit, it was not until Keith Moon joined them in July 1964 that the newly rechristened The Who really took off.

1964

August–October: THE HIGH NUMBERS

With Moon in place behind the drums, the transformation within the band was remarkable. Slightly younger than the others, Moon exuded a confidence that rubbed off on his band mates. A new publicist was in the offing too, when Pete Meaden, a mod evangelist, saw a chance to take the band and mould it for a mod audience. A change of look, a change of musical direction and even a change of name – from The Who to The High Numbers – rapidly followed, as the band became the focal point of the mod movement. A single, 'Zoot Suit'/ 'I'm The Face', was released but sold a dismal 500 copies.

October: SIGN WITH ORBIT

The professional relationship with Meaden quickly faltered when Kit Lambert and Chris Stamp bought the band out of their contracts. Initially seeing the band as an ideal centrepiece for a documentary, the two men soon recognized much greater potential. Reverting to the name The Who, the group entered the recording studio in November, this time with one of Townshend's own compositions – 'I Can't Explain'. Decca producer Shel Talmy, who had worked with The Kinks, was chosen to produce the record, and The Who signed a four-year deal with his production company Orbit Music. It was a decision that eventually cost them dearly.

November: LIVE AT THE MARQUEE

The band had gained a reputation for their destructive stage act, albeit one that had started accidentally. Lambert and Stamp knew, however, that to progress The Who must succeed in the West End, so they set about turning the Marquee Jazz Club, situated in Wardour Street, into a residency for the band. The club allowed them to play on Tuesdays – traditionally the worst night of the week – and their first night, 24 November 1964, hardly made a dent at the box office. Spurred on by inspired promotional activities, though, the band broke the house attendance record within three weeks.

1965

January: 'I CAN'T EXPLAIN'

'I Can't Explain' was released in the UK on 15 January 1965. Despite little publicity from the record company (Decca in the US and its subsidiary Brunswick in the UK), it reached No. 8 in the UK charts, although it only just nudged the Top 100 in the US. Lambert and Stamp took it upon themselves to publicize the record with TV and radio slots, but even with a Top 10 success it became clear that the contracts signed with Decca and Orbit were restrictive and not in the band's favour. Certainly little was coming back in the way of royalties.

January: *READY, STEADY, GO!*

The Who made their TV debut on the seminal show *Ready, Steady Go!* on 29 January 1965. Lambert – ever the opportunist – managed to talk the producer into recruiting the audience from the Marquee for the taping of the show, guaranteeing the band a fantastic reception. It worked magnificently and The Who became regulars on the programme right up until the final show, *Ready, Steady, Goes!*, in December 1966. *RSG!* allowed the band to be seen by audiences outside their London stronghold and played an important role in popularizing the band both in the UK and abroad.

May: 'ANYWAY, ANYHOW, ANYWHERE'

Described by Townshend as 'orderly disorder', 'Anyway, Anyhow, Anywhere' – released in the UK on 21 May 1965 – was the perfect aural description of The Who's anarchic stage act. Townshend began to see himself as a mirror of his audience, and whereas 'I Can't Explain' had delved into the insecurities of the teenagers he found himself performing to on stage, the new record was a two-and-a-half-minute exploration of the bravado and newfound confidence of British youth, happy to cast aside the shackles of previous generations. The single charted at No. 10.

August: RICHMOND JAZZ FESTIVAL

The Who appeared at the prestigious Richmond Jazz and Blues Festival on 6 August 1965. Earlier the same day they had recorded another slot for *Ready, Steady, Go!* without singer Roger Daltrey, who had been taken ill with glandular fever a few days previously. However, the evening show took place with the band at full strength. They had recently recorded a segment for *Shindig!*, a US music show whose crew were also filming at the festival. Footage of the band appeared on the *Shindig! Goes To London!* special, which aired in the US on 9 December 1965.

September: DALTREY DEPARTS

Internal conflicts within the band were becoming more public, which of course helped raise the band's profile. However, the tensions were serious enough to threaten their survival. The hostilities came to a head during a riotous September tour of Denmark, when founding member Roger Daltrey was fired following a backstage fight which saw the singer flush Keith Moon's supply of drugs down the toilet. Out of the band and living in the back of his van, Daltrey had a change of heart, swallowed his pride and asked to be taken back, vowing to change his ways.

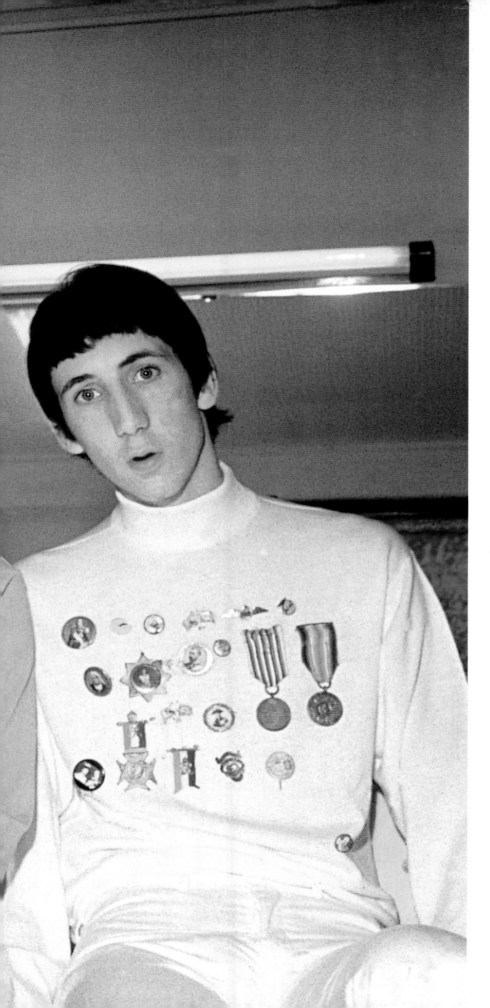

October–November: *MY GENERATION*

With the singer reinstated, the band members set about recording their next single and their debut album. The title track – containing the now-immortal and oft-cited line 'I hope I die before I get old' – was recorded on 13 October 1965 and sold over 300,000 copies, eventually reaching No. 2 in the UK. The album, released the following month, was a mixture of original compositions and cover versions, and peaked at No. 5. However, the group's growing disenchantment with Talmy led to them disowning the album almost instantly, setting the tone for what was to follow.

1966-68

The Who became embroiled in legal proceedings with their record company and producer. Finally extricated from a restrictive contract, the group launched into a period of creative brilliance, spurred on by Townshend's eloquence and knack for writing the perfect pop single.

Encouraged by Lambert and influenced by classical composers such as Purcell and Scarlatti, Townshend experimented with elaborate arrangements and extended works. His first piece, the spoof 'Gratis Amatis', set the tone for what was to come. A project provisionally entitled *Eccentrics* was cherry-picked for the band's first mini-opera *A Quick One, While He's Away*. 'Rael', on the third album, allowed Townshend to hone his skills further. At the same time, non-stop touring saw the band forge a fine reputation, although backstage bust-ups still occurred with alarming alacrity. During their first tour of America, The Who performed at the Monterey Festival, establishing themselves as headline artists.

After Monterey, Townshend renounced drugs and looked instead towards a more spiritual outlet; he discovered the teachings of Meher Baba, which he found inspirational. A new writing project, begun in 1967, took shape the following year. The band was perilously in debt, however, and although touring kept the wolf from the door it could not pay the bills. Despite this, Daltrey, Entwistle and Moon allowed Townshend the luxury of time to work on the project, in the hope he would pull a rabbit out of the hat. The explosive result was *Tommy*.

THE WHO
65.004

A LEGAL MATTER   *Brunswick*   INSTANT PARTY

1966

January: TOWNSHEND'S DRUG CONFESSION

The Who's hedonistic lifestyle and use of illicit substances were already newsworthy. Their mod fans embraced drug use as part of their lifestyle and it seemed only fitting that a band mirroring its audience should follow suit. Daltrey had already discovered – to his cost – the extent of the problem, and Townshend elaborated on it further when he appeared on the first edition of the TV show *A Whole Scene Going* on 5 January 1966. In front of a live audience, he stated that the band used drugs regularly and were 'blocked' a lot of the time. The confession created a minor furore.

March: 'A LEGAL MATTER'

Despite efforts by Lambert and Stamp to improve the contractual situation with Decca and Talmy, the duo felt stymied at every turn. As a last-ditch measure they consulted lawyers and decided to break the contract, signing a temporary agreement with Robert Stigwood for record distribution on his Reaction label in the UK and with ATCO in the US. The first release was the Townshend-produced 'Substitute' instead of the intended Talmy production 'Circles'. Talmy sought an injunction and, three days after the release of 'Substitute', The Who's original label released 'A Legal Matter' – no doubt completely unaware of the irony.

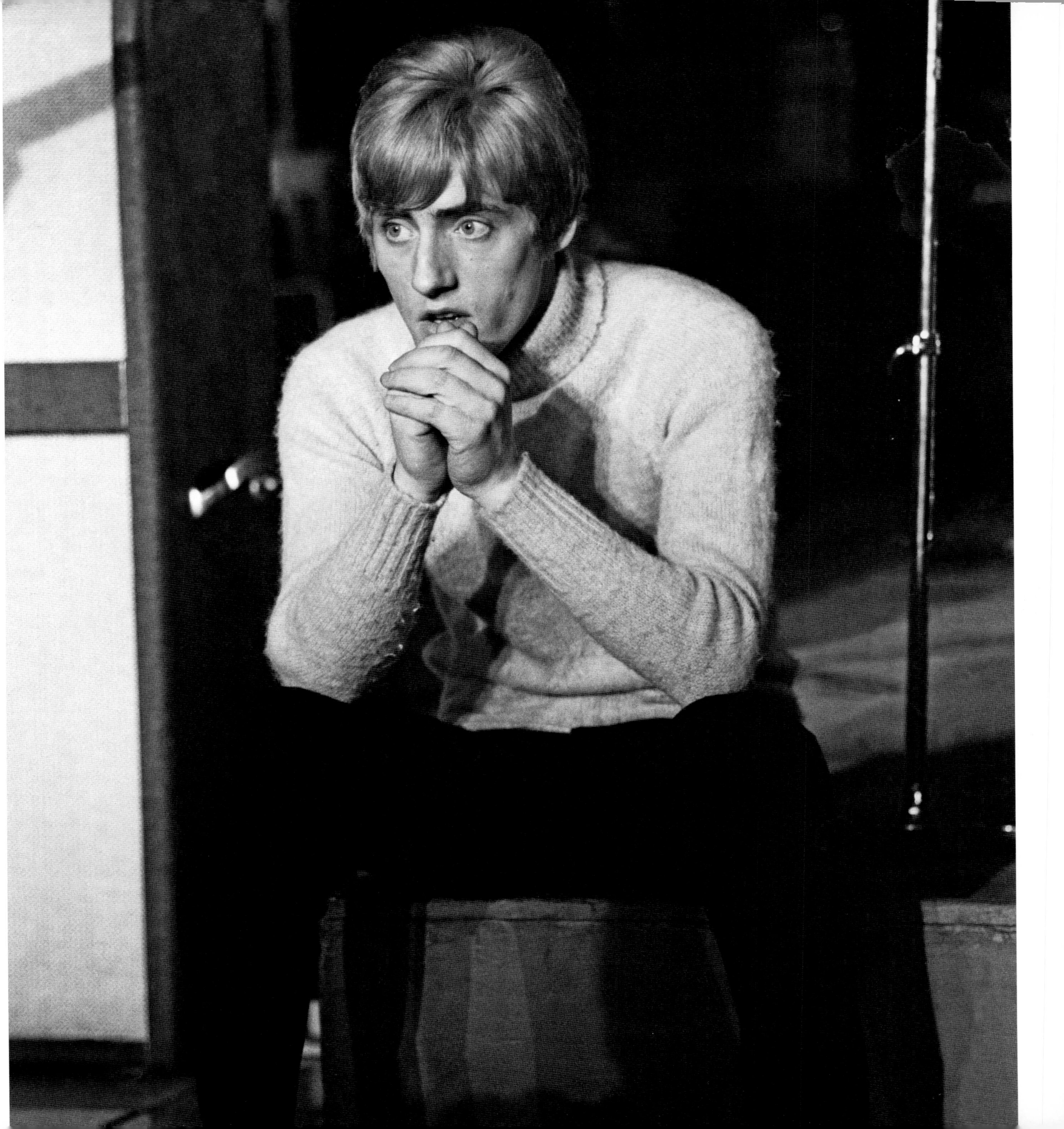

March: BATTLE WITH TALMY

After the promise of the previous year, 1966 proved to be one of frustration, with a prolonged court battle that effectively stopped the band releasing any new material for more than five months – a lifetime as far as the charts were concerned. Despite flirting with Rolling Stones representatives Andrew Oldham and Allen Klein, The Who managed to extricate themselves from Talmy's grasp in August 1966. The price of freedom was dear, however – an out-of-court settlement which included an agreement that Talmy would receive five per cent on all Who recordings over the following five years. It was a millstone the group begrudgingly accepted.

March: MOON MARRIES

Although the magazine *Disc* ran an article on 19 March stating that Keith was going to be engaged to a dancer from *Ready, Steady, Go!*, this was nothing more than a subterfuge, as he had actually married his girlfriend Kim Kerrigan two days earlier at Brent Registry Office. Kim was pregnant at the time, and their daughter Amanda Jane (Mandy) was born on 12 July, when Keith was still only aged 19. Marriage and fatherhood didn't stop him being a face around the London party scene, however, and the couple split in 1973. The divorce was finalized in April 1975.

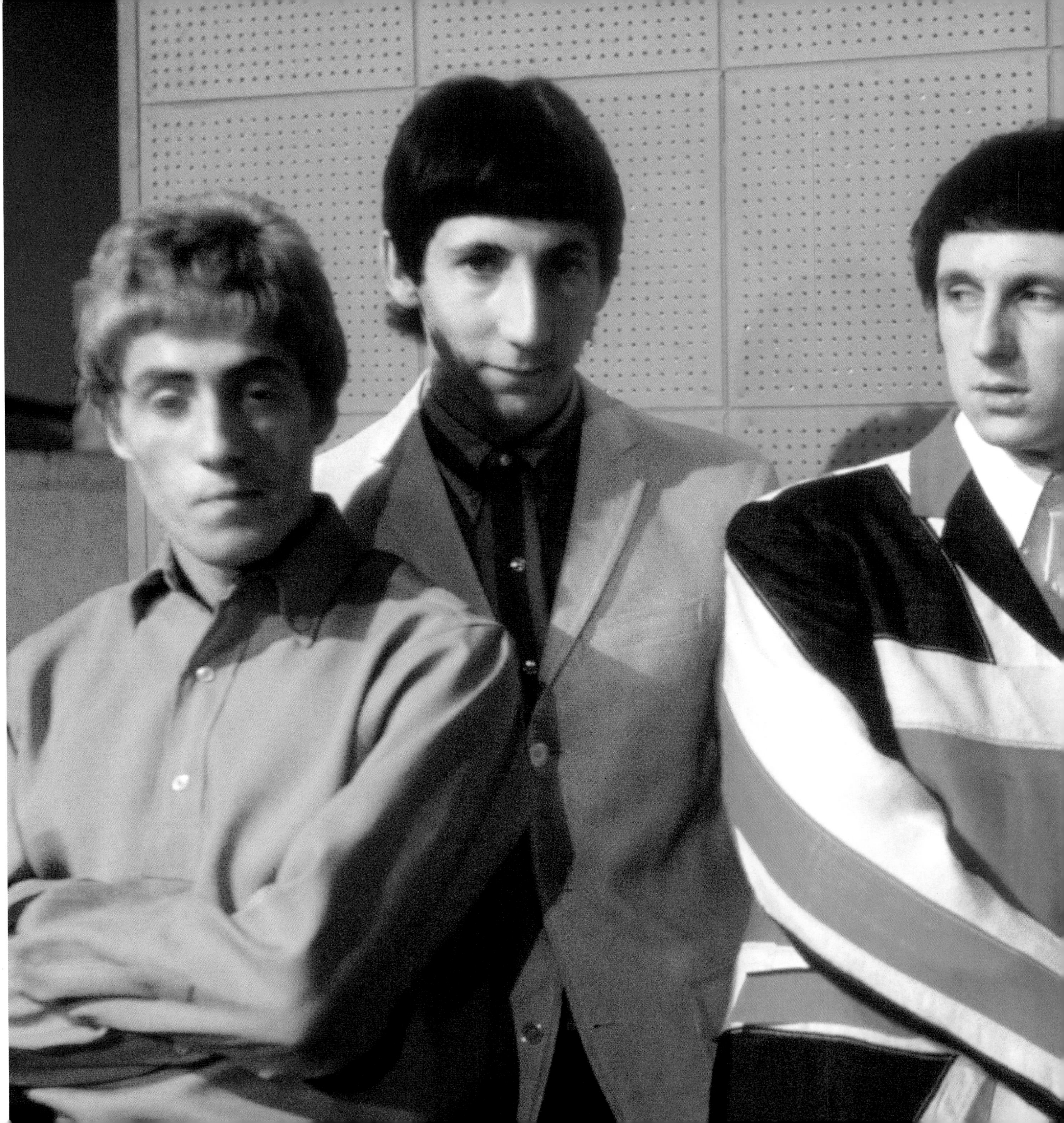

March–April: LIVE GIGS

With the enforced studio layoff, The Who continued their relentless schedule of live work. At the time there was little option as it was their main revenue stream. In between gigs they fitted in TV work, including shows filmed in France. On 20 March they also appeared on the cover of the *Observer* Sunday supplement, photographed by Colin Jones, with Townshend sporting a Union jacket. In April they set out on their second package tour of the UK, topping the bill with support from the likes of The Spencer Davis Group.

May: NME POLL-WINNERS CONCERT

The Who performed on a bill that included The Beatles and The Rolling Stones for their only appearance at an annual NME poll-winners concert, on 1 May 1966 at the Empire Pool, Wembley. A two-song set, consisting of 'Substitute' and 'My Generation', saw Moon kick over his kit and Daltrey storm off stage. Tensions between members were running high again, and the band was close to implosion. May proved a difficult month, with missed shows, Moon 'quitting', Entwistle threatening to join him, and some physical fighting – not to mention the IRA threatening to blow them up...

August: 'I'M A BOY'

With the dust hardly settled from the court proceedings, The Who released a new Townshend composition, 'I'm A Boy', on Reaction on 29 August. It resulted in a welcome return to the Top 10, reaching No. 2 exactly a month later. 'I'm A Boy' introduced both Lambert's debut as unconventional producer and signified a new direction for Townshend. With overtones of Purcell, the song was taken from an extended piece of work called *Quads*, which was set in the year 2000. Although the work in its totality remains unheard, this was an important stepping stone in Townshend's songwriting evolution.

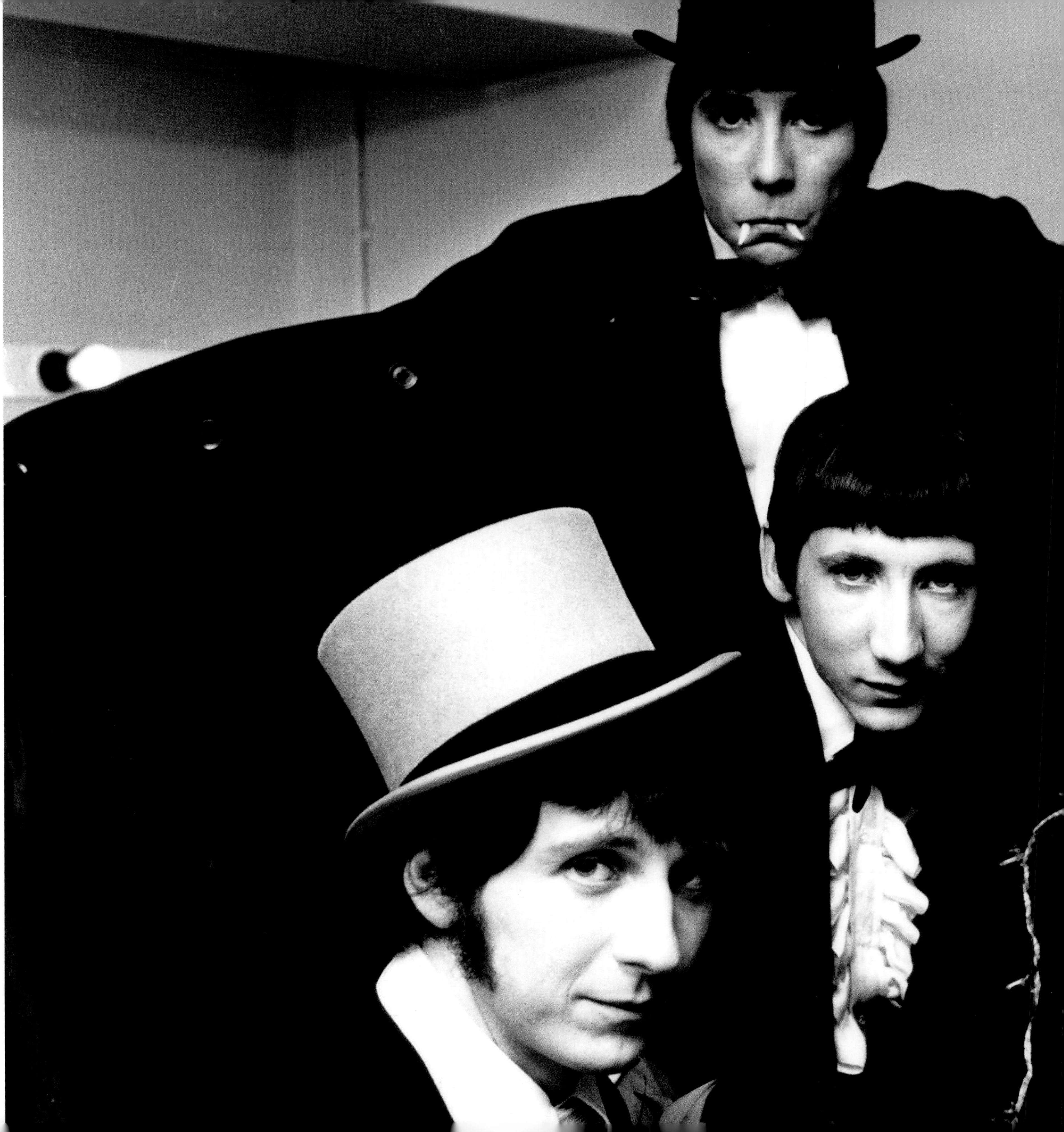

December: A QUICK ONE

The Who's second album, complete with Pop Art sleeve, was released in December 1966. With songwriting contributions from all four members (thanks to a publishing deal that richly rewarded their efforts), the release was a far cry from their debut just a year earlier. The album culminated in a whimsical six-song mini-opera entitled *A Quick One, While He's Away*, showcasing the group's mock operatics. It was released the following year in the US, retitled as *Happy Jack*. The year finished with the band's representatives flying to the US to drum up support in advance of their first visit stateside.

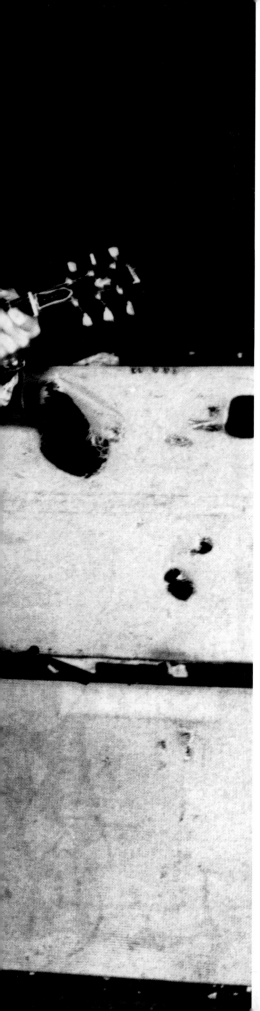

1967

January: SAVILLE THEATRE CONCERTS

With a new record label (Lambert and Stamp's Track Records) and the lure of America ahead, the year started well. The Who appeared at the Saville Theatre in Shaftesbury Avenue for one of Brian Epstein's Sunday Soundarama shows. Playing two performances on 29 January, the supporting bill included Track stablemates The Jimi Hendrix Experience, who had become the label's first signing a couple of weeks earlier. This would not be the last time the two giants would share a bill, leading to some interesting encounters. The shows saw the band debut the mini-opera *A Quick One, While He's Away*.

March: US DEBUT

The Who arrived in New York for their US debut as part of Murray Kaufman's Music In The Fifth Dimension concerts at the RKO Radio Theatre on 58th Street. The concerts ran over nine days and The Who were expected to perform a gruelling five times a day. Although singing only a couple of songs at each gig, every show was expected to climax with the destruction of their tools of trade. America was finally taking notice and The Who returned in June for their first proper tour, which began at Ann Arbour, Michigan.

April: 'PICTURES OF LILY'

'Pictures Of Lily' became The Who's first release for their new home, Track Records, in April 1967. Inspired by a postcard of theatre producer Lilian Baylis, and often referred to as an ode to masturbation, the song once again highlighted the band's – and in particular Townshend's – mastery at producing sublime, witty and adventurous three-minute masterpieces. The single peaked at No. 4 in the UK and No. 51 in the US when it was released there two months later. A couple of days after its UK release the band recorded a couple of instrumental tracks, including Edvard Grieg's 'Hall Of The Mountain King'.

June: MONTEREY FESTIVAL

Days after arriving in the US, The Who flew to San Francisco for the first Monterey International Pop Festival. The line-up included Jimi Hendrix, who was now incorporating his own brand of auto-destructive art into his act. It was clear that neither wanted to be accused of copycatting by following the other on stage. The matter was settled by a coin toss – Townshend won and The Who went on first. The band finished their 30-minute set with total destruction and Hendrix his by ritually burning his guitar. Townshend subsequently experienced a shocking LSD trip, which changed his attitude towards drugs forever.

June: ENTWISTLE WEDS

On 23 June 1967 John Entwistle became the third member of the band to marry. His bride was long-term partner Alison Wise, and they married at the Congregational Church in Acton, where eight years earlier he had first performed with Pete Townshend. The original promotional film for 'I Can't Explain' includes film of the couple kissing. Their honeymoon meant that John missed the sessions for the band's versions of 'Under My Thumb' and 'The Last Time', which were hastily recorded as a show of support for Mick Jagger and Keith Richards, who had been arrested during a drugs bust.

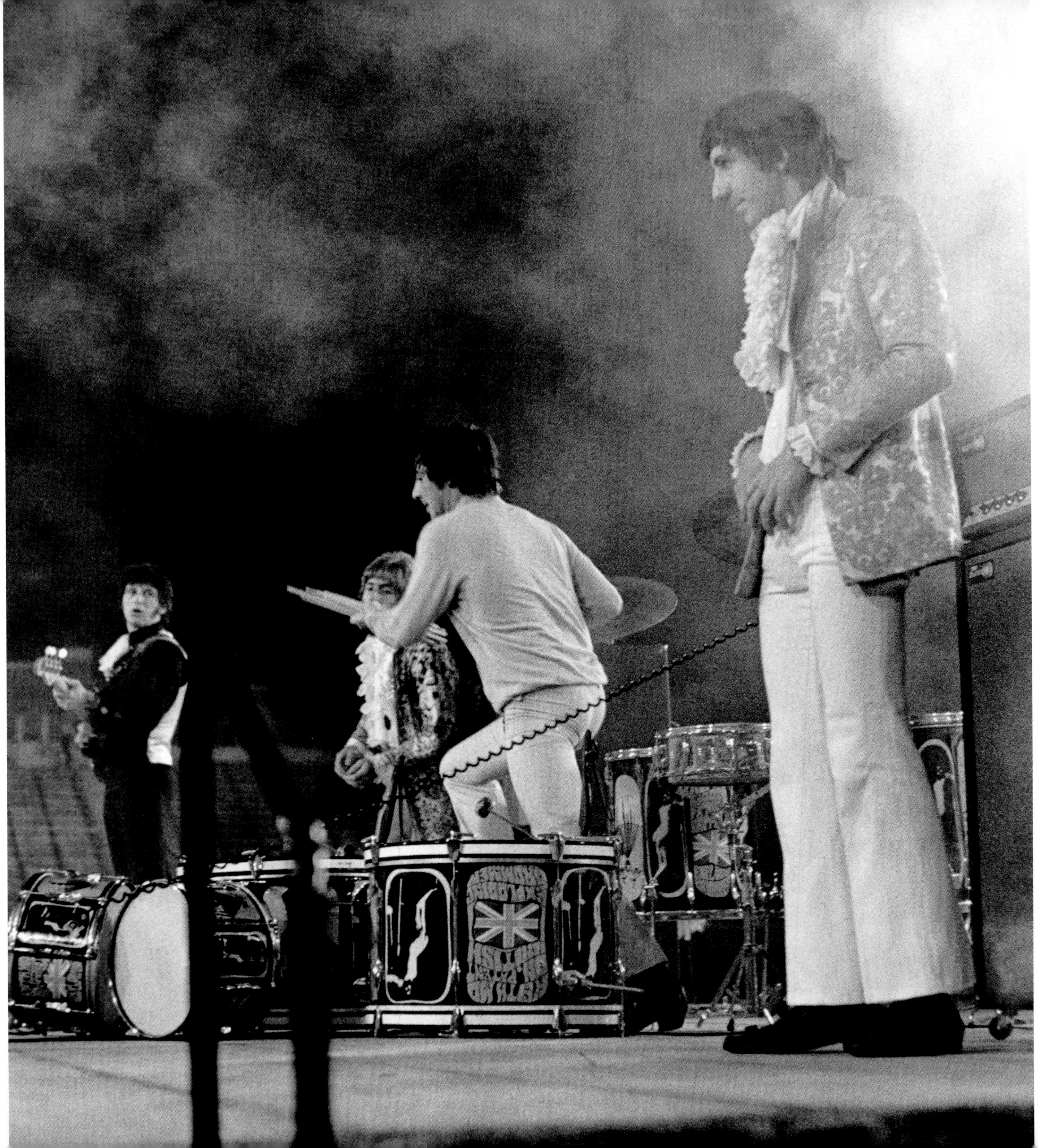

July–September: TOUR OF NORTH AMERICA

Building on the success of their previous visit, the band returned to America in July for shows that included a 10-week coast-to-coast tour as the unlikely support act for the squeaky-clean Herman's Hermits. The tour also took them to Canada and, ultimately, Hawaii – the band's only visit there for 37 years. Billed as 'Stars of Monterey Pop Festival', the band were exposed on this tour to a vast audience across North America, which helped cement their reputation as a live act. This period wasn't without controversy, however, and they returned to the UK in September greatly in debt.

August: MOON'S 21ST BIRTHDAY

Twenty-third of August 1967 will always be remembered in rock'n'roll folklore. Although reports vary, what is undisputed is that Keith Moon's infamous birthday party in Michigan culminated in police action, physical damage and a hotel ban. With the party in full swing a midnight curfew was imposed, which resulted in the hotel manager and the local sheriff literally ending up with cake on their faces. The resulting chaos involved car damage, television sets in the swimming pool and Moon losing his front teeth in the mayhem. A night in prison and a bill for $5,000 were just two of the presents Moon received.

September:
'I CAN SEE FOR MILES'

If one was to search for the perfect single, 'I Can See For Miles' would surely be a contender. Written the previous year, the progressive track was recorded in London in May 1967 and mixed whilst The Who were on the road in the US. It premiered during their infamous appearance on *The Smothers Brothers Comedy Hour* TV show, in which the host joined in the guitar-smashing. Released in the US in September – a month before the UK – 'I Can See For Miles' just forced its way into the British Top 10. This led Townshend to reassess his attitude to singles' releases, resentful that his tour de force was not sufficiently appreciated.

December: *THE WHO SELL OUT*

Legitimate radio in the UK was a pretty bland affair. New broadcasting legislation led to a major upheaval, outlawing supportive 'pirate' stations. Looking for a change of direction, The Who came up with the idea of making the next album an homage to these illegal stations. *The Who Sell Out* mixed unauthorized real and spoof jingles with the new songs, including the majestic 'Rael', running at almost six minutes, and included a 'psychedelic' poster with initial copies. Failing to capture the imagination of the record-buying public at the time, it is now seen as a masterpiece of its era and a template for what was to come.

1968

January:
TOUR OF AUSTRALIA AND NEW ZEALAND

A promising tour of Australia and New Zealand – with The Small Faces and Paul Jones – turned into a horror trip, as The Who were relentlessly vilified by both press and politicians. Before the band even set foot in the Antipodes, the Fourth Estate was drumming up bile against foreign entertainers, and things only became worse once they were there. Even the Australian prime minister got in on the act, labelling the group hooligans. Mayhem ensued, including a fine example of hotel 'refurbishment', while poor stage equipment meant that the performances were below standard. Despite vowing never to return, the band finally succumbed 36 years later.

February: HEADLINE IN THE US

A few weeks later the band returned to the US, where a more pleasant welcome was guaranteed. Their performance at the Opera House in Peoria was filmed by Tony Palmer and included in his music documentary *All You Need Is Love*, which aired later that year. The tour included shows at the legendary Fillmore West and Fillmore East, both recorded for a possible live album. The Fillmore East show in New York, though, was overshadowed by the shooting of Martin Luther King. The authorities were naturally a bit twitchy around a band known for its violence and often liberal use of explosives.

May: TOWNSHEND MARRIES

Pete Townshend became the last of the group to tie the knot when he married Karen Astley, three years his junior, at Didcot Registry Office on 20 May 1968. The couple had met at art college in Ealing five years earlier. Her father, Edwin (Ted) Astley, was a successful composer and arranger, most noted for his work on TV musical scores in the Sixties and Seventies, such as *The Saint* and *The Champions*. Her brother John would later work with The Who as engineer and producer. The couple had three children before separating. Divorce proceedings began in 2009.

June: 'DOGS' FLOPS

Knowing how fickle the singles market was – and still reeling from the disappointment of 'I Can See For Miles' – the band released 'Dogs', a strange, charming and at times just plain weird vignette of life in and around the greyhound racing circuit. The single harked back to earlier, less complex arrangements such as 'Happy Jack', but again failed to impact on the charts, peaking at No. 25. 'Dogs Part 2' would follow the next year, providing an equally unusual experience for the listener. The B-side, 'Call Me Lightning', was recorded in Los Angeles along with a promotional film for the track.

August: CLASH WITH THE DOORS

The Who returned to the US and Canada in June. This time, due to their increasing popularity, they stayed for three months. By the group's standards the tour was relatively incident-free, but the show at Flushing Meadows, where they shared the bill with The Doors, was an exception. Stage problems led to delays, and the two groups clashed after claims that The Who had accidentally damaged some of The Doors' equipment while in the process of (deliberately) damaging their own. During The Doors set, a young female stage-invader fell. The incident prompted Townshend to write the song 'Sally Simpson', which later appeared on *Tommy*.

September: MAGIC BUS

With no new material ready, The Who revisited an earlier effort and released 'Magic Bus' as a single. But the song, written during the 'My Generation' era, fared no better than its two predecessors. The release prompted Decca – against the group's wishes – to release *Magic Bus – The Who On Tour* as an album in the US. Despite its title, the release was a hotchpotch of studio recordings that did little to appease fans eagerly awaiting new material. Pete Townshend already had that in hand, though, and was teasing the press throughout the year with what was to follow.

September: THE BIRTH OF *TOMMY*

Whilst it is impossible to pinpoint exactly when *Tommy* was conceived, it's fair to say that Townshend had certainly spent much of 1968 preparing the ground for its birth. He had already begun writing for the new project in 1967, with the pivotal song 'Amazing Journey'. Musical motifs that appeared on 'Rael' would also resurface. Inspired by his following of Avatar Meher Baba, Townshend set out to write a spiritually enriched body of work. Various titles for the project were discussed, and recording began on 19 September for the then-entitled *Deaf, Dumb And Blind Boy* album at IBC Studios in London.

December: ROCK AND ROLL CIRCUS

With an abundance of A-list talent *The Rolling Stones Rock And Roll Circus* was recorded over two days at Wembley. A gruelling schedule, in which The Who were allotted 10 minutes to perform the mini-opera from *A Quick One*, went woefully over time, with The Stones not reaching the stage until the early hours. Although it was destined for TV and a possible tour, The Stones, unhappy with their performance in comparison with others, blocked its transmission. The Who, undoubtedly the stars of the production, negotiated the right to show their performance in the 1978 movie *The Kids Are Alright*.

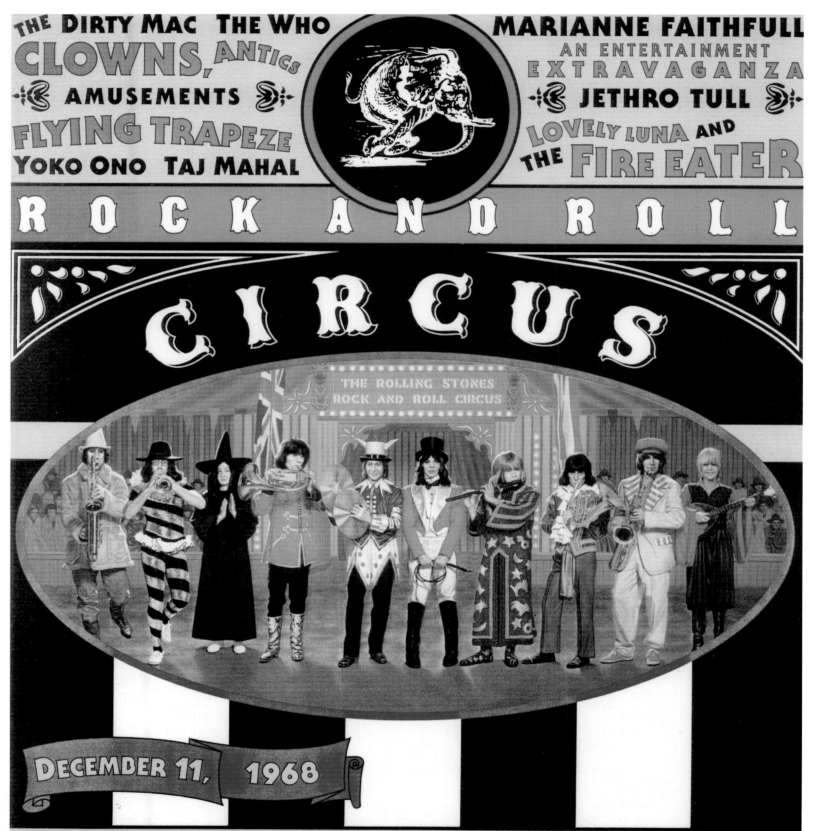

ROCK GODS: 1969-78

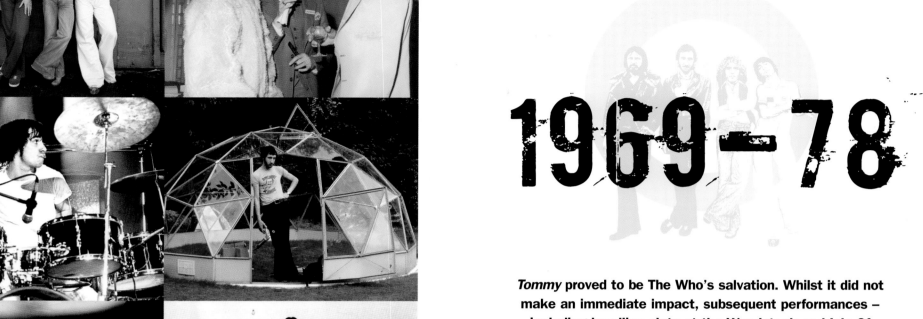

1969–78

Tommy proved to be The Who's salvation. Whilst it did not make an immediate impact, subsequent performances – including headline slots at the Woodstock and Isle Of Wight festivals – catapulted the group into superstardom. They rewrote the rule book when it came to live shows, and raised the rock bar so high that few could follow.

The intended follow-up, *Lifehouse*, could have been their *meisterwerk* but it was smothered by technology and indifference. It was abandoned, much to the frustration of its originator, but the album picked from its remains, *Who's Next*, is still considered one of the greatest rock albums of all time.

Finally the band had financial security. With it came the trappings of luxury – some good and some bad. Drink and drugs began to take their toll and eventually led to tragedy. Keith Moon was the first member to outwardly show the extent of the problem during the 1973 *Quadrophenia* tour in America. The production was magnificent in the studio but unwieldy on stage. This, together with the failure of *Lifehouse*, led Townshend to despair. He began to reassess his and the band's position. As they began to take longer breaks from the road, they became more interested in solo activities. Moon suffered most from not playing and relocated to LA, where his partying became infamous. On his return to the UK in 1978 he was woefully out of shape and, despite appearing indestructible, he died that September.

1969

March: 'PINBALL WIZARD'

After all the talk about *Tommy*, the first recording, 'Pinball Wizard', was released on 7 March 1969 in the UK. Reaching No. 4 in the charts, it failed to topple Peter Sarstedt's 'Where Do You Go To (My Lovely)?'. In the US, the single was released in a picture-cover sleeve that stated 'from the soon to be released Rock Opera TOMMY'. The single was branded 'distasteful' by Radio 1's Tony Blackburn – a statement he would later rue. In April, when Blackburn introduced the band on *Top Of The Pops*, Moon handed out his own retribution by flicking drumsticks at the hapless DJ.

May: LIVE PREVIEW OF *TOMMY*

Ahead of the album's release, the band played a live preview of *Tommy* to the press at Ronnie Scott's in London, although they had already broken in the new songs the previous week with some live shows, having rehearsed the new stage production in April at Hanwell Community Centre. The hour-long preview saw Townshend give an in-depth explanation of the story, before the band played at a deafening volume in a venue more used to the relaxing sounds of jazz. The show was met with unanimous critical acclaim, and set up The Who well for their upcoming American tour.

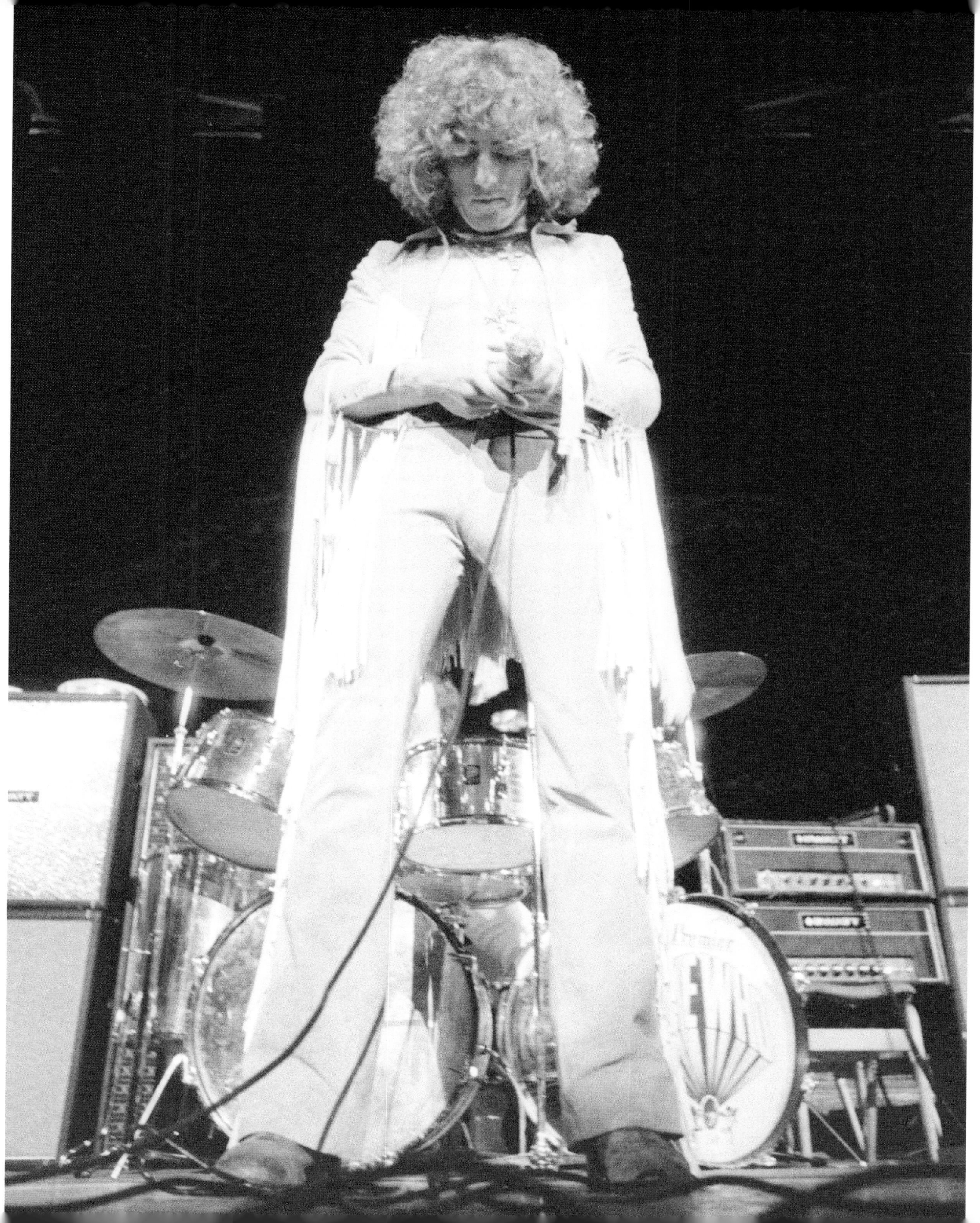

May: THE TOMMY TOUR

In May The Who set off for a two-month tour of America. Performing *Tommy* marked a shift in the group's live persona, with the spotlight thrust firmly on Daltrey as frontman. The performances also grew longer, reaching over two hours as the band played a tripartite act with *Tommy*, delivered almost in its entirety, sandwiched between two sections of hits. The shows mesmerized audiences, with state-of-the-art light and sound equipment adding to the atmosphere. In New York, Townshend was booked and fined $75 for unceremoniously kicking off stage a policeman who had come to warn the audience of a nearby fire.

May: TOMMY RELEASED

The album was released in America two weeks into the US tour. The UK release followed a week later. A lavish affair, it was housed in a triptych sleeve, designed by fellow Baba devotee Mike McInnerney, together with a libretto, which gave the album a different feel to most records of the time. Although Townshend's baby, the album had been a real group effort in the studio. Some of the less savoury aspects of the story were handed over to Entwistle, and even Moon threw in some ideas and lyrics. The subsequent exposure from *Tommy* would mark a shift in the band's fortune.

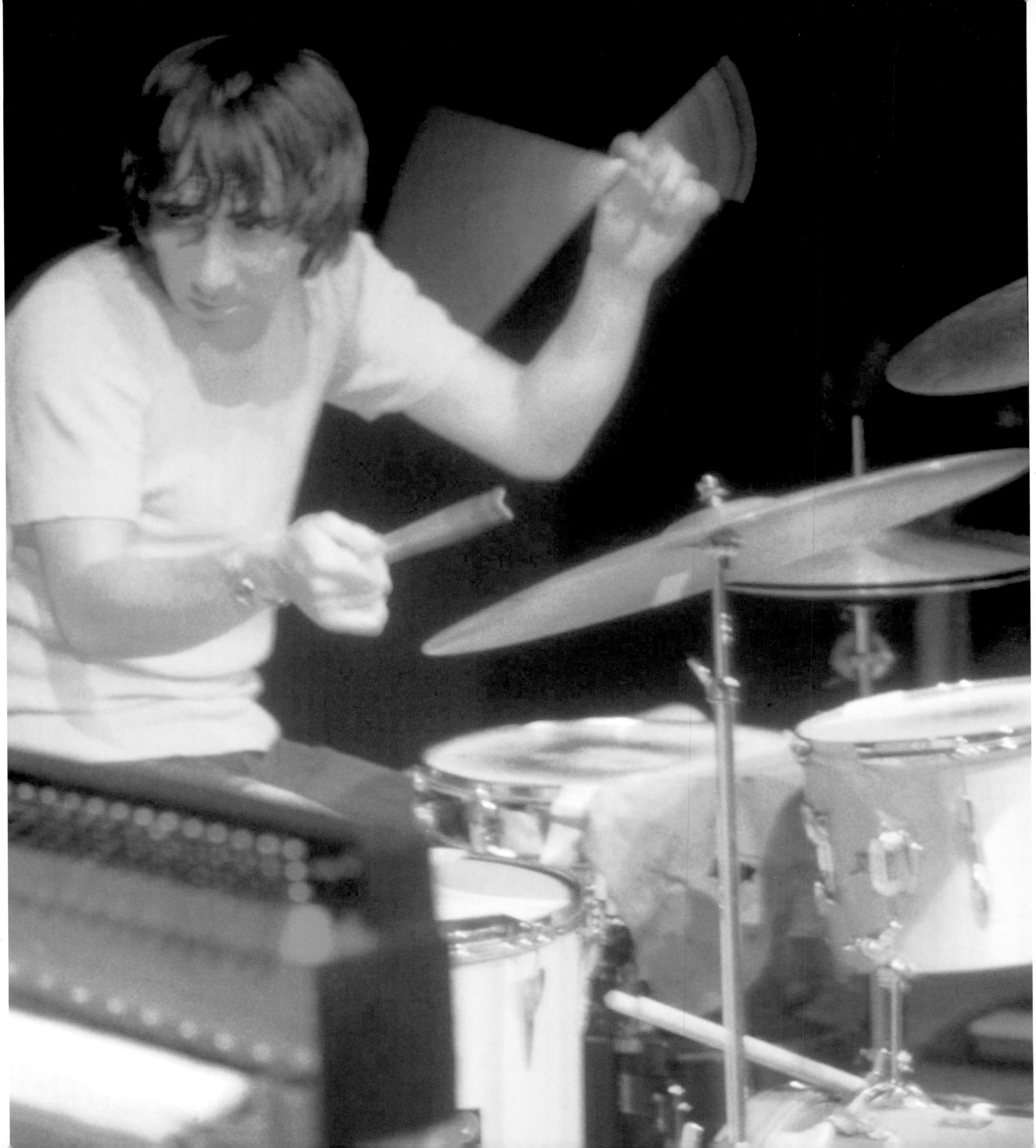

July: POP PROMS

After the success of the American tour, The Who returned home and appeared on the last night of the Royal Albert Hall's Pop Proms on 5 July. Billed as the 'First London Pop Gala', the week-long event also boasted performances by Led Zeppelin and Fleetwood Mac. The Who shared the bill with Chuck Berry, alternating as headliners, for two performances. Trouble during both sets was aimed at The Who by Berry's Teddy Boy followers, and the police were forced to intervene. The show took place on the same day as The Rolling Stones played their free concert in nearby Hyde Park.

August: WOODSTOCK FESTIVAL

Returning to the US in August, the band played two festivals – the Tanglewood Music Festival, attracting an audience of 23,000, and the Woodstock Music And Arts Fair, the legendary event where musicians found themselves appearing in front of an estimated half a million people. Scheduled to appear at 10 p.m. on the Saturday, The Who actually hit the stage at 4 a.m. the following morning, with the sun rising as they finished their set. Hated by Townshend, loved by Daltrey, the show – and the ensuing movie – turned the band into a household name in the US and cemented their reputation as the premier live rock act.

August: ISLE OF WIGHT FESTIVAL 1969

After a couple of low-key shows back in the UK, the group performed at the second Isle Of Wight Festival of Music on 30 August. Arriving by helicopter, they had assembled the largest PA possible and erected signs warning the audience to stay at least 15 feet away. As support act to Bob Dylan, the band spent little time at the festival itself, instead choosing to leave the island immediately after their performance, thus missing Dylan's first major appearance in three years. With the successes of America behind them, the group was confident that they had found a winning formula performing *Tommy*.

October: BACK IN THE USA

Consolidating their successes, The Who crossed the Atlantic in October for their second tour of the year. A record-breaking residency at New York's Fillmore East saw the band play eight shows over six nights. No group had previously played the venue for more than two nights, and the shows grossed $75,000 – from which they received over $50,000. Guests included luminaries such as Bob Dylan and Leonard Bernstein, who waxed lyrical to Townshend about the gigs. Led Zeppelin, who had opened for The Who at a show on the previous tour, were present at the opening-night party at Max's Kansas City nightclub.

December: THE COLISEUM

Back on home turf the band fitted in five concerts before the year was out, including one at the home of the English National Opera, the Coliseum in London. Although Townshend admitted to being embarrassed at playing there, it wasn't evident in his performance. The performance was filmed (as were all five shows) for a possible *Tommy* project, but the footage remained unused until the making of *The Kids Are Alright* movie eight years later. The idea of playing at landmark venues such as this subsequently became commonplace for the band. An extended DVD of the show was released in 2008.

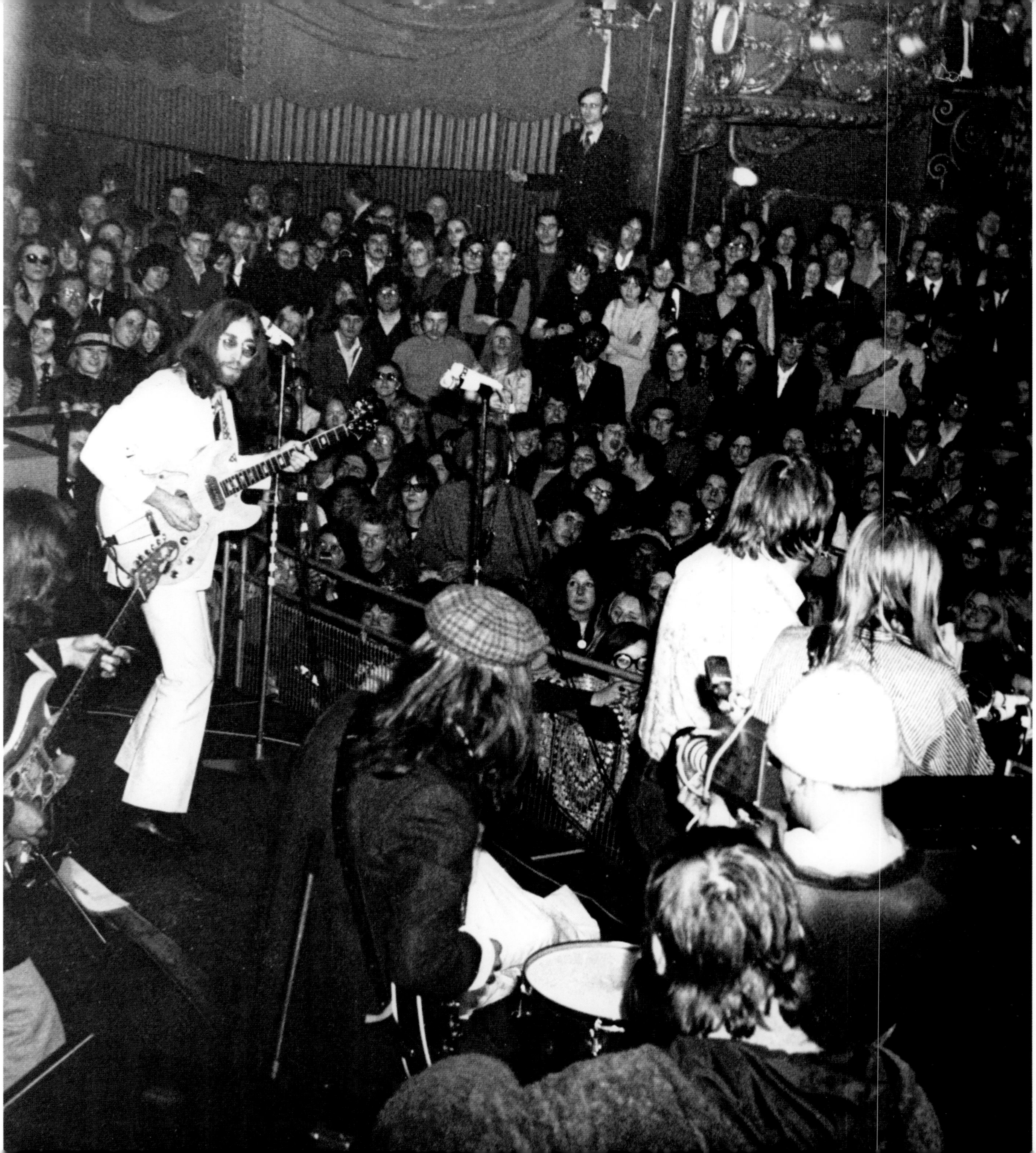

December:
MOON PLAYS WITH THE PLASTIC ONO BAND

In between the UK shows, the irrepressible and inexhaustible
Keith Moon managed to find time to play a charity show with
The Plastic Ono Band. The concert, in aid of UNICEF, took place
at the Lyceum in London on 15 December and was billed as
'Peace For Christmas'. As well as Moon on sticks, John Lennon
and Yoko Ono had assembled an all-star line-up that included
George Harrison, Eric Clapton, Klaus Voormann and Billy Preston.
The performance was released in 1972 as part of John and
Yoko's *Sometime In New York City* album.

1970

January: MOON'S CHAUFFEUR KILLED

The highs of the Sixties quickly dissipated at the onset of the
new decade. On 4 January, Keith Moon attended the opening
of a nightclub in Hertfordshire. When he was leaving, a group of
youths began kicking his car. The driver, Cornelius 'Neil' Boland,
jumped out to clear a pathway and was knocked to the ground.
Accounts vary as to the exact circumstances, but the car
accelerated, dragging Boland underneath. He was pronounced
dead on arrival at hospital. Although Moon admitted driving, a
verdict of accidental death was returned and no sentence was
imposed. The incident, however, had a lasting effect on Moon.

May: LIVE AT LEEDS

The *Tommy* bandwagon moved on, and in January it was performed at some of Europe's most prestigious opera houses. However, the success of the rock opera had left its creators with a dilemma – how to follow it. The answer was to record a live album as a stopgap. Although many of the shows in the late Sixties had been recorded for possible live release, the band had never been happy with the results and so two shows – played at Leeds and Hull – were arranged and recorded in February. The subsequent album *Live At Leeds*, released in May 1970, is generally regarded as the seminal live recording by any artist.

June: TOMMY IN NEW YORK

A new single, 'The Seeker', was released in March and *Live At Leeds* in May, before the band returned to the US in June. Having played the European opera houses it was only natural that they should perform at the Metropolitan Opera House in New York. The two shows on 7 June attracted 8,000 fans and sold out within hours of tickets going on sale. No other rock band – before or since – has been allowed to tread the hallowed boards of the Met, and the shows grossed $55,000. Snippets of the performance were broadcast on CBS news reports.

August:
ISLE OF WIGHT FESTIVAL 1970

The Met shows were intended to mark the end of *Tommy* as the focal point of the stage show, and new material was introduced into the act. The relentless touring continued and The Who returned to the Isle Of Wight Festival in August, this time as headliners. The Aquarian festival dream of Monterey and Woodstock had already been destroyed by the darkness of Altamont, and the Isle Of Wight added to this. Fences were torn down, making the concert a free-for-all that resulted in The Who playing to an estimated 600,000 people.

September–December:
EUROPEAN TOUR

The rest of the year continued in a similar vein, with more shows in Europe and the UK. Townshend had, however, begun working on the follow-up to *Tommy*, and the band fitted in recording during the heavy touring schedule throughout the year. Some of the songs, such as 'I Don't Even Know Myself', 'Naked Eye' and 'Water', had made it into the live set, but *Tommy* still dominated. This series of shows, running from September to December, marked the end of the *Tommy* period, as the band embarked on the next project, *Lifehouse*.

December: *TOMMY'S CURTAIN CALL*

A single comprising four new tracks was proposed for release at the end of 1970 but was cancelled, although an EP of *Tommy* tracks was released in November. A week later the band began rehearsals for *Lifehouse*, the ambitious follow-up. *Tommy* had helped the band achieve worldwide stardom and financial stability, but was becoming a millstone around their necks, and the pressure had long been on Townshend to produce a follow-up. The band appeared on the BBC 1 New Year's Eve special *Into '71* performing two songs, neither of which, tellingly, was from *Tommy*.

1971

January–March: *LIFEHOUSE SESSIONS*

Lifehouse was to be a multi-media, multi-sensory experience that would meld fiction with live performance. Well, that was Pete Townshend's intention at least. In December 1970 the press had announced that the band would embark on two film projects: *Tommy* and the provisionally titled *Barrel One And Barrel Two*, which later evolved into *Lifehouse*. In January a press conference was held at the Young Vic Theatre in London, at which Townshend began to outline his story and the interaction with live audiences at a series of experimental shows at the theatre. However, there were machinations going on behind his back of which he was blissfully unaware.

May: ENTWISTLE'S SMASH YOUR HEAD AGAINST THE WALL

Frustrated by the limitations for his own songs within the band, Entwistle became the first member to break ranks and release a solo album. *Smash Your Head Against The Wall* was recorded at the end of 1970, in between *Lifehouse* sessions and other gigs, but was not released until 14 May 1971. It was everything you would expect from a John Entwistle album – morbid, macabre and very humorous. The first of seven solo studio albums by Entwistle, it was not a critical success, but it laid the foundation for the four members to explore their own musical direction in the future.

May-June: LIFEHOUSE SESSIONS PART 2

It's fair to say that Townshend's ideas for *Lifehouse* were way ahead of their time. Visions of 'The Grid' and 'Experience Suits' were pretty accurate predictions of the Internet and virtual reality – but this was 1971 and the technology wasn't as advanced as Pete's imagination. No one other than Townshend seemed to fully grasp the ideas. The Young Vic sessions proved unsatisfactory. Kit Lambert had also been trying to sell a *Tommy* script without Townshend's knowledge, causing a huge rift between the two. Frustrated and depressed, Townshend lost interest and the group reassembled in the studio in May to pick at the bones of the fledgling project.

June: 'WON'T GET FOOLED AGAIN'

The band started to record *Lifehouse* in New York in March. Lambert, though, struggled to mix the tracks back in London, and Glyn Johns, who had assisted Shel Talmy years earlier, was recruited to help. He suggested starting over and in April 'Won't Get Fooled Again' was recorded at Stargroves mobile studio, with additional work done at Olympic and Island studios. The track would eventually close the resultant album, *Who's Next*, running at over eight minutes, but an edited version was released as a single in June and reached No. 9 in the UK charts. In the US the label read 'From the motion picture *Lifehouse*'.

July: DALTREY'S SECOND MARRIAGE

On 19 July 1971 Roger married his long-term girlfriend Heather Taylor, an American model he had met whilst on tour in 1968. The quiet wedding took place near their East Sussex home at Battle Registry Office and was officiated over by the improbably named registrar Daisy Field. This was Daltrey's second marriage; he first tied the knot in March 1964 with Jacqueline Rickman at Wandsworth Registry Office. Although a divorce was applied for in January 1968, it took over two years for it to be granted.

July: US TOUR 1971

The band's reputation as the most exciting live rock'n'roll band had been consolidated by the *Tommy* tours and the release of *Live At Leeds*. As a result The Who were booked to play much larger venues in the US when they returned in July. Opening with two shows at Forest Hills Tennis Stadium, the band seamlessly incorporated the new songs into the set. However, the second show at the venue was marred by the fatal stabbing of an usher. The 12 performances on this leg of the tour grossed over $1.25 million.

August: WHO'S NEXT

Whereas *Lifehouse* failed to work either on stage or in the studio, the album pulled from its remnants is judged by many to be the band's greatest achievement. *Who's Next* was released in the US on 14 August, and it reached No. 14 in the charts. Released in the UK two weeks later, it hit the coveted top spot. The album was an instant hit on US rock radio stations, where its anthemic and innovative compositions proved to be hugely popular. Although dispirited by the rejection of the *Lifehouse* project, Townshend would never turn his back on it, and eventually released *The Lifehouse Chronicles* in 2000.

November: RAINBOW THEATRE GIGS

The band had planned a triumphant return to London with a huge free show in Hyde Park, but the idea was rejected by the authorities. The group did, however, play a show to benefit the Bangladesh relief fund at the Oval Cricket Ground on 18 September. In October they embarked on a short UK tour, culminating in the opening three nights at the Rainbow Theatre in Finsbury Park. The band took to the stage behind a chorus of dancing girls, with Townshend resplendent in a silver boiler suit. With a capacity of 3,500, the venue somehow managed to squeeze in 4,000 each night.

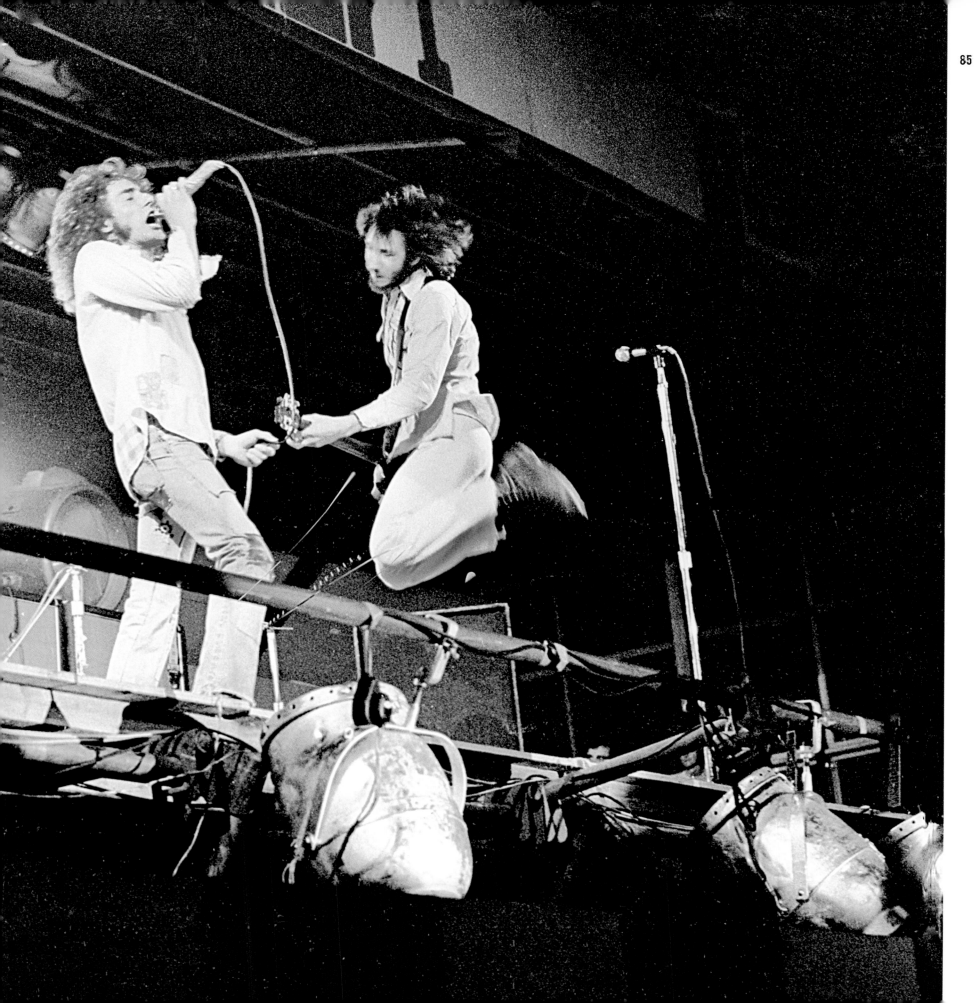

1972

November–December: US ARENA TOUR

The final leg of the 1971 US tour began in North Carolina on 20 November. The West Coast shows resulted in the band breaking box-office records, but also saw Keith Moon leave the Los Angeles area in a wheelchair after deciding to excessively mix brandy and barbiturates. During the next show, in San Francisco, Moon – still visibly suffering – was propped up behind his kit thanks to the occasional morphine injection. The effect was short-lived, though, and the drummer soon returned to his 'usual' self. The shows were recorded and tracks have been released intermittently over the years.

January: PETE'S PILGRIMAGE

Financial stability afforded the opportunity of relaxation after years of unremitting live work. For Townshend in particular, the previous couple of years had been exhausting. He spent much of the first part of 1972 occupying himself with Meher Baba, and in January he travelled to Arangaon, India, where he paid an emotional visit to Baba's tomb, performing Cole Porter's 'Begin The Beguine'. *I Am*, the second album devoted to Baba, was released and included Townshend's original demo for 'Baba O'Riley' as well as an adaptation of 'O Parvardigar', the Avatar's universal prayer. He also recorded a German version for the opening of a European Baba centre.

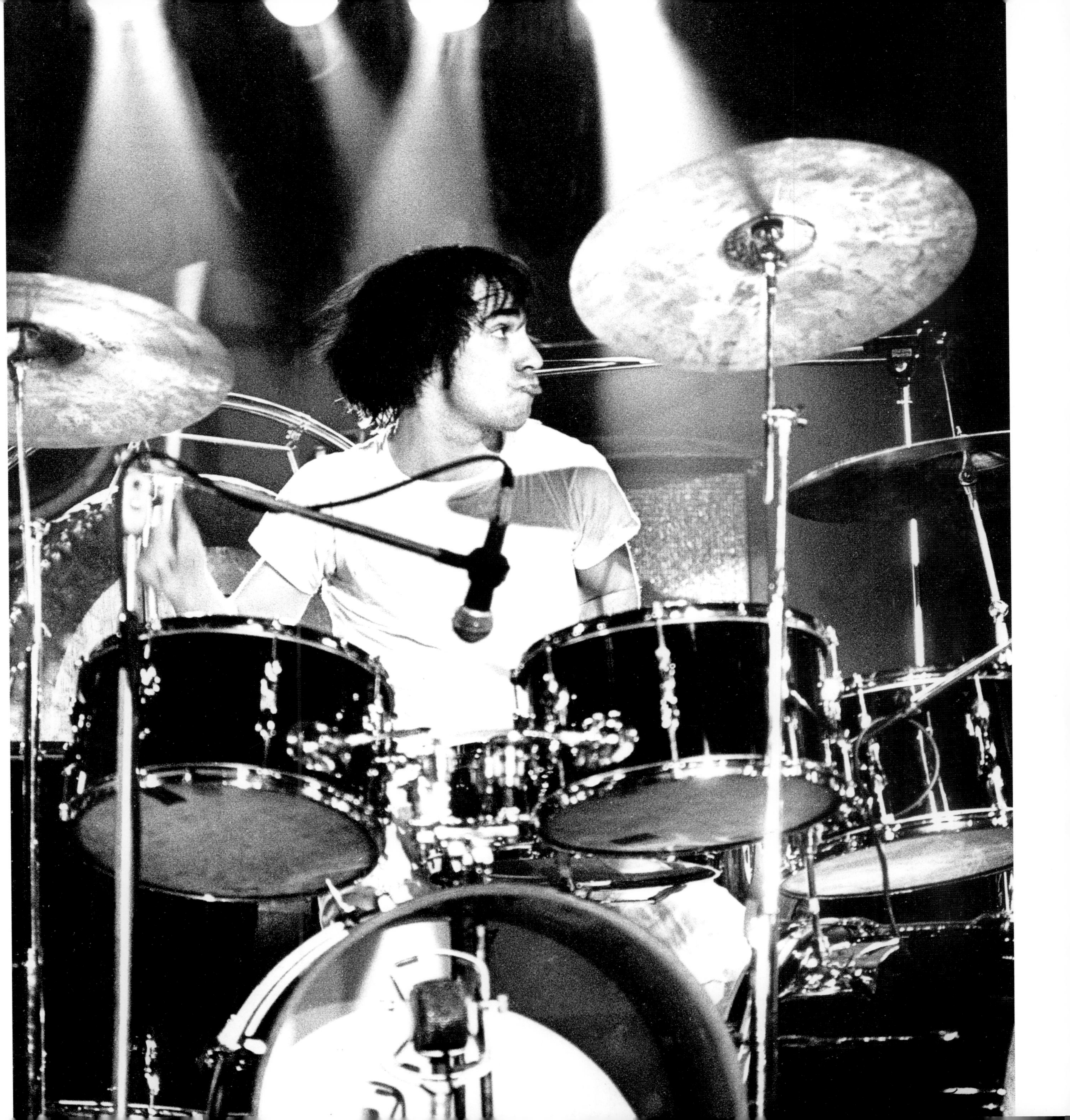

August: EUROPEAN TOUR 1972

The Who returned to the stage for the first time in eight months when they began their first European tour in two years in Germany. They had kept themselves busy with solo activities and the occasional foray into the studio for their new project, provisionally entitled *Rock Is Dead – Long Live Rock*. A single, 'Join Together', was released in June, together with a promotional film shot in front of fan-club members at London Weekend Television studios. The tour took in nine countries in one month.

September: FÊTE DE L'HUMANITÉ

The largest show on the tour took place in Paris, where The Who performed in front of 400,000 people at the annual Fête De L'Humanité at La Courneuve. Whilst people speculated about their political stance – particularly over songs such as 'Won't Get Fooled Again' – the band had never expressed any real political direction. The concert, however, was held by the French Communist Party and The Who took to the stage to a shower of red roses. The performance was filmed and shown the following year during the documentary *Pop Galérie*. A rehabilitating Eric Clapton travelled to the event at Townshend's invitation.

September:
TOWNSHEND'S *WHO CAME FIRST*

Townshend became the second band member to release a solo album when *Who Came First* was launched on 29 September 1972. Ostensibly a devotional album for Meher Baba, the recording also included demos intended for the *Lifehouse* project. Although he called on a few fellow Baba devotees for assistance, the album was a true solo record which saw Pete playing almost all of the instruments, as well as taking on engineering and production duties. This was the first of seven studio albums (excluding live, compilations and the *Scoop* trilogy) and Townshend was to become the most critically successful solo performer within the band.

December: ORCHESTRAL *TOMMY* LIVE

If the band thought that they had seen the back of *Tommy* they were mistaken. Earlier in the year the first approved stage production was mounted at the Aquarius Theatre in LA, after a run at the University of Southern California. Lou Reizner released his orchestral interpretation in November, and on 9 December a star-studded cast – many reprising their roles from the album – appeared in two shows at the Rainbow in aid of the charity SOS. The performances were relocated from the Royal Albert Hall after the management reneged on the booking, citing the 'unsavoury' nature of the subject.

1973

January: ERIC CLAPTON COLLABORATION

As in the previous year, The Who began 1973 in virtual hibernation. Pete Townshend had agreed to help Eric Clapton go through some Derek And The Dominoes tapes a year earlier, but Clapton was engulfed in a heroin addiction at the time, and Townshend now started to take a leading role in helping his friend kick the drug. After 10 days of rehearsals, which Clapton found gruelling, they eventually took to the stage on 13 January for two shows at the Rainbow. Backed by a supergroup that included Townshend, Ron Wood and Steve Winwood, the shows were ostensibly arranged to mark Britain's entry into the Common Market.

April: DALTREY RELEASES *DALTREY*

The unusual period of band inactivity led Roger Daltrey in the direction of his own solo album. Recorded at the start of 1973 and released in April, the eponymous *Daltrey* was the first major solo success for any of the band members, even spawning an unexpected hit single in 'Giving It All Away'. The material was far removed from what he had become accustomed to in The Who, leaning more towards pop. Daltrey saw this more as a learning process to improve his vocal abilities rather than a serious move away from the band he had founded. In all, Daltrey has produced eight solo studio albums.

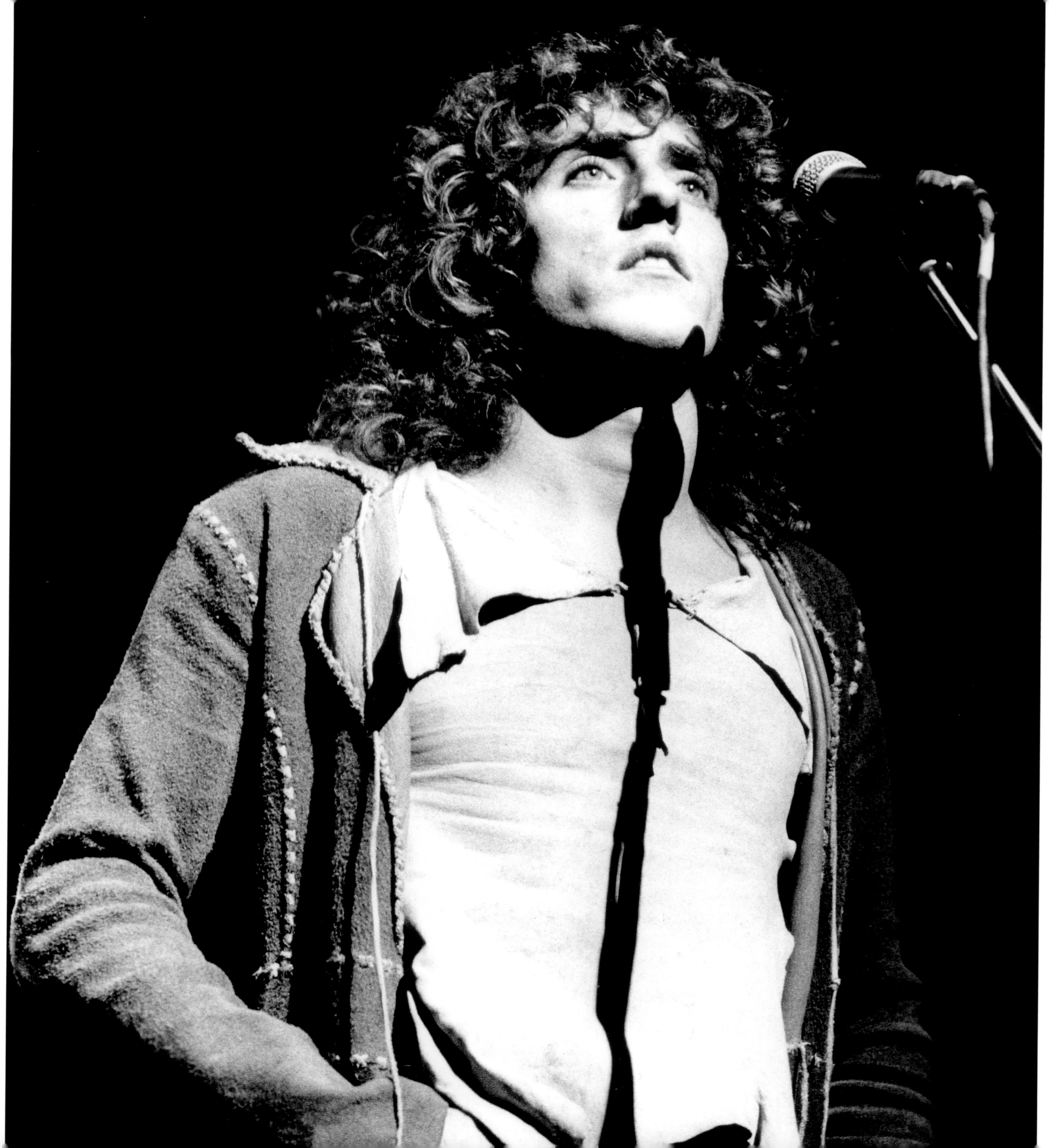

May–June: QUADROPHENIA SESSIONS

The *Rock Is Dead* idea floundered and Townshend reused some of the themes to fashion a new story that harked back to the band's origins. *Quadrophenia* told the tale of a London mod and his quest for identity and salvation. Recording began in May at Ramport Studios, The Who's own studio in Battersea, which was still under construction during these recording sessions. In June they filmed a sequence at the Rainbow Theatre, intended for use as a backdrop to the later live shows. During this period, Ken Russell visited the studio to discuss the film version of *Tommy*, which he would direct the following year.

October: '5.15'

The first fruit of the *Quadrophenia* sessions was the release of '5.15' on 5 October 1973. Two days earlier the band had appeared on the 500th edition of *Top Of The Pops*, a show that would further enhance their hell-raising image. Annoyed by BBC rules, the band ended the performance by destroying the set and, having earlier emptied out the prop room, distributing the contents into the audience. Townshend finished by giving a two-finger salute. It was a tightly edited version that was transmitted the following night. The single reached No. 20 in the charts and the ban the incident had incurred was later lifted.

October–November: 10-DATE TOUR

Rehearsals for the tour were fraught, and at one point Daltrey
felled Townshend with a single punch, sending him to hospital
with amnesia. As before, the band embarked on the tour before
the new album was released. However, unlike *Who's Next,
Quadrophenia* was a complete piece, and the sequence of songs
was interrupted with explanations of the story, which somewhat
stifled the flow. The shows also relied heavily on backing tracks,
which consistently refused to co-operate, leaving soundman Bob
Pridden in an unenviable situation. Tracks were dropped and the
show reworked before the tour reached its climax at London's
Lyceum Theatre.

QUADROPHENIA
QUADROPHENIA
QUADROPHENIA
QUADROPHENIA
WHO
113

November: *QUADROPHENIA*

The album was recorded to a backdrop of uncertainty and frustration. Kit Lambert and Chris Stamp were under scrutiny, and were effectively replaced as managers by Bill Curbishley around this time. Both Entwistle and Daltrey complained about the final mix, as Townshend assumed control over the production, whilst Lambert – who was supposed to be producing – was reduced to bringing in 'trays of food'. Through all this adversity, though, Townshend had produced yet another masterpiece. *Quadrophenia* was released on 2 November in the UK, reaching No. 2 in the charts. In the US it was released a week earlier, and achieved the same position.

November: KEITH COLLAPSES

A week after the chaotic UK tour ended, The Who returned to North America. Here things went from bad to worse. At the opening show in San Francisco, Moon collapsed as a result of imbibing horse tranquilizers with his drink. Midway through the gig, he began to falter and collapsed completely during 'Won't Get Fooled Again'. The band left the stage for 15 minutes, with Moon taking up his post on their return. However, after a brief respite he was once again carried off. Townshend asked for volunteers from the audience, and 19-year-old Scott Halpin finished the show on drums.

December: A DAY IN JAIL

Less than two weeks later, The Who landed in Montreal. High jinks on the plane ended with a warm reception, but things turned decidedly darker after the show. The record company had arranged a party at the Bonaventure Hotel, but here things got out of hand when Moon started destroying artwork, gold discs and pretty much anything else he could lay his hands on. Interior redecoration then took place, with items of unwanted furniture occupying the swimming pool. A night in jail for the entire entourage (minus Daltrey, who had retired early) was the outcome, resulting in them almost missing the next show in Boston.

December: WHO'S CHRISTMAS PARTY?

In December, Roger Daltrey appeared alongside an all-star cast for *Tommy* at the Rainbow. The year finished with three concerts in north London under the banner 'Who's Christmas Party?'. Tickets were sold by mail order only, in an attempt to avoid the chaotic scenes that had taken place when the Lyceum shows were announced. In the two months since the tour began, the *Quadrophenia* element of the show had been reduced by a third, as the band began to fill in with older favourites.

1974

February: TOUR OF FRANCE

The year kicked off with the *Tommy* film soundtrack recording sessions at Ramport. In February these were interrupted by a six-date tour of France, where The Who were supported by long-term Townshend cohort Speedy Keene. On the second date, the doors to the venue had to be opened eight hours early because of the pressure on them from the swell of the crowd, which had already been queuing for hours for the best positions. Only nine songs from *Quadrophenia* remained in the act, and this tour would be the last time it would feature so heavily for 22 years.

April: FILMING BEGINS ON *TOMMY*

During preparations for the film of *Tommy* Pete Townshend immersed himself in the role of musical director, which exacerbated his drinking habits. On 14 April he performed a solo charity show at the Roundhouse, his first public appearance outside the confines of the band. Ken Russell began filming *Tommy* on 22 April at Harefield Grove, Middlesex, and continued until August. This included a specially arranged concert sequence in May at the King's Theatre, Portsmouth, for the 'Pinball Wizard' scene. The band would return to Portsmouth later that month to play a full concert as a thank you to the students who had appeared in the film.

May: CHARLTON FOOTBALL GROUND

Filming had taken up much of the year, but The Who decided to return to the live scene with a performance at Charlton Athletic Football Club on 18 May, where Alan Curbishley – brother of the band's manager Bill – was a player. Billed as Summer of 74, the all-day event attracted a huge audience. The official limit was set at 50,000 but, due to security problems, more than twice that amount crammed into the valley-like amphitheatre. The performance was filmed by the BBC and an edit was shown on *2nd House*, a new arts programme hosted by Melvyn Bragg.

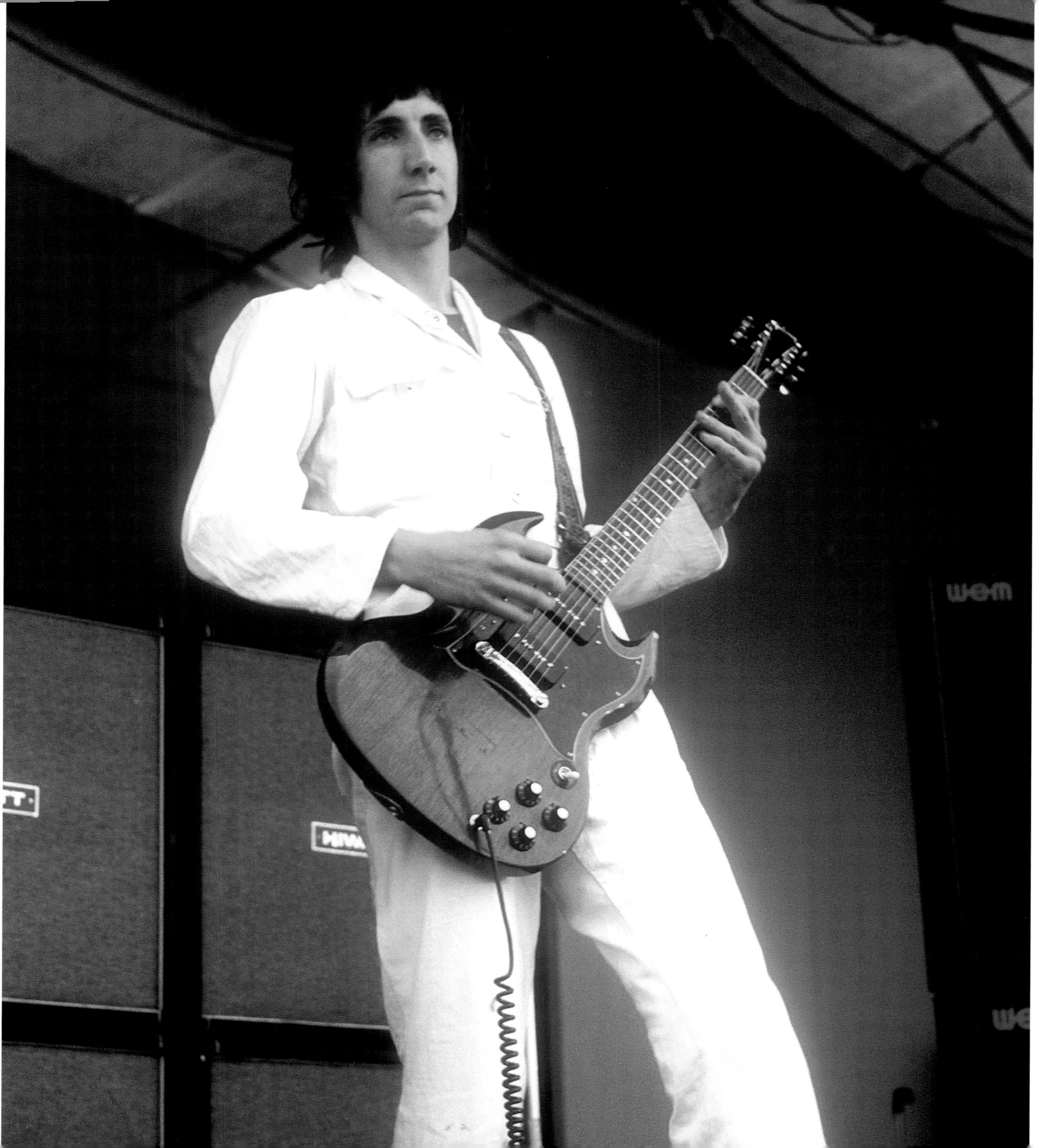
wem

June: MADISON SQUARE GARDEN

The Who also snatched some time between filming *Tommy* to visit New York, their first attendance there in three years, where they played four shows at Madison Square Garden. As far as the band members were concerned, the Charlton show had been a lacklustre affair, and Townshend in particular had suffered, feeling little more than a caricature of his former self. The NYC shows did little to assuage his or the rest of the band's feelings. The penultimate gig finished chaotically, with the audience ready to riot. And the final show saw Townshend smashing three guitars – graciously allowing Moon the pleasure of a fourth.

October: ODDS AND SODS

With Townshend and Daltrey fully occupied on *Tommy*, the rhythm section found themselves with time on their hands. Keith Moon recreated his role as J.D. Clover for the film *Stardust*, and decided to relocate to LA with trusty sidekick 'Dougal' Butler. John Entwistle stayed at home to work on a collection of rarities entitled *Odds And Sods*, which he completed in July. The album was released the following October and included comprehensive notes on each track, written by Townshend. Fed up with the inactivity, Entwistle took his own band, Ox, on the road in December.

1975

March:
MOON RELEASES *TWO SIDES OF THE MOON*

Despite no evident vocal
abilities, having seen
the others release solo
albums Keith Moon
saw no reason why
he shouldn't follow
suit. Recording began
in August 1974 and a
single – 'Don't Worry
Baby' – was released
in the US the following
month. The record
company hated it
and ordered a complete

rethink for the album. The album was originally entitled *Like
A Rat Up A Pipe* but Moon began re-recording *Two Sides Of The
Moon* in November, with up to 60 guest musicians. It was finally
released in the US in March 1975 and in the UK the following
month, but failed to make any impact on the charts.

T the MOVIE mmy

Your senses will never be the same.

Columbia Pictures and Robert Stigwood Present A Film By Ken Russell "Tommy" By The Who Based On The Rock Opera By Pete Townshend
Starring **Ann-Margret** As The Mother **Oliver Reed** As The Lover **Roger Daltrey** As Tommy And Featuring **Elton John** As The Pinball Wizard
Guest Artists **Eric Clapton, John Entwistle, Keith Moon, Paul Nicholas, Jack Nicholson, Robert Powell, Pete Townshend, Tina Turner & The Who**
Associate Producer Harry Benn, Musical Director Pete Townshend, Screenplay By Ken Russell, Executive Producers Beryl Vertue And Christopher Stamp
Produced By Robert Stigwood And Ken Russell, Directed By Ken Russell, Original Soundtrack Album on Polydor Records [   ] and Tapes

March: PREMIERE OF *TOMMY*

In short, the release of *Tommy* the movie was huge. The promotional campaign was unprecedented, and the three US premieres on 19 and 20 March cost $100,000. Showing in just 13 theatres across America, the film grossed $2 million in one month. The European premiere took place at London's Leicester Square Theatre on 25 March and broke box-office records, taking over £26,000 in its first week. In a move ironically reflecting the film's climax, you could buy *Tommy* T-shirts, mirrored badges and other merchandise. 'We're Not Going To Take It' indeed….

April–June: *THE WHO BY NUMBERS SESSIONS*

The band reconvened in April to begin recording the next album, *The Who By Numbers*. The sessions had been due to begin a fortnight earlier, but Moon stayed on in LA longer than planned. Both his and Townshend's drinking had become noticeably worse, and Moon tried to go on the wagon in time for the recordings – but failed. After the success of *Tommy*, Daltrey was away filming *Lisztomania* with Ken Russell, and Entwistle appeared to be the only one ready to rejoin the fold with any enthusiasm. In Daltrey's absence, the other three spent time jamming at Shepperton Studios.

October: *THE WHO BY NUMBERS*

The album was released in October, just in time for the UK tour.
Prior to that, Moon and Entwistle previewed the tracks on John
Peel's show, admitting that they had not heard the final mixes
and that last-minute changes by Pete meant they could be in
for as much of a surprise as the radio audience. The album
reflected Townshend's physical and mental state – with brutally
honest lyrics and almost minimalist arrangements. In contrast,
the chosen single 'Squeeze Box' was a jolly ditty reminiscent
of his ebullient writing a decade earlier.

October: RETURN TO LIVE PERFORMANCE

A three-month tour of Europe and North America started the day the album was released. Initially the band appeared under-rehearsed, but the shows were a marked improvement on the lacklustre ones 18 months earlier, and they picked up pace quickly. The performances reintroduced a large *Tommy* element and marked the debut (at certain venues) of their groundbreaking laser light show. Being The Who, of course, the tour did not pass without incident, and Moon was arrested in Scotland after damaging airline equipment. As a result they were banned from commercial flights and had to charter a jet for the European shows.

December: HAMMERSMITH ODEON

The tour concluded with The Who's Rock'n'Roll Christmas Show, over three nights at Hammersmith Odeon. Demand for tickets was so great that they were allocated by lottery. Those lucky enough to receive tickets were also welcomed with Christmas gifts from the band – balloons, streamers and badges – ensuring a party atmosphere. Moon descended onto the stage via harness from the gods. The tour proved once and for all that The Who was the rightful keeper of the title 'The Greatest Rock'n'Roll Band in the World', and they played with a renewed vigour and enthusiasm.

1976

February: *BY NUMBERS* TOUR

The previous year had re-established The Who's reputation as *the* premier live band. At the start of 1976 Townshend undertook a second pilgrimage to Meher Baba's tomb, while a deteriorating Moon was admitted to hospital after suffering an epileptic fit caused by alcohol withdrawal. Mirroring events 10 years earlier, the band members also found themselves tied up in legal matters, this time with Kit Lambert and Chris Stamp, who had filed court papers against them. Consequently, the reliance on live work dominated once again. At the end of February the *By Numbers* tour continued for a few dates in Europe.

March: KEITH'S SECOND COLLAPSE

The European shows were followed by a further trip to the States, where the band would spend much of the year. Here, history repeated itself, and the opening night of the tour in Boston proved memorable for the wrong reasons. During the second song, Moon collapsed behind his kit and had to be removed from the stage. Unlike in San Francisco, though, no volunteers were sought as a replacement and the show was cancelled, causing riotous behaviour from the crowd. At the time, the publicity machine gave out that Moon was suffering from flu, but this is unlikely to have been the real cause of his collapse.

March: THE TOUR CONTINUES

The second show of the tour was put back a day to allow Moon to recover, and they took to the stage once again at Madison Square Garden on 11 March. The drummer found himself the centre of attention but played as if nothing had happened. Standing ovations and ecstatic reviews followed, and this became the norm for the rest of the tour, as American cities welcomed the band with open arms. However, Moon's downward spiral – which began with the death of Neil Boland and intensified with his break-up from Kim – was becoming more evident.

June: WHO PUT THE BOOT IN CONCERTS

Having helped pioneer stadium rock in the US, The Who arranged three huge shows back in the UK, playing at football stadia under the banner Who Put The Boot In. The mini-tour opened on 31 May with a return to Charlton Athletic and the show earned the band the title of 'World's Loudest Pop Group' in the *Guinness Book Of Records*, although the event was spoiled by overcrowding and violence. The other shows took place in Glasgow and Swansea, the latter marking the last time Keith Moon would play with The Who on home turf before a paying audience.

August–October: US AND CANADA TOUR

The second tour of North America began in August. Moon's health was still a major cause for concern, and he was hospitalized in Miami for eight days after collapsing in his hotel room, suffering from 'nervous exhaustion'. He later admitted that his drinking had become out of hand and that he was trying to cut back on doctor's orders. Unlike previous tours, the shows didn't sell out, mainly because of high ticket prices, but this did not stop the band from putting in some of their best performances. The tour concluded in Toronto on 21 October, a gig that fatefully marked Moon's curtain call.

1977

December: KILBURN STUDIOS

After a 14-month live-show hiatus, The Who agreed to stage a show that would be filmed for *The Kids Are Alright* documentary, which had begun production some six months earlier. The show was announced at the last minute and a single mention on Capital Radio resulted in over 800 fans turning up within half an hour of broadcast. Accounts say that the band was rusty and under-rehearsed but pretty 'well-oiled'. Little of the footage was used in the film, although when finally released 30 years later it showed, with hindsight, that the critics had been a little harsh in their reviews.

1978

May: LAST SHOW WITH MOON

Disappointed with the results at Kilburn, director Jeff Stein requested a further shot at capturing the band's live prowess on film. On 25 May the cameras once again rolled as the band performed a private show at Shepperton Studios. Originally scheduled for just three numbers, the band went on to play a complete show, on much better form. The audience, which included members of The Sex Pistols, The Rich Kids and The Pretenders, not only witnessed the band firing on all four cylinders but were also, unknowingly, watching the last show at which the original members would ever perform together.

July: 'WHO ARE YOU'

The first new material in almost three years hit the shops on 14 July with the release of the single 'Who Are You'. Moon had returned to live in Britain and, with the film wrapping up and a new album in the can, the band's future looked assured for the first time in a number of years. On 1 August Townshend and Moon attended 'Who's Who', an exhibition at the ICA to mark the group's 15th anniversary. It was a bittersweet event, as the news filtered through that Pete Meaden, the influential figurehead from those early days, had died a few days previously, aged just 36.

August: WHO ARE YOU

Recording for the album had commenced the previous September but turned out to be a prolonged affair. Townshend had publicly stated that he no longer wished to undergo long tours with the band. Moon moved back to London but was woefully out of shape in the studio. Entwistle provided three songs for the album, a contribution that underlined Townshend's growing disenchantment. Daltrey took his frustrations out on Glyn Johns, who he insisted was overproducing the record. Released almost a year after the sessions began, the cover shows Moon sitting in a chair marked 'Not To Be Taken Away'.

September: QUADROPHENIA FILMING BEGINS

Production on the long-awaited celluloid version of *Quadrophenia* had started earlier in the year when Bill Curbishley picked up the reins from Chris Stamp. After considering various directors he settled for Franc Roddam, who had impressed him with his work on TV. Although none of the band was to star in the film, the image and sound of The Who would loom large. Virtually unknown actors were cast in the roles and *New Musical Express* ran competitions for fans to star as extras. The soundtrack was overseen by Entwistle, Daltrey and Townshend as musical directors.

September: DEATH OF KEITH MOON

Seemingly having more lives than the proverbial cat, Keith Moon finally succumbed to his excesses on 7 September. Having attended the premiere of *The Buddy Holly Story* in London, Moon and his girlfriend, Annette Walter-Lax, left the event early to return to their rented flat in Mayfair. He retired after taking Heminevrin, which had been prescribed to help kick his alcohol addiction. At 3.40 p.m. Annette found him dead. An open verdict was recorded at the inquest 11 days later, as there was no reason to suspect suicide even though he had taken 32 sedatives. Rock music had lost the best 'Keith Moon type drummer in the world'.

THE WHO REMIXED: 1979-82

1979-82

The band's decision to continue, with Kenney Jones on drums, raised a few eyebrows. At first they proved the sceptics wrong by demonstrating that The Who were still an unstoppable live force. The honeymoon period came to an abrupt halt at the end of 1979, however, when tragedy struck in Cincinnati and 11 fans died.

The new line-up released two albums but neither received the critical acclaim of the group's previous efforts. They also invested heavily in the British film industry, releasing three movies, starting with the biopic *The Kids Are Alright*. Further successes came with a screen adaptation of *Quadrophenia* and *McVicar*, the story of one of Britain's most notorious gangsters. Daltrey carved out a respectable acting career as a sideline. Meanwhile, Townshend had started using drugs regularly and was drinking to excess. He seemed intent on emulating Moon's 'hellraiser' reputation, and ended up in hospital after taking a near-lethal cocktail of drugs. Entwistle and Jones had their share of personal issues too, as their marriages dissolved.

A radical shake-up was needed, and Townshend entered rehab. Tensions within the band resurfaced and Daltrey vented his frustrations towards Jones, making for unworkable relationships. Daltrey also believed that Townshend was sacrificing The Who in favour of his own solo work. A crisis meeting was held at Bill Curbishley's house, at which they discussed shutting down the band in 1983. As events progressed, though, it became clear that closure would take place earlier than expected.

1979

January: KENNEY JONES JOINS THE WHO

The Who without Keith Moon was hard to imagine. No other drummer in the history of rock music had treated the drums so badly and yet played them so well, turning them into a lead instrument. He was surely an impossible act to follow. Daltrey, Townshend and Entwistle thought otherwise, and quickly decided that they would continue. In December 1978 they announced that Kenney Jones, a long-time friend and ex-Small Faces drummer, would join the band as a permanent member.

May: LIVE AT THE RAINBOW

The Rainbow Theatre in Finsbury Park was the unassuming venue chosen for the debut of new Who, eight months after Keith Moon's death. Although the choice of Jones had been questioned in some circles, their arrival back on the live stage was eagerly anticipated. The mod revival was peaking, and the streets around the venue were speckled with scooters and fishtail parkas – and a whole new audience. Alongside Jones, John 'Rabbit' Bundrick completed the new line-up on keyboards. Some of the faces may have changed but on stage it appeared that very little had, as the band ripped through their back catalogue.

June: THE SECRET POLICEMAN'S BALL

At the end of June Pete Townshend appeared at Amnesty International's 'Secret Policeman's Ball' at Her Majesty's Theatre in London. An inebriated Townshend performed two solo numbers, 'Pinball Wizard' and 'Drowned', before being joined by classical guitarist John Williams for 'Won't Get Fooled Again'. The following month he put in an appearance with a one-off band at the 'Rock Against Racism' show at the Rainbow, which raised funds for the legal defence of youths arrested at an anti-racism demonstration in London.

June: THE KIDS ARE ALRIGHT

The film biopic had endured a tortuous production schedule and turned out to be an unhappy shoot for everyone involved, resulting in accusations and counter-accusations for years to follow. With Moon's death, however, it also acted as a tribute to a man whose antics had provided the newspapers with countless headlines. The film reinforced what many of them had missed – that Moon's talent outshone those often-lurid stories. Its London premiere in June saw a crowd of 4,000 gathered outside the Rialto Cinema.

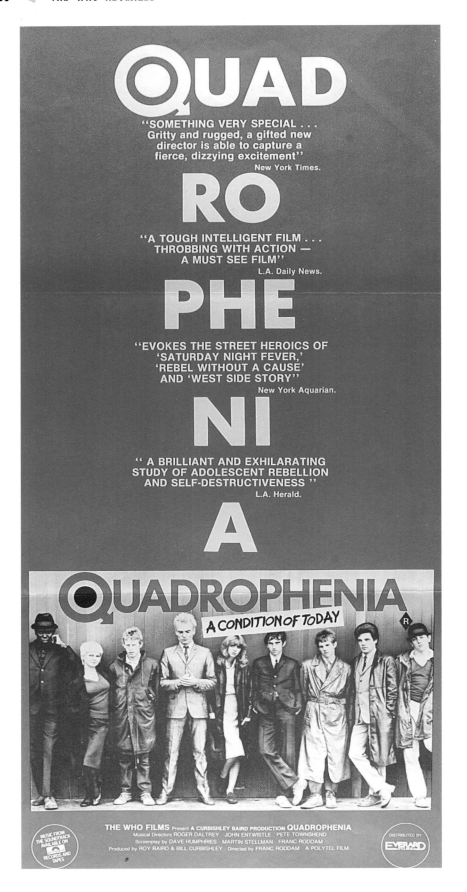

August: QUADROPHENIA FILM RELEASED

Three months later, The Who Films released their next venture, *Quadrophenia*. The fruits of the band's investment in the British Film Industry were beginning to show, and *Quadrophenia* was released with perfect timing, catching the *zeitgeist* of the mod revival gripping the UK. Bands such as The Jam and The Lambrettas appeared in the charts, ensuring a ready-made audience for Townshend's tale of teenage angst. A huge hit in UK cinemas, its transition across the pond was less successful than that of its predecessor, due mainly to the leading characters' broad cockney accents.

August: HEADLINING AT WEMBLEY

To celebrate the new line-up and a return to the road, the band played a huge show at Wembley Stadium on the August bank holiday weekend, supported by AC/DC, The Stranglers and Nils Lofgren. Tickets were priced at £8. The band played well enough, but the cavernous stadium, together with nitpicking local council officials, did little to help. The state-of-the-art sound system had limitations placed on it by the Greater London Council, as did the planned laser show. This was probably a result of The Who's open-air show at Charlton in 1976, at which the band had contravened numerous by-laws.

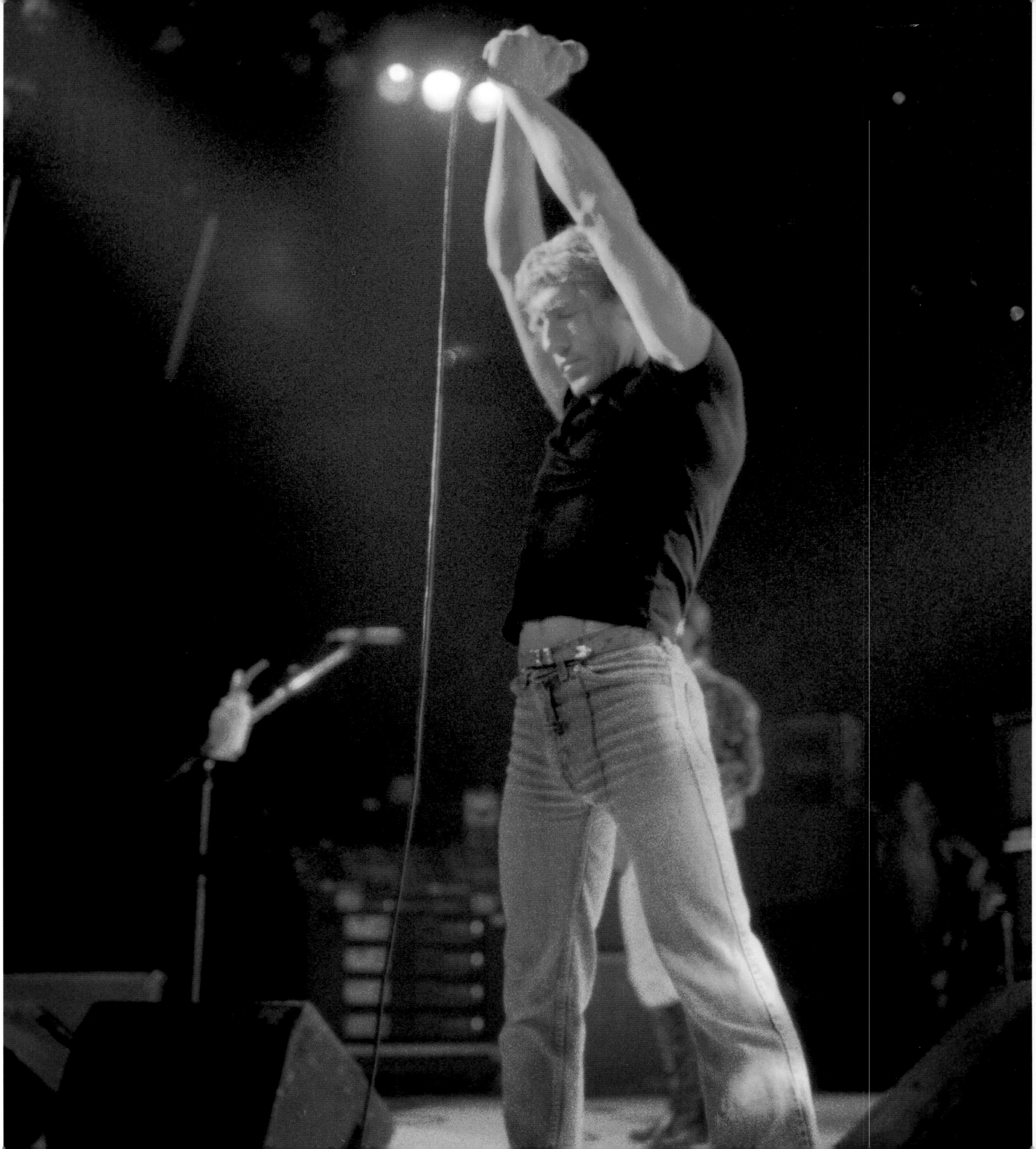

September: FIVE NIGHTS IN NEW YORK

The following month The Who returned triumphantly to the US for seven shows, five of them at Madison Square Garden. Demand for the shows meant that all 100,000 tickets for the New York performances sold out in record time, and the last show culminated in a pie fight on stage. In November they performed a few low-key dates back in the UK before embarking on the second leg of the US tour, kicking off in Detroit, where the band had begun their US love affair in 1967.

December: TRAGEDY IN CINCINNATI

Three shows in – on 3 December – the tour stopped off at the Riverfront Coliseum in Cincinnati. A large crowd had gathered in the early afternoon because much of the venue was general admission, with no reserved seating. When the doors opened the crowd pushed forward, causing mayhem and tragically resulting in 11 fans being trampled to death. Unaware of what had happened, the band performed the full gig, and were only informed of the situation afterwards. At the next show, Roger Daltrey commented, 'We lost a lot of family yesterday. This show's for them.' It was a sad end to a year that had begun with so much promise.

1980

December: CONCERT FOR KAMPUCHEA

Three weeks after the Cincinnati disaster, The Who played one night at the Hammersmith Odeon as part of the week-long Concerts For The People Of Kampuchea. Arguably the best gig the band played in the UK during the Kenney Jones era, the show could just as easily have ended in another tragedy. Daltrey, commenting that the audience seemed a long way away (author's note: they weren't, I was in the front row), 'invited' them on to the stage. With bodies clambering, people scrambling and security in a panic, the singer realized his folly and told everyone to return to their seats.

March: EUROPEAN TOUR

The concerts the year before had gained critical acclaim. The new line-up, complemented by a horn section, had allowed the band to be less structured on stage, and they set off on another short European jaunt in March. This time, though, the band return to a more rigid set list and some of the previous opportunities for improvisation had disappeared. Off stage, Pete Townshend picked up where Keith Moon had left off and began to party heavily – delving deeper into the world of drugs and alcohol. He also moved into a new flat in King's Road rather than return to his Twickenham family home.

April: TOWNSHEND'S *EMPTY GLASS*

The ailing songwriter released *Empty Glass* in April 1980. Whereas his previous solo efforts – *Who Came First* and *Rough Mix* – were collaborations or devotional in nature, this one was full of new Townshend compositions that were powerful, emotional and honest, highlighting his own demons and struggles. The album had been written over the previous two years and represented a move away from his traditional writing for the band, although its release would cause a disturbance within it. A single, 'Let My Love Open The Door', became a Top 10 hit in the US. Townshend dedicated the album to his wife Karen.

April–July: TOUR OF THE US AND CANADA

The opening show of the North American tour, on 14 April, coincided with the UK release of *Empty Glass*. That show at the PNE Coliseum in Vancouver reportedly received enough requests to fill 3.2 million seats (with only 16,000 available) and was a testament to the band's box-office credentials. The venue owners even applied to have it included in the *Guinness Book Of Records* as the largest mail-order response to a single music event. Townshend's drug use became noticeable on stage during the tour, causing performances that were both erratic and brilliant.

1981

January–March: LONGEST UK TOUR

Despite Townshend's difficulties, the band announced their longest-ever UK tour beginning in January. Although they could fill the largest venues in the world they chose to play smaller ones at home, and visited towns that had often been missed off their previous itineraries. With a new album about to be released, the set list was reworked to include the first new material for three years. At a charity show at the Rainbow in aid of victims of domestic violence, Townshend's unpredictability came to the fore as he played extended solos and harangued the audience, prompting the others to storm off stage.

March: *TOP OF THE POPS*

A single from the forthcoming album was released in February. 'You Better You Bet' was coupled with the John Entwistle composition 'The Quiet One', and became the band's last single to make the Top 10 in the UK. A black-and-white video of the band performing the single in the studio was released, and became the fourth video to appear on the fledgling MTV network. The band made a rare appearance on *Top Of The Pops* miming to the track on 5 March, a day before the release of the album *Face Dances*.

March: *FACE DANCES*

The Who had signed a three-album deal with Warner Brothers as part of a $12 million contract. The first of these three albums, *Face Dances*, reached No. 2 in the UK charts and No. 4 in the US when released there a month later. Recording, however, was not an enjoyable affair. As well as Townshend's problems, both Entwistle and Jones were watching their marriages dissolve and were also partial to the lure of the bottle. Daltrey, conversely, was riding a wave of success for his acclaimed film characterization of the eponymous villain McVicar. But he was critical of Townshend, believing that some of his better work appeared on *Empty Glass* rather than The Who's latest offering.

March: ESSEN GRUGAHALLE IS TELEVISED

Amidst rumours of a split, the UK tour continued. A further date in Germany on 28 March saw their performance broadcast live across Europe as part of *Rockpalast*, a popular TV programme, to an estimated 50 million people. A full European tour in May was mooted but Townshend had already told Bill Curbishley that he would not participate. On 7 April Kit Lambert was found dead, a fall down the stairs of his mother's home resulting in a brain haemorrhage. The following month, an inebriated Townshend performed in London at the culmination of the People's March For Jobs campaign.

1982

September: *IT'S HARD*

It was an apt title for a band on the verge of collapse. The previous September, almost exactly three years to the day that Moon had died, Pete Townshend was rushed to hospital as a result of taking heroin. Only the quick reactions of his driver, Paul Bonnick, saved him. He was a mess and decided that he needed treatment, so he moved back in with Karen before checking into a Californian clinic. The band held a crisis meeting and decided to release two more albums before dissolving the band. In fact, only one more album saw the light of day. *It's Hard* was released in September 1982.

September: BIRMINGHAM GIGS

Pete managed to clean himself up for the recording sessions and the upcoming tour. He even managed to fit in a solo charity performance at the Dominion Theatre, where he looked fit and confident. He also released another solo album. In September, The Who booked two nights at the NEC arena in Birmingham to loosen up for the forthcoming US tour. It had, after all, been almost 18 months since their last live performance together at Essen. The shows were competent, highlighting songs from the latest album as well as signalling Daltrey's return as a guitarist for the first time in 20 years.

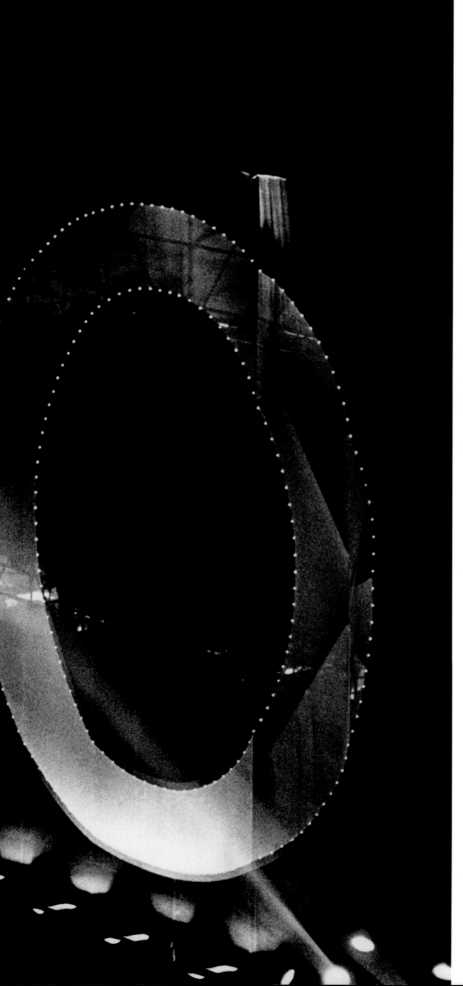

September–December:

FAREWELL TOUR IN THE US

On 22 September the band returned to North America for what
was to be their final tour. On stage the magic was still there,
but backstage the tensions were as evident as ever. Surprisingly,
in light of Townshend's alcoholism, the tour was sponsored by
Schlitz beer. The 40-date term smashed box-office records and
included two nights at Shea Stadium, where they were supported
by The Clash. The final show took place at the Maple Leaf
Garden, Toronto, and was beamed live as a pay-to-view event
across the continent, as well as being released later as
a live album. The Who had left the building.

1985– PRESENT

After the farewell tour of 1982, Pete Townshend made it clear that he wanted out of the band and a complete break-up followed. Despite misgivings, they agreed to play Live Aid in the summer of 1985 and, although a messy affair, the gig did get the band talking again and the subject of 25th anniversary celebrations were raised. No more was said for a further two years, until Townshend – of all people – resurrected the idea.

Becoming aware of the dire financial situation his long-time friend John Entwistle found himself in, as well as acknowledging his own money problems, Townshend agreed to a small tour. The lucrative *The Kids Are Alright* tour eventually took in 40 shows and afforded the opportunity for philanthropy, with charity performances of *Tommy* in the US and UK. At Daltrey's insistence, Kenney Jones was replaced on drums.

Once the tour was over the three surviving members once again retreated to their solo activities. The Nineties saw the emergence of Britpop, and with it a new respect for The Who. This resulted in a charity performance of *Quadrophenia* at Hyde Park in 1996, and the members enjoyed the experience enough to take the production on the road. They returned to full active duty in 1999 and have been touring regularly ever since. An album, *Endless Wire*, was released in 2006 and marked the first recording of new material for 24 years.

1985

July: LIVE AID

Two and a half years after the final show of their farewell tour, The Who reunited to play Live Aid at Wembley Stadium on 13 July 1985. The worldwide event, masterminded by Bob Geldof's Band Aid charity, was to raise money for famine relief in Ethiopia. The band's four-song performance was little short of shambolic at times, and was completely under-rehearsed. The live TV transmission failed during their set for the only time during the day, but somehow it all felt right. Never let it be said that The Who ever did anything the easy way.

1988

February: BPI LIFETIME ACHIEVEMENT AWARD

Live Aid would prove to be the band's only live outing for a further three years. They once again reunited on 8 February 1988 to receive the Lifetime Achievement Award from the British Phonographic Industry. The ceremony, at the Royal Albert Hall, included a three-song set comprising 'My Generation', 'Substitute' and 'Who Are You'. Again the performance was rough, the band over-ran their allotted time and the TV transmission was cut short to accommodate the nine o'clock news. The shambles was typical of the whole ceremony that year, though. The performance was notable as being Kenney Jones's last one with the band.

1989

June–September: 25TH ANNIVERSARY TOUR

The Who reformed for a lucrative tour to celebrate their 25th anniversary and the 20th anniversary of the release of *Tommy*. The US leg saw them perform 40 shows over four months and play to capacity crowds. In New Jersey alone they played to nigh on a quarter of a million people over four nights, grossing $5 million. Kenney Jones was replaced on drums by Simon Phillips, and the band employed a further 11 musicians to boost the sound. Two charity performances of *Tommy* also took place. In Tacoma Townshend damaged his hand and the band finished the show without him.

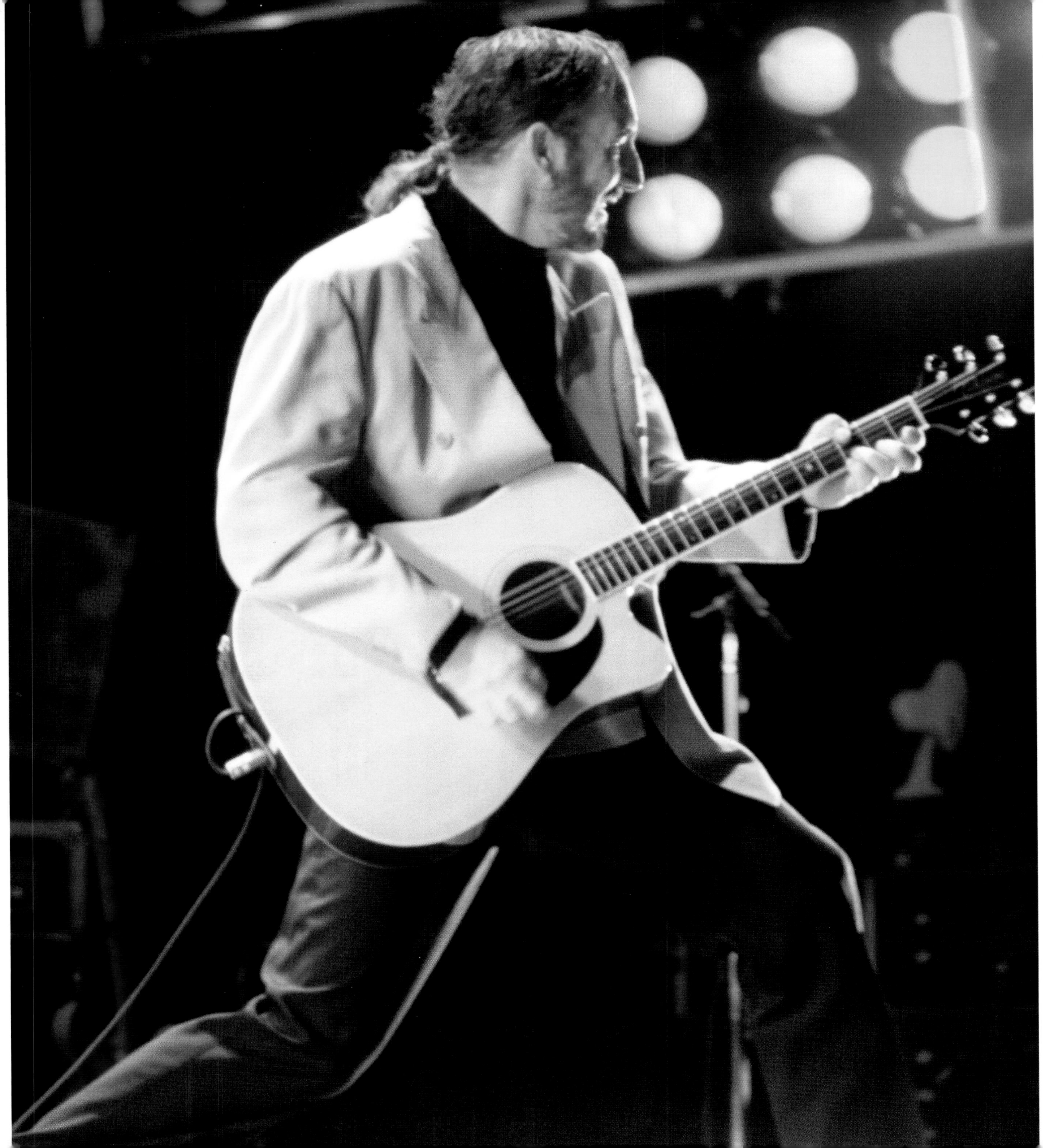

October: RETURN TO THE UK LIVE

For the UK leg they played a four-night stand at the Birmingham NEC, followed by four nights at Wembley. Two charity performances of *Tommy* at the Royal Albert Hall concluded the tour. Although Townshend admitted they did the tour for the money, it is hard to deny that the band gave the audiences value for theirs. Most shows on *The Kids Are Alright* tour clocked in at three hours plus, and included songs never played before or since. Each founder member was given space to perform solo or cover material and, unusually for The Who, they had rehearsed around 70 songs.

1990

January: ROCK AND ROLL HALL OF FAME

The band was inducted to the Rock And Roll Hall Of Fame in New York on 11 January, and during the evening they performed 'Pinball Wizard'. All three members were present, and after two fairly strange speeches by Daltrey and Entwistle, Mandy Moon, Keith's daughter, accepted on behalf of her father. Pete Townshend's speech was articulate and heartfelt, and ended with him saying that he did not know where the future lay for the band but – referring to the music around him – tellingly said: 'It's not up to us to try to understand it. It's not even up to us to buy it. We just need to get the fuck out of the way.' And that's exactly what The Who did.

1993

April: TOMMY ON BROADWAY

Townshend had adapted his *Iron Man* album for the stage in the late 1980s, and decided to work with director Des McAnuff on a new stage version of *Tommy*. The show debuted in July 1992 at the La Jolla Playhouse in San Diego. It moved to Broadway the following year, where it premiered at the St James Theatre on 22 April. The show was a box-office smash, picking up many awards, and ran for over two years. In the same year, Townshend made his first solo tour of the US in support of his *Psychoderelict* album.

1994

March: *THIRTY YEARS OF MAXIMUM R&B*

To all intents and purposes The Who was dead. Roger Daltrey did his best to keep the flame alight, but Pete Townshend attempted to blow it out at every opportunity. Their back catalogue had suffered badly at the hands of record executives looking to make a quick buck from compilations, and their legacy appeared in danger. Journalist and long-time fan Chris Charlesworth took action and talked the band, management and record company into allowing him to compile a four-CD retrospective of their stage and studio recordings. The acclaimed box set was well received and helped to reignite interest.

1995

February: *LIVE AT LEEDS REMASTERED*

The box set was the trigger for all the band's albums to be re-released with additional tracks. The first one to receive this treatment was also probably the most anticipated. *Live At Leeds* remixed and remastered was released in February 1995, and contained the entire show from Leeds with the exception of *Tommy* (which followed in a further release in 2001). The record companies had realized that fans wanted quality as well as quantity, and produced immaculate packaging to match the product. Although the reissue programme was to have its detractors, it proved to be a success.

1996

September: THE WHO FAN CONVENTION

The Who's old haunt of Shepherd's Bush was an apt area to hold the UK's first fan convention. A group of six English fans spent 12 months putting together the day-long event at the Bottom Line, which culminated in a two-hour performance by Roger Daltrey and John Entwistle, together with Zak Starkey and Simon Townshend. The large audience of fans from around the world, including the cream of the contemporary Britpop scene such as Noel Gallagher and Elastica, witnessed a gig that turned out to be the catalyst for the band reuniting and returning to the stage with *Quadrophenia* a few months later.

March: TOMMY ON THE LONDON STAGE

After the success of *Tommy* on Broadway, Pete Townshend moved the production to London's West End, where it opened at the Shaftesbury Theatre on 5 March. During rehearsals in North Acton, Pete took time out to give a lengthy interview to *Naked Eye* fanzine, in which he spoke about the production and The Who in what was his most revealing dialogue in a long time. The show emulated its success on Broadway, garnering many theatre awards, with the *Independent* labelling it 'a brave, outlandish, unmissable show'. It ran at the Shaftesbury until 8 February 1997.

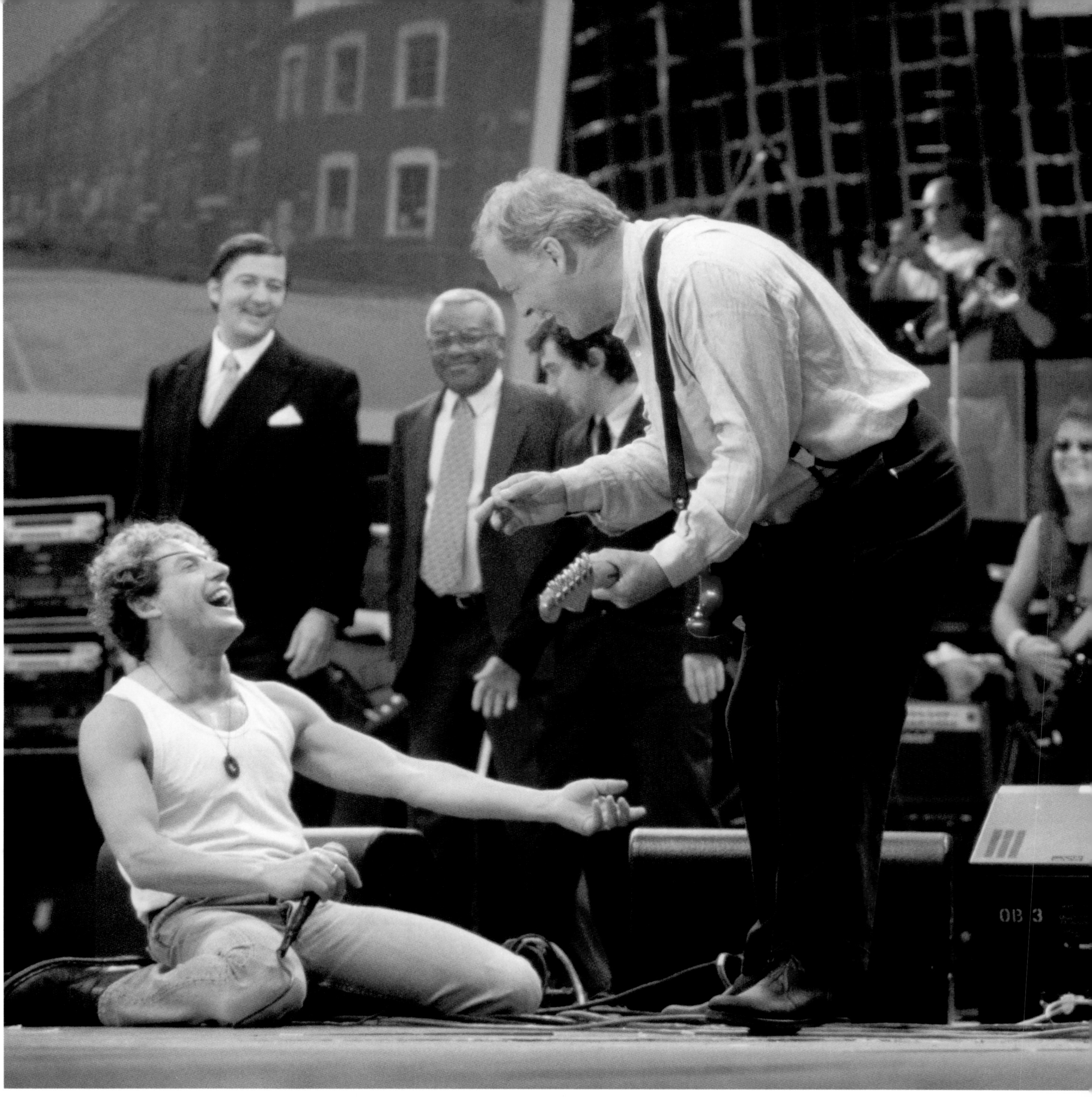
OB 3

June: QUADROPHENIA IN HYDE PARK

The Who reunited to perform *Quadrophenia* for The Prince's Trust charity in Hyde Park on 29 June 1996. However, at no stage was the band's name mentioned in the advertising or on stage. It was simply billed as *Quadrophenia*. It was, however, performed by an all-star band that included Townshend, Entwistle and Daltrey (TED for short), as well as Zak Starkey and Simon Townshend, amongst others. It was the first time that the band had attempted the piece in its entirety live. The day-long event also included performances by Bob Dylan and Eric Clapton.

October: *QUADROPHENIA ON THE ROAD*

Although the Hyde Park show was initially planned as a one-off event, it sparked a six-night residency at Madison Square Garden in the band's spiritual home of New York. The success of those shows convinced the band – still nameless at this point – to take the production on the road. Not using their name posed problems for local promoters trying to sell seats, however, and some resorted to producing posters with 'The Who' boldly emblazoned across them. Townshend, now suffering hearing problems, mainly played acoustic guitar, although he progressed to electric as the tour went on.

1997

April–August: *QUADROPHENIA CRAZY*

Quadrophenia went back on the road the following year. Tour itineraries had been produced under the subtitle TED In The Shed but it was decided that the tour would continue under the name of The Who. The 1997 production was smaller than that of the previous year and included a change in guest stars, with Gary Glitter and Billy Idol replaced by P.J. Proby and Ben Waters. Kicking off with some European shows in April, the band continued through to August, finishing in Florida. In total they performed the piece at over 70 concerts in a 14-month period.

1999

October–November: BACK IN THE USA

The Who returned to the stage in October 1999, with five shows in the US that mixed charity with a lucrative payday. They had slimmed down to a five-piece, with Zak Starkey on drums and John 'Rabbit' Bundrick continuing on keyboards, a seat he had occupied since 1979. The band played two shows in California as part of Neil Young's annual Bridge School benefit concert, followed by two shows in Chicago in aid of the Maryville Academy. Prior to these they performed at the MGM Grand in Las Vegas as part of an elaborate launch for start-up Internet company Pixelon.

2001

December: BACK IN THE UK

Encouraged by the reaction to the US concerts, the group announced two Christmas shows back in London at the Shepherd's Bush Empire. These performances were a return to form – and noticeably louder than the *Quadrophenia* tours, with Townshend predominantly playing electric guitar throughout the show. The venue was packed to the rafters on both evenings and there was an edge both on stage and in the audience, with the first show culminating in Townshend smashing a guitar. Although all three founder members were under the weather with flu, the gigs are acknowledged as the beginning of The Who renaissance.

October: CONCERT FOR NEW YORK

In the aftermath of the 9/11 tragedy in New York City, The Who showed their affiliation to the American people by performing at the Madison Square Garden benefit show the following month. The band delivered an emotionally charged, powerhouse performance of four tracks, which was undoubtedly the highlight of the whole event. Regular Townshend collaborator Jon Carin stood in for Bundrick on keyboards for the show. Coincidentally, Pete Townshend had been due to fly to New York on 12 September to collect the Yahoo Internet Pioneer Award for his website.

2002

January–February: CHARITY GIGS

The year began on a bright note, with the announcement of two shows at the Royal Albert Hall in aid of the Teenage Cancer Trust, together with three warm-up shows, the first of which saw Townshend destroy his guitar and throw it to his son, watching from the front row. In June the band reconvened at Townshend's Oceanic Studio for tour rehearsals, which included two new compositions as well as outings for some rarely played older tunes. Some of the rehearsals were streamed live on Townshend's website. This was to be the last time that John Entwistle would play with the band.

June: JOHN ENTWISTLE DIES

John Entwistle, whose constitution had earned him the nickname of 'The Ox', died of a heart attack in his room at the Hard Rock hotel, the night before the band was due to open its North American tour at The Joint, in the very same hotel. The tour commenced instead on 1 July at the Hollywood Bowl, after a difficult and sad weekend of rehearsals in Burbank, for which Pino Palladino was drafted in on bass. As with the death of Keith Moon, the tabloids concentrated on the more lurid details of John's death, often overlooking his sublime artistry as a musician.

July: US TOUR BEGINS

The band continued the tour in the shadow of John's death, with 27 concerts in North America spread over four visits between July and September. The shows were understandably emotionally charged, as Daltrey and Townshend came to terms with the loss of their childhood friend. After the first leg, the band returned to the UK for Entwistle's funeral, which took place on 10 July in his home village of Stow on the Wold. The tour finished in Toronto, the location of the band's final show in 1982 before they split. A similar feeling of finality surrounded them this time.

2003

May: TOWNSHEND'S POLICE CAUTION

On 11 January 2003 the *Daily Mail* newspaper published an article linking an unnamed rock star with child pornography. Pete Townshend immediately issued a statement saying that it was him the article referred to, and that he had visited a site as research for a book he was writing. He stated he had informed the police and various child-protection agencies of his intentions. Two days later the police took away all Townshend's computers for analysis but, after a lengthy investigation, found no evidence to convict. On 7 May he was told that he would face no charges, but he accepted a formal caution.

2004

June: THIRD TIME AT THE ISLE OF WIGHT

The Isle of Wight Festival had resumed in 2002 after a break of 32 years, and The Who returned to play their third gig there on 12 June 2004. The 35,000-strong audience was far smaller than the 600,000 that had witnessed their last visit to the island in 1970. A strong supporting bill, including Manic Street Preachers and Jet, meant that they needed to be at the top of their game. The band did not disappoint – proving that they could still command and satisfy large outdoor audiences as well as indoor arenas.

2005

July: JAPAN AND AUSTRALIA

The Who played 19 shows in 2004, and after the Isle Of Wight Festival flew to Japan to perform their first ever shows in the country. As part of the Pacific Rim tour they played two shows in Japan (one in Yokohama and the other in Osaka, sharing the bill with Aerosmith). They followed this with three shows in Australia, two in Hawaii and two in California. The Australian shows marked a return to the country that Townshend had vowed never to revisit after their treatment at the hands of the media and politicians in 1968.

July: LIVE 8

Cajoled into appearing at Live 8 in order to raise awareness of global poverty, and marking 20 years from the original Live Aid concerts, The Who performed in Hyde Park on 2 July. This was to be their only performance of the year (save for a private gig for Samsung in New York the previous month). Although overshadowed by the Pink Floyd reunion, the band was in fine form and the event once again allowed them to showcase their live prowess to a worldwide TV audience as well as to the estimated 200,000 people who had gathered in the park.

2006

June: LEEDS PERFORMANCE

With news of a new album in the offing, The Who embarked on a year-long tour across Europe and the US. An initial show, in aid of the Teenage Cancer Trust, was held at Knebworth House, and the second was the eagerly awaited return to Leeds University, their first visit since recording the seminal live album *Live At Leeds* in 1970. Prior to the show, Daltrey and Townshend unveiled a commemorative plaque in honour of the band's performance there. This was just the beginning of an intense period of live activity for the band, which saw them play 110 concerts in 12 months.

June–July: FESTIVALS OF EUROPE

The Who had generally shied away from playing festivals since the Seventies, mainly due to Townshend's indifference at the time and his feelings of separation from the audience. In fact, after the tragedy at Cincinnati they rarely played non-seated shows. They had, of course, played a few festival-type shows but 2006 saw them embrace the festival circuit wholeheartedly, playing most of the major European gigs throughout the year, before returning to the arenas of North America. There were proposals to take the tour to South America and the Far East – including China – but these plans never came to fruition.

September–October: CONCERTS IN AMERICA

The American fans had been stalwart supporters of The Who since the late Sixties, and the band toured coast to coast during October 2006 and March 2007 to rapturous receptions. The marked difference between these shows and those on previous tours was the inclusion of new material. With songs from the album *Endless Wire* (released in October) as well as the single 'Wire & Glass' to call on, The Who finally gave fans what they had hoped for as they changed their standard repertoire to incorporate the new material.

October: ENDLESS WIRE

It took 24 years, but The Who did finally release an album of new material on 30 October. Preceded a few months earlier by a new Townshend mini-opera entitled *Wire & Glass*, the new disc was based on a novella, *The Boy Who Heard Music*, which Townshend had been working on for a number of years and a large part of the album was based on a song cycle entitled 'The Glass Household'. It was released in various formats, including bonus CDs and DVDs. *Endless Wire* charted at No. 9 in the UK and No. 7 in the US.

2007

June: GLASTONBURY

Having played all the major historical rock festivals, The Who eventually made it to a traditionally wet and muddy Glastonbury on 24 June 2007. Belting out a career-spanning set, the band headlined a day of top British acts that included the Kaiser Chiefs and Manic Street Preachers. The set finished with the poignant 'Tea and Theatre' from *Endless Wire*, with Roger Daltrey clutching a mug of tea. Pete Townshend, who has a long association with the festival, addressed the audience: 'We waited a long time to come here. We are so pleased to be here. Thanks for sticking with us.'

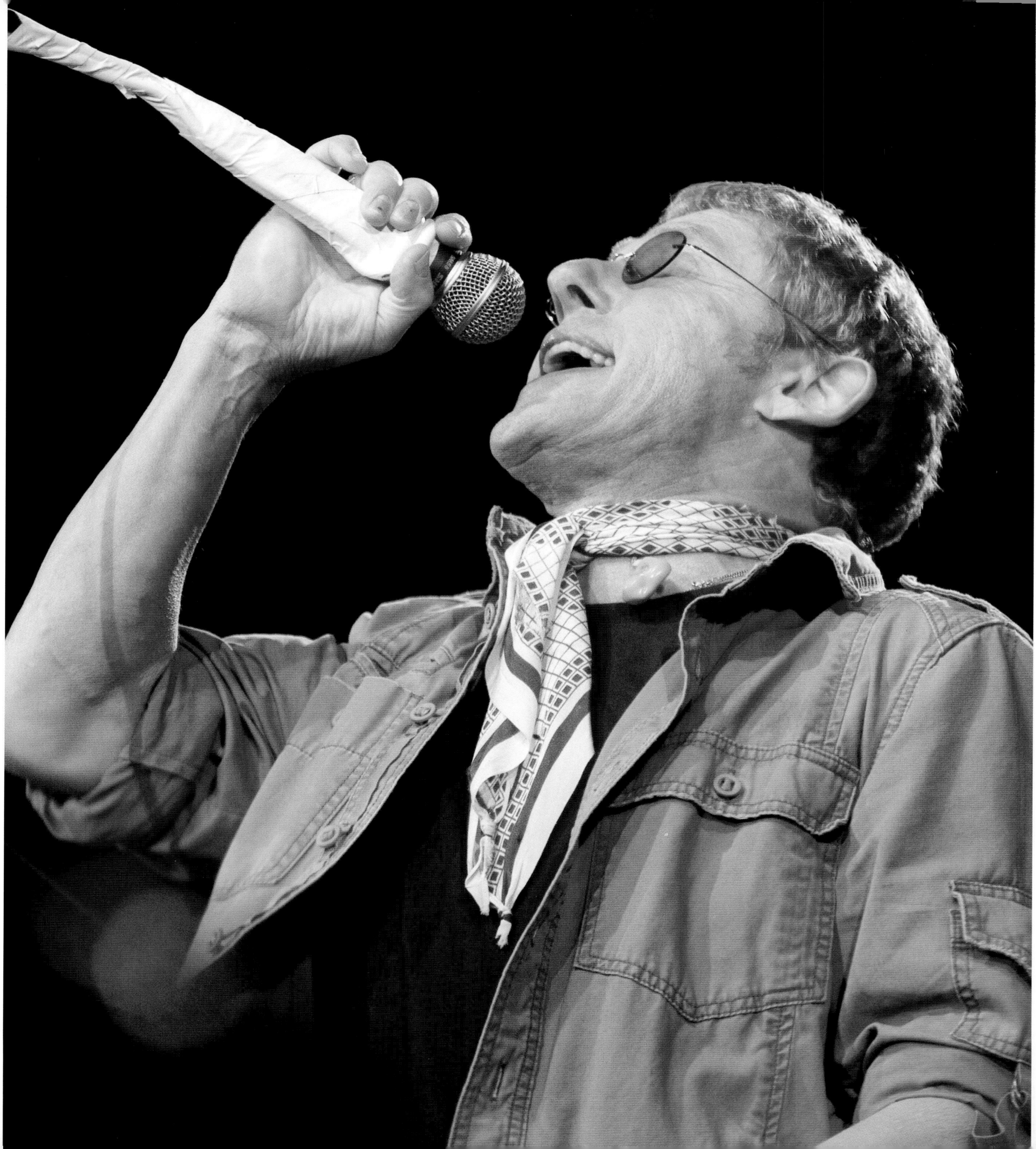

2008

December:
DALTREY AND THE TRANS-SIBERIAN ORCHESTRA

In December 2007 Roger Daltrey made a surprise guest appearance with the Trans-Siberian Orchestra at two of their shows: the Nassau Coliseum in Long Island and the Izod Arena in New Jersey. Coming on stage towards the end of their set, Roger played three Who songs – 'Behind Blue Eyes', 'Pinball Wizard' and the 'See Me Feel Me/Listening To You' finale of *Tommy*. He also joined the orchestra on guitar for a rendition of 'Christmas Eve In Sarajevo'. Always keen to play live, Daltrey is no stranger to performing with other acts.

May: TOWNSHEND WINS BMI AWARD

The *CSI* TV franchise provided good exposure and a whole new outlet for Pete Townshend's music, and all three shows used his compositions for their title tracks. As a result, from 2001, he was consistently awarded BMI (Broadcast Music Inc.) Awards in recognition of that body of work. The 2008 BMI Annual Film And Television Awards, held at the Beverly Wilshire Hotel, were no different, with Townshend picking up awards for all three variations. Also honoured was songwriter Mike Post, who Townshend himself had honoured with an eponymous song on the *Endless Wire* album.

July: ROCK HONORS TRIBUTE SHOW

The VH1 Rock Honors show began in 2006 and has become an annual event, paying tribute to artists who have shaped and influenced modern music. On 12 July 2008 it was The Who's turn in the spotlight, as the band became the first single band or artist to be honoured. The show took place at the Pauley Pavilion at UCLA, and an edited version was broadcast five days later. The Who themselves performed five songs and watched other bands, including Pearl Jam, Foo Fighters, Flaming Lips, Tenacious D and Incubus perform own versions of Who classics.

2009

December: USA AND JAPAN

The Who's second visit to Japan took place in November. Having enjoyed the trip four years earlier, the band members were keen to return, playing four shows for the Japanese fans. Prior to this, they enjoyed a 10-date tour of the US, starting at the perennial favourite Detroit, before criss-crossing the country and finishing in LA. The shows received a fantastic welcome from both fans and critics alike. The year finished with three Christmas shows at Indigo, a small venue in London's O2 arena complex.

March–April: BACK DOWN UNDER

The band's visit to Australia in 2004 seemed to have settled the bad blood between them and the locals that had simmered for over 35 years. Having agreed to perform at the 2009 Australian Grand Prix – the inaugural event in the Formula One season – they took the opportunity to arrange further shows, turning it into a six-date mini-tour. The Grand Prix performance took place on 29 March at the Melbourne circuit in Albert Park, and The Who sang out a 20-song set. It was the culmination of a good day for the Brits – earlier in the day, Jensen Button had won the race.

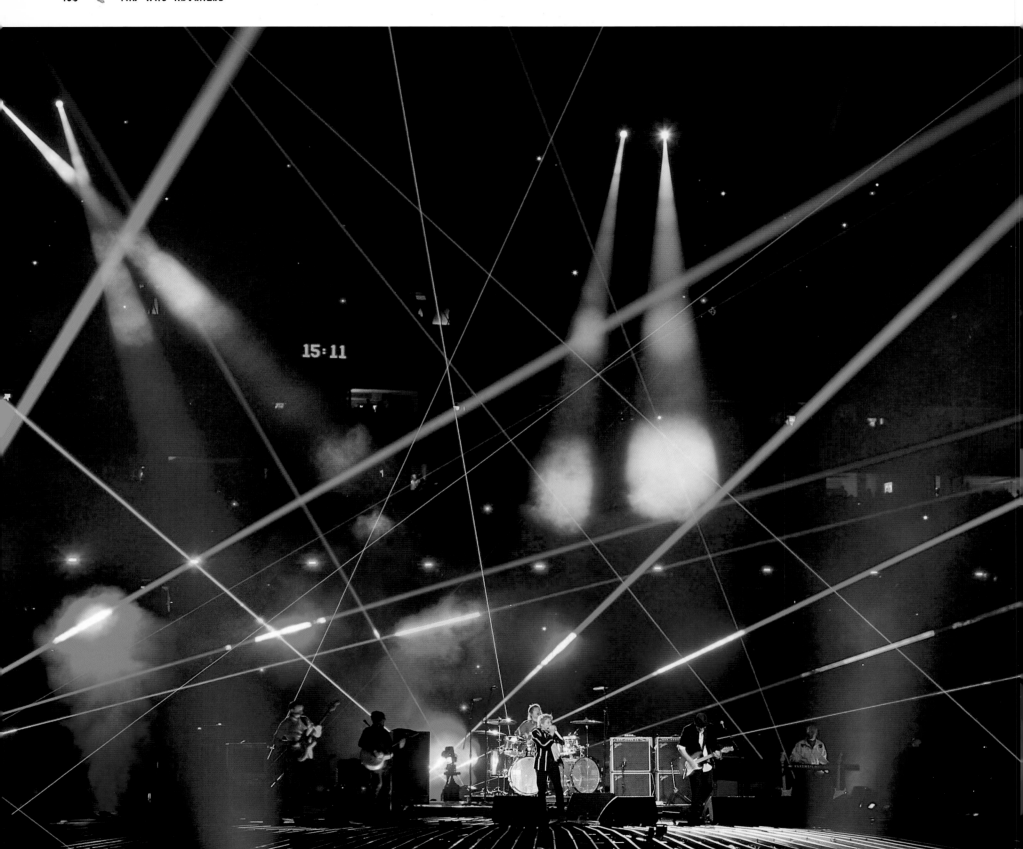

2010

February: SUPER BOWL XLIV

The Who performed the half-time showcase at the 44th Super Bowl, held at the Sun Life Stadium in Miami, in February 2010. It included a 12-minute medley of crowd-pleasers, namely 'Pinball Wizard', 'Baba O'Riley', 'Who Are You', 'See Me Feel Me' and 'Won't Get Fooled Again' in front of 74,000 spectators and an estimated 121 million TV viewers. With the crowd joining in on backing vocals, the show was a spectacular mix of sound, light and pyrotechnics, and proved that The Who still commanded the top ranks of live rock performers.

March: TEENAGE CANCER TRUST

The band celebrated the 10th anniversary of the Teenage Cancer Trust shows at the Royal Albert Hall with a performance of *Quadrophenia*. They were joined by special guests Eddie Vedder (as The Godfather) and Tom Meighan (as The Ace Face), together with a horn and string section, and performed the piece in its entirety for the first time in 13 years. Due to reported problems with tinnitus, a perspex barrier was placed behind Pete Townshend (they had performed the same trick on the 1989 tour). However, this did not impinge on a memorable performance, which was rapturously received by audience and critics alike.

INDEX